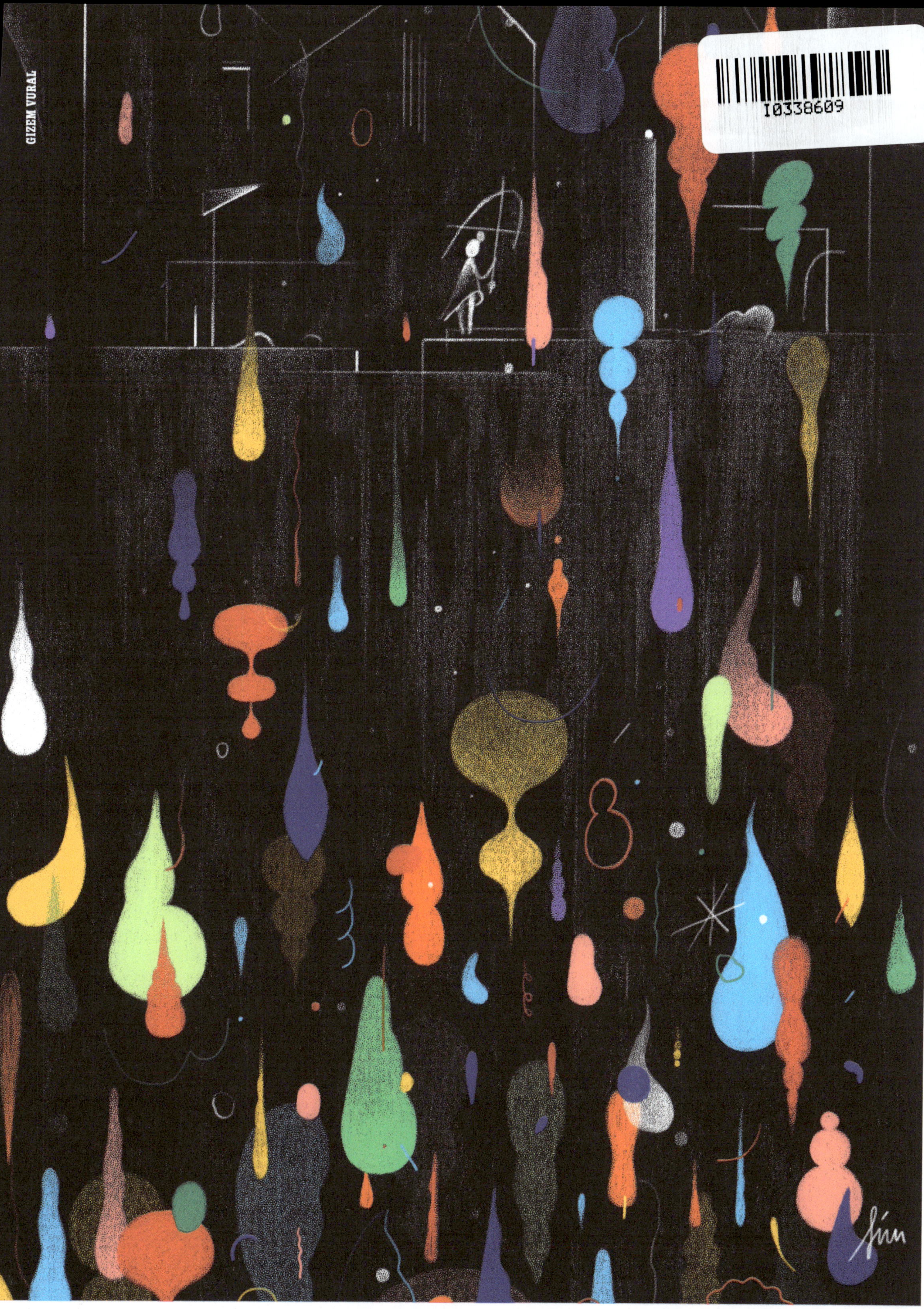
GIZEM VURAL

PUBLISHER'S LETTER
BY MICHAEL GERBER

MY FIRST CHRISTMAS MEMORY
Too Aware Too Young—where's the 12-Step group for us, dammit?

The first Christmas I remember is actually a Christmas Eve. It was 1975, and my mother and I were living in the top floor of an old mansion in the Central West End of St. Louis. She was working her way through art school; I was working my way through childhood. We both felt we were making satisfactory progress, but this was definitely a minority opinion. My grandma thought I needed a dog; my mom's friends thought she needed a husband; I thought we needed an endowment.

December 23rd had been typical: Mom used a smoke break to pick me up from school, and together we went back to Webster College's painting studio, where I drew quietly and made small talk with the naked person. Then we went to O'Connell's, and she worked a shift while I sat at the bar, fiddling with dominoes and drinking Shirley Temples. My presence among the barflies elicited no comment; O'Connell's was an unofficial commissary for both the *Globe-Democrat* and *Post-Dispatch*, and the sight of a six-year-old in a tavern was nothing remarkable to a newspaperman; surely some of them had been that kind of child themselves. Anyway, Mom and I arrived back home around eight, had a quick dinner, and collapsed into bed.

Our lives were so busy, it was like being in a trance. Then suddenly the trance lifted, and it was the night before Christmas. I remember we had a small tree, and that it was beautiful.* We weren't religious, the family downstairs was Jewish, and St. Louis produces only sleet until January. Sure, you get "dustings," but those are merely camouflage for the daily slip-and-falls (an art in which, as a kid with cerebral palsy, I was already a master).

But for all my bruises and skinned palms, I wasn't complaining; far from it. I was an adored child, and already knew how rare that was. I had my heart set on one toy, a *Six Million Dollar Man* action figure, but Mom had seen something on the news as she made our dinner that night. "Mike," she said, "don't be too disappointed if you don't get Steve Austin."

"I won't," I said, and meant it. My mom, my aunts, my Grandma, everybody was working so hard. Cutting them some slack was the least I could do.

MICHAEL GERBER (@mgerber937) is Editor & Publisher of *The American Bystander*.

---

* My mother can make anything beautiful, even dead bugs or a pile of rocks, but it's like a spell: if you want the magic, you must follow her directions exactly. 1975 was the year of "blue and green lights only." At six I was outraged; at forty-nine I am man enough to admit it worked.

After we finished our fish sticks and salad, Mom took a *thirty-minute* bath—utter decadence. When she emerged, she said, "Get into your pajamas, I have a surprise for you."

I changed, intrigued. "What are we going to do?"

Mom pulled back the covers. "You'll see." I got in.

Mom left the room, and I heard her, *click-click-click*, turning off all the lights in the apartment. When she came back in, she held a candle, which she put by the side of the bed.

"Scoot over," she said. "I'm going to read you a book." This wasn't so unusual; for efficiency's sake, Mom would often read me her assigned texts—W.B. Yeats, or *Alice in Wonderland*. But a whole book? She pulled out a small orange-spined paperback. "Comfortable?"

I nodded, practically delirious with pleasure—cuddle-time with Mom was precious. Usually she smelled like smoke, from the studio or the pub; tonight it was Jean Naté. This was a special occasion.

Mom began to read. "'I endeavor in this Ghostly little book to raise the Ghost of an idea…'"

A Christmas Carol is a pretty heavy trip, to use the language of 1975; I don't think I've ever really recovered from it. Though my family was never Crachit-poor, in those days there were about three women for every man still living, and then as now that doesn't lead to prosperity. There was a lot of love, but not a lot of money; thank God nobody had credit cards.

I remember identifying a lot with Tiny Tim. In the Spring of that year, I'd gotten a big operation on my legs, which kept me in the hospital for a week, and in a waist cast for six more. After all that smelly, itchy plaster got cut off, I learned to walk again, and wore heavy braces for a while. Thankfully for my vanity and popularity, that process was mostly finished by the time school started up again. But I was different, inside.

Of course I reveled in Scrooge's transformation, but as I drifted off to sleep, *A Christmas Carol* troubled me. Not the supernatural part—Mom had assured me that there was "no such thing as ghosts." It was deeper. Even at six, I didn't like the implications of an economic system that had to rely on ectoplasmic do-gooders to prevent children from starving to death. Seems sub-optimal. Seems like something to fix. I remember thinking, "What about all the *other* Tiny Tims? What about all the *other* Scrooges, the ones that didn't change? And you know that sooner or later, this Scrooge'll get pissed off at something and change back!"

If it seems unbelievable to you that a six-year-old would think such things, please be assured that it is the single most accurate portion of this article. I should have "Too Aware Too Young" tattooed across my back, where Roger Stone keeps his Nixon.

As Mom read, I thought of all the other children in Shriner's Hospital, all of us getting free surgeries, the burns and handicaps fixed as best they could be. I thought of the kids I'd met who didn't have even a mother, the ones who cried all night and never got visited. What about those people? Who will take care of them? *Spirits?*

The question haunts me still, and not just on Christmas.

Mom slept with me all night, something she never did. At 10:00 A.M., we left for Grandma's house. Around noon, people started to arrive—first my Aunt Mary, then as now my favorite person in the world.

"Did you?" Mom whispered.

Mary rolled her eyes. "Only took about fifteen stores."

"What are you guys talking about?"

"Oh, big ears!" Mary scolded. "You'll see soon enough."

When it came time to open presents, I grabbed Mary's first. "Is this what I think it is?" I could tell by her face that it was. I couldn't open the package fast enough; with my legs, *The Six Million Dollar Man* wasn't just a TV show, it was something between a life goal and a religion. I hugged Mary so hard she made a fake choking sound.

"Will you be able to sleep with this one?" Mom asked wryly. The year before, I had gotten a four-foot model of *T. rex*; its glow-in-the-dark teeth and claws had proved too much for the man.

I didn't answer; I was way too busy for idle chitchat. I looked through Steve's bionic eye; rolled the fake skin on his arm up and down; took the plastic diode thingy out of his forearm. As I played with my doll, I felt a kind of satisfaction, a completeness, that I didn't feel again for years. But there was something else, something left over from the night before.

The story of *A Christmas Carol* isn't simply about a miser having a change of heart; it portrays a world where the virtuous rich benevolently take care of the rest of us. Even at six, I knew this was a pretty slim reed upon which to hang civilization. I wasn't about to let me and mine suffer, not if I could help it. I saw my doll, that Mary had driven all over to get, and all the other presents, big and small, so thoughtful. I loved my family so much; I determined that I would be my own Scrooge—I would be strong, and powerful, and have plenty of money to take care of them with. Six million dollars should be enough. Could I do it? I had to—after all, *there's no such thing as ghosts.*

As I stood there with my doll, I knew the world was full of people who weren't opening any presents; people who were sick, and poor, and brokenhearted; people without any love at all. Feeling all that, and feeling so unequal to doing anything about it, perhaps that's the beginning of adulthood. I think it came too early for me. Or maybe not, but I've always remembered it—my first **Christmas memory.**

"When you put on a magic silk hat, things can get out of hand pretty quickly."

TABLE OF CONTENTS

DEPARTMENTS
Frontispiece: "Rain" *by Gizem Vural* 1
Publisher's Letter *by Michael Gerber* 2
Poetry Corner: Clerihews-Who *by David Chelsea* 8
Spotlight: Ghost Porn *by Rich Sparks* 10
Errata *by Steve Young* 97
Crossword: *"Shakespearean Holiday Gifts"*
  by Matthew Matera & Alan Goldberg 100

GALLIMAUFRY
Lydia Oxenham, Mike Shear, David Etkin, Penny Barr, Patrick Kennedy, Matthew Disler, Alex Schmidt, Phil Witte, Adrian Bonenberger, Thatcher Jensen, Jonathan Zeller, David Chelsea.

SHORT STUFF
So Be Good For Goodness' Sake *by Victor Juhasz* 5
Menasha Skulnik *by Drew Friedman* 7
I Believe in You *by Alicia Kraft* 25
Seasons Greetings From the Steinbeck Family
  by Riane Konc 26
Health Food Hell *by Dave Hanson* 28
Unsubscribe Me *by Risa Mickenberg* 30
Merry Mithras, One and All *by Mike Reiss* 32
No, Virginia *by Tim Harrod* 34

The AMERICAN BYSTANDER
#9 • Vol. 3, No. 1 • Fall 2018

EDITOR & PUBLISHER Michael Gerber
HEAD WRITER Brian McConnachie
SENIOR EDITOR Alan Goldberg
CONTACTEE Scott Marshall
ORACLE Steve Young
STAFF LIAR P.S. Mueller
INTREPID TRAVELER Mike Reiss
AGENTS OF THE SECOND BYSTANDER INTERNATIONAL
Craig Boreth, Matt Kowalick, Neil Mitchell, Maxwell Ziegler
MANAGING EDITOR EMERITA
Jennifer Boylan

CONTRIBUTORS
Lila Ash, Penny Barr, Ron Barrett, Charles Barsotti, Tracey Berglund, Adrian Bonenberger, George Booth, M.K. Brown, Roz Chast, David Chelsea, Tom Chitty, Joe Ciardiello, Olivia de Recat, Matthew Disler, Nick Downes, Bob Eckstein, Ivan Ehlers, David Etkin, Xeth Feinberg, Emily Flake, Katie Fricas, Drew Friedman, Rick Geary, Sam Gross, Tom Hachtman, Kaamran Hafeez, Lance Hansen, Dave Hanson, Tim Harrod, Ron Hauge, Thatcher Jensen, John Jonik, Victor Juhasz, Patrick Kennedy, Riane Konc, Alicia Kraft, Ken Krimstein, Stephen Kroninger, Peter Kuper, Sara Lautman, Stan Mack, Merrill Markoe, Matt Matera, Zoe Matthiessen, Risa Mickenberg, P.S. Mueller, David Ostow, Lydia Oxenham, Marc Palm, Matt Percival, Jonathan Plotkin, Denise Reiss, Mike Reiss, Ellis Rosen, Laurie Rosenwald, Alex Schmidt, Jonathan Schwarz, Cris Shapan, Mike Shear, Mike Shiell, Jim Siergey, Rich Sparks, Nick Spooner, Ed Subitzky, Tom Toro, P.C. Vey, D. Watson, Shannon Wheeler, Phil Witte, Steve Young, Cerise Zelentz, Jonathan Zeller & Jack Ziegler.

THANKS TO
Kate Powers, Kate Ingold, Rae Barsotti, Lanky Bareikis, Jon Schwarz, Alleen Schultz, Diane Gray, Molly Bernstein, Joe Lopez, Eliot Ivanhoe, Neil Gumenick, Michael Thornton, Ben Orlin, Greg and Patricia Gerber and many, many others.

NAMEPLATES BY
Mark Simonson
ISSUE CREATED BY
Michael Gerber

Vol. 3, No.1. ©2018 Good Cheer LLC, all rights reserved. Proudly produced in California, USA.

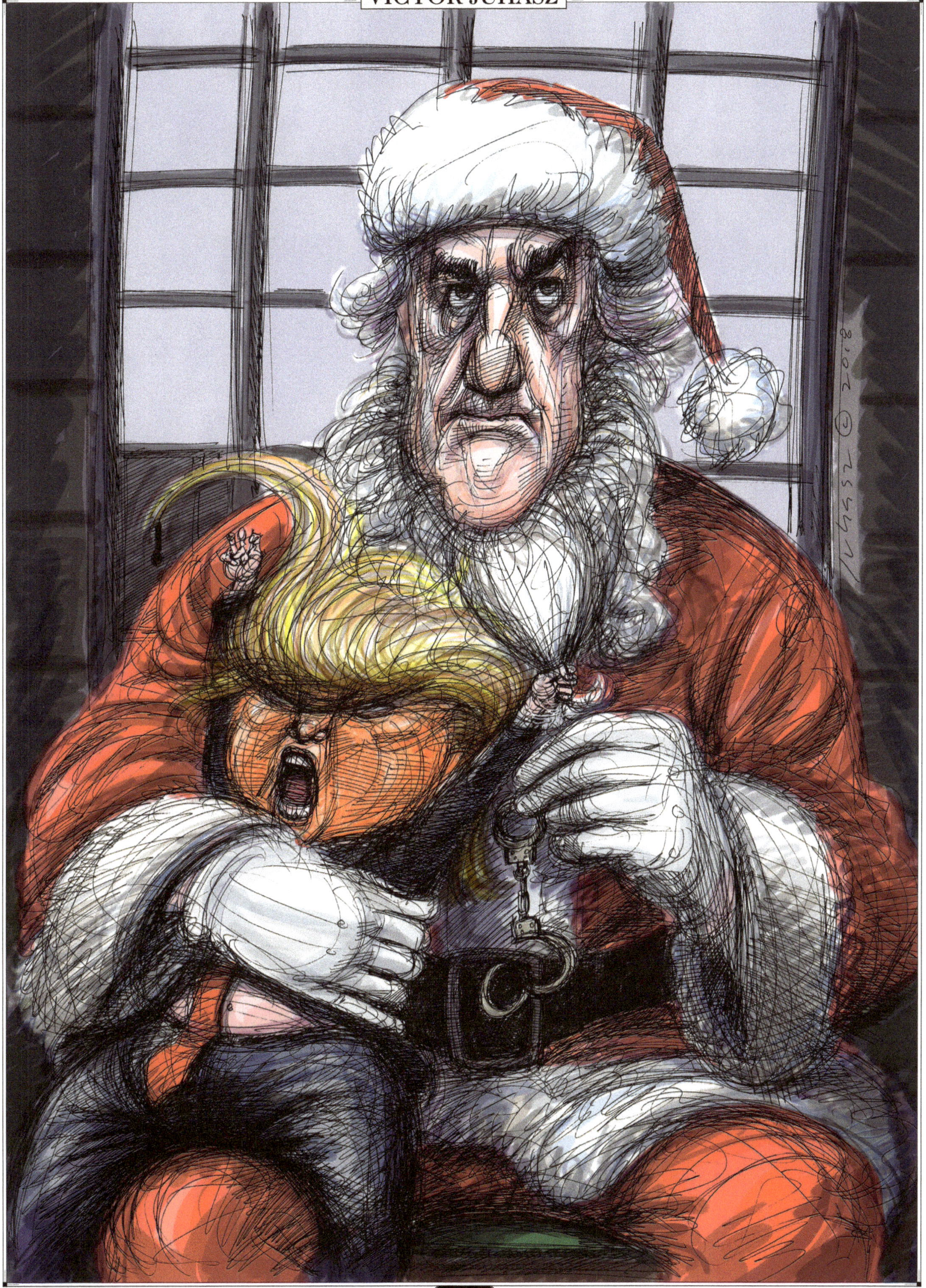
Juhasz © 2018

FEATURES
Spaghetti Westerns **by Joe Ciardiello**..................37
Enormous Blonde Herring-Scented Nauseatingly Fair-Minded Nymphomaniacs in Clogs **by Laurie Rosenwald**..................42
Gertrude's Follies **by Tom Hachtman & Sam Gross**............46
A Turkey for Lewis **by Merrill Markoe**....................47
Why Are Things Not What They Seem?
  by Rick Geary..................49
A Christmas Peril **by Michael Gerber**...................50
Don't Teach Your Grandmother to Suck Eggs
  by Ron Barrett..................83

OUR BACK PAGES
Letter From Melania **by Emily Flake**...................85
Joan's Other Kitchen: "Baseball Is Hunting"
  by Brian McConnachie..................87
What Am I Doing Here?: Rio Stole My Heart and Wallet
  by Mike Reiss..................95
Errata **by Steve Young**..................99

CARTOONS & ILLUSTRATIONS BY
Lila Ash, Penny Barr, Ron Barrett, Charles Barsotti, George Booth, M.K. Brown, Tracey Kleinman Berglund, Roz Chast, David Chelsea, Tom Chitty, Olivia de Recat, Nick Downes, Bob Eckstein, Ivan Ehlers, Xeth Feinberg, Kate Fricas, Drew Friedman, Rick Geary, Michael Gerber, Sam Gross, Tom Hachtman, Lance Hansen, Ron Hauge, Kamraan Hafeez, John Jonik, Victor Juhasz, Ken Krimstein, Stephen Kroninger, Peter Kuper, Sara Lautman, Stan Mack, Zoe Matthiessen, P.S. Mueller, David Ostow, Marc Palm, Matt Percival, Jonathan Plotkin, Denise Reiss, Ellis Rosen, Laurie Rosenwald, Jon Schwarz, Cris Shapan, Mike Shiell, Jim Siergey, Marc Simonson, Rich Sparks, Nick Spooner, Tom Toro, P.C. Vey, D. Watson, Shannon Wheeler, Cerise Zelentz and Jack Ziegler.

"Just as I feared. Tariffs."

COVER

In addition to his civilian fans, **Rick Geary** is one of those illustrators that other illustrators love, and I am with them all 1000%. This drawing, entitled "New Mexico Christmas," appeared in my inbox mere moments after I'd given Rick the assignment—which is why editors love him, too! Thank you, my friend; next year, lunch at Comic Con is on *Bystander*.

ACKNOWLEDGMENTS

All material is ©2018 its creators, all rights reserved; do not reproduce or distribute it without written consent of the creators and *The American Bystander*. The following material has appeared previously, and is reprinted here with permission of the author(s): Stan Mack's "Great Gran'ma's Gospel" first appeared in *The Village Voice*. Riane Konc's "Seasons' Greetings From The Steinbeck Family" was published online by *The Toast*. A verison of Merrill Markoe's "A Turkey for Lewis" appeared in *The Wall Street Journal*. Matt Percival's cartoon "Transitioning" appeared in *The Spectator* (UK).

THE AMERICAN BYSTANDER, Vol. 3, No. 1, (978-0-578-42873-4). Publishes ~4x/year. ©2018 by Good Cheer LLC. No part of this magazine can be reproduced, in whole or in part, by any means, without the written permission of the Publisher. For this and other queries, email *Publisher@americanbystander.org*, or write: Michael Gerber, Publisher, *The American Bystander*, 1122 Sixth St., #403, Santa Monica, CA 90403. Subscribe at www.patreon.com/bystander. Copious additional info can be found at www.americanbystander.org.

DREW FRIEDMAN

Menasha Skulnik
(1890-1970)
Yiddish comedian and
Broadway star

FLU REVIEWS — *Mike is usually pretty easygoing, but in November he got the flu and spent 24 hours watching TCM and dealing hard truths on Facebook:* **A CLOCKWORK ORANGE** *"Just a movie about a bunch of assholes in the future."* **THE BIG SLEEP** *"Rich people from Pasadena are always more trouble than they're worth. Ditch 'em and keep boinkin' that bookstore chick."* **THE MAGNIFICENT AMBERSONS** *"I don't usually advocate violence, but somebody needs to break a foot off in that kid's ass."* **A NIGHT AT THE OPERA** *"The musical numbers are making my body aches worse."* **THE FRENCH CONNECTION** *"Look, don't blame French people because New York got shitty."*

POETRY CORNER
BY DAVID CHELSEA
CLERIHEWS-WHO
"A short comic verse in two rhyming couplets, with lines of unequal length, and referring to a famous person"

DAVID CHELSEA *has been a cartoonist/illustrator for decades, but never a published poet until now. His next book is* **Are You Being Watched?**, *a graphic novel from Dark Horse.*

Passing for Human

Liana Finck

Dare to be Different

"PASSING FOR HUMAN IS ONE OF THE MOST EXTRAORDINARY MEMOIRS I'VE EVER READ."
— ROZ CHAST, AUTHOR OF *CAN'T WE TALK ABOUT SOMETHING MORE PLEASANT?*

"NO ONE DRAWS LIKE LIANA FINCK, AND NO ONE ENCHANTS LIKE HER EITHER."
— STACY SCHIFF, AUTHOR OF *CLEOPATRA*

A Random House Hardcover

@lianafinck

SPOTLIGHT
GHOST PORN
BY RICH SPARKS

Recent work from one of our favorite cartoonists

HEDUSA

ONANDONODON.

NUDE DESCENDING A STAIRCASE

BATMANAGER

RICH SPARKS *has appeared in* **The New Yorker**, **The Wall Street Journal** *and other places. A collection of his cartoons,* **Love and Other Weird Things**, *will be published by Yoe Books in 2019.*

Gallimaufry

*"December used to be a month—
now it's a whole year."*
Seneca

PREGNANCY PRESS CONFERENCE.

Thank you all for coming. As the spokesperson for the mother-to-be, I've been getting a lot of very specific and personal questions about her well-being, and so I've decided to answer them all at once instead of individually, and repeatedly, *ad infinitum* really, over the next few months.

She's resting at home now, and I will pass along any kind words shared here today. First question.

Hi, I'm Linda, from next door. I'd like to know: How is she feeling?

Absolutely fine. We thank you for your concern.

This is Bill, I'm her uncle on her mother's side. She hasn't gained any weight at all. How does she do it?

Bill, while we appreciate your suggestion that female weight gain is always negative, we won't be revealing her weight at this time.

But she hasn't gained any weight, right? I know what pregnant women should look like.

She has gained an undisclosed amount of weight, which, I can assure you, is totally healthy.

I'm Katie, her college roommate. I disagree. She's gained an inordinate amount of weight. Her ankles have completely disappeared. I think she's having twins.

Quiet down, please. I can confirm that she is not having twins.

Well, my sister thought she wasn't having twins, and then she did, so…

Next question.

Sheila, the mother-to-be's yoga instructor. Is she about to pop? She looks like she's about to pop.

We ask that you keep any observations about her weight and/or circumference to yourself.

I'm Pam, her coworker. How is she feeling?

Asked and answered, Pam.

This is Alison, cashier at T.J. Maxx. She's just so brave for wearing such tight clothing at this stage in her pregnancy.

Do you have a question, Alison?

No, I just think she's very brave to show her body in this unusual state.

I'll pass that along.

Darla, Whole Foods produce section. Is she eating the right things? And does she plan to feed her baby the right things? And by "the right things" I mean the things that I have determined to be the right things.

ROZ CHAST

Next question.

This is Courtney, her sister-in-law on her husband's side. When is she due?

Excellent question! March 1st.

So you're saying she had intercourse on…

Please do not attempt to calculate or visualize the moment of conception.

This is a stranger, from her local Walmart. Can I touch her belly?

You cannot, nor should you want to. That's an abnormal feeling, and a completely inappropriate invasion of boundaries that most psychologists say stems from deep childhood trauma and lack of human contact. Next question.

I'm Brittany. I'm just an acquaintance. My sister had a miscarriage. So it's pretty common. Can you tell her that miscarriages are common and I'd be happy to console her should she experience a miscarriage?

I will not.

This is Sheryl. Let's call me a concerned citizen. How is she feeling?

I've already answered this today, Sheryl! Any subsequent utterances of "how are you feeling?" should be reserved for medical practitioners.

I'm Denise, her other college roommate. My sister also had complications. It was a rare yet totally preventable thing that probably won't happen, but I think I should tell you anyway.

…

I have a follow up question: how is she feeling?

—Lydia Oxenham

MUSIC NOTES ON THE ROUGH CUT OF *BOHEMIAN RHAPSODY*.

0:00 Opening with "Under Pressure." I like it. Makes the film feel high stakes.

5:43 This is a little on the nose. Everyone knows that Queen's going to win the 1970 Ealing Art College Battle of the Bands. Do we really need to underscore that with "We Are the Champions"? Let's give our audience a little credit.

12:11 Oooh, really interesting how you use "Crazy Little Thing Called Love" to showcase Freddie Mercury's relationship with his fans.

18:22 You probably know this, but you're using "Under Pressure" again here. That said—the band sure is under a lot of pressure at this point in the film! I guess the good news is that the song works in both places. Pick either one; you can't go wrong!

27:11 That other one really did bite the dust in that scene!

35:12 Look, you can't just keep playing "Under Pressure" over and over. You're only supposed to use each song once in the movie.

42:45 I want to make sure we're on the same page here. "Radio Ga Ga" isn't supposed to be *literal*. It's a metaphor—it doesn't mean John Deacon's car radio only plays the phrases "ga ga" and "goo goo" on a loop.

50:14 I get it! The band is under pressure! That's what movies are about! Characters under pressure! But you can't just play a song about being under pressure every time someone in the movie is under pressure! Your job is to find new and interesting ways to dramatize that pressure on screen!

52:13 Son of a—if you're going to keep using that song, at least give us a reason! Maybe "Under Pressure" is Freddie's motif? It was the lullaby his mother sang to him every night. What if each member of the band has his own motif based on a different Queen song? Like how each animal has its own instrument in *Peter and the Wolf*. Let's definitely circle back to this on the conference call. But no more "Under Pressure"!!!

56:49 We finally made it to the big bicycle race set piece, and you assholes are playing "Under Pressure."

1:02:11 Why is Freddie Mercury giving a speech about how he'll never record a song with David Bowie no matter how much pressure he's under? The existence of the song itself (actually used to pretty good effect here) refutes this argument.

1:05:11 Okay, this is better. The band are all best friends again after a rocky patch, and they're singing "You're My Best Friend." A little on the nose, but at least it's not…

1:06:52 What the fuck?! A mashup of "You're My Best Friend" and "Under Pressure"? (That said, DJ Khaled's guest verse is killer.)

1:10:52 Weeee willll weeee willll rock you! [CLAP] [CLAP]

1:18:11 I don't know where to start. We're at the point in the film where Freddie Mercury is under the most pressure. He's coming to terms with his upbringing in Zanzibar, he's about to perform at Live Aid, and he's concerned for his best friend Ronald Reagan, who's undergoing last-minute life-or-death colon surgery. But, at this crucial moment, you went with… "Pressure" by Billy Joel.

1:20:12 I mean, Billy Joel has a song called "Zanzibar." Why don't you just play that over the closing credits? For fuck's sake. I'm going to lose my job over this movie.

1:21:23 You know, a *lot* of us are under pressure.

1:22:11 I've been under pressure my whole life.

1:22:13 Pressure to do well in school. To follow the rules. To be a success, as if anybody ever bothered to tell me what the definition of success was.

1:22:22 That's *right*, Billy Joel! All my life was channel 13! *Sesame Street*! What did that mean!?

1:30:38 The song is "Flash" not "Flesh." This whole montage needs to be reworked.

1:46:00 Did we run out of Queen songs? For the last 15 minutes, it's been footage of Brian May lecturing a Freshman physics class about how, in an ideal gas, volume and temperature directly influence the gas's pressure. We're really going to need a killer closing number to save this.

1:46:01 "Killer Queen"! Nailed it!

1:52:11 The movie's over? You never played "Bohemian Rhapsody"! If you don't find a place for it in the next cut, we're hiring a new editor. No pressure.
—*Mike Shear*

GRIFTING.

Monsieur, madame, welcome to Lé Strap. I can seat you immediately. Please, both of you follow me to the VIP entrance. No need to go in the front, like the riff-raff. Just around here…and a bit farther around please…

We are almost there—the veal medallions are exquisite tonight; the chef has a veal farm on the roof…First date? You both have that "what will happen" look. But I know what will happen to both of you tonight.

Ha, ha, no I simply meant that you will fall in love. It is written on your faces. Did you park on the street? *Sacré bleu!* We must rectify that *immédiatement*. Sir, I shall not sleep until your car is safely in the tender care of our finest valet. His name is Henrí, and he would die of a sudden aneurism were he to learn you had eschewed his services for…*le rue merde*.

No, no, do not concern yourself; it is but the work of a moment. Henrí waits behind this door day and night. Simply drop your car keys through the mail slot like so, yes? Now sit here, next to the cluster of gentlemen absorbed at craps. You are lucky, *monsieur*, *madame*, as typically our *al fresco* facilities are reserved for captains of industry and heads of state. I shall scurry to alert the chef to your presence and commence the slaughtering of our most contented veal calf. *Adieu*—no, of course I meant *au revoir*. My bad.

• • •

Come over here, sir! This is the Sterling Select Priority TSA checkpoint. No line as you can see. It is my privilege to curate your TSA experience today. Forgive the façade of informality given off by the mufti; we find uniforms… *gauche*. My uniform is the smile on my face and the song in my heart. You and your new bride—

Really? You both have a glow—you can both keep your shoes on, just until we get to the van.

Ah! Our most commonly asked question: it is unmarked to establish a sense of understated elegance. Sterling Select members are driven from curbside directly to the tarmac in one of several luxury vans. The security screening process occurs en route.

I see that you have a dog in a carrier—either that or a very small, very cleverly disguised police officer. I am joking of course, as almost no police officer could fit into that bag. I will assume that it is a service animal; let us not speak of it again. Now this helpful gentleman is Henry; he will be our driver.

He is armed to protect our clients, high-net-worth individuals. Are you comfy? Now we can begin—standard procedure: please place everything into the plastic tray.

Your watch looks to have a platinum band, one which I am sure a thief would covet so highly that he would not hesitate to break your wrist if it gave him even an instant's advantage in obtaining it. Your seatbelt is jammed? Let me help you. But first: would you like some brandy? I would, but I'm on duty. I will try some ether however. The only way to fly, I say. Care for some? I insist—here you go.

• • •

First time getting your wrist x-rayed? Well, you came to the right place, an orthopedist's office, which is what this is. Please sit down right here. Now, I must ask that you take off any rings, as they would interfere with the procedure. I apologize for the décor—we are in the midst of renovation. Quite heavy renovation. We are putting in a water slide, which will liven up our waiting room in a daring yet not unprofessional way. You saw the sign on the door, yes? It clearly states that this space is in fact an orthopedist's office. Now, if you please: rings, watches, and yes, that MedicAlert bracelet for your penicillin allergy. Me? Ha, ha, no I'm not the doctor, just a lowly x-ray technician. That man in the corner is your physician. His name is Dr. Henry. I would ask that you not disturb him; he is going over the latest research on cases such as yours. Your wife? She looked pregnant, so we sent her to our resident OB/GYN at no charge to either of you. Now, I will keep your items safely here in my pocket until the procedure is over. We have had some robberies, can you believe it? You have been robbed? Twice? *Quel dommage!* Well, nothing like that will happen to you while in our care. Oh, this piece looks like an antique—a family heirloom? I will keep it extra-safe. Now, I will x-ray your wrist with this machine that is clearly labeled as an x-ray machine. No, Dr. Henry and I must step into the other room, to protect ourselves from the radiation. When this door closes it sounds like a bolt is being thrown, but it's just the hinges, which need oiling. I'm sweating? You don't look so good yourself sir, I suggest we get your wrist fixed *immédiatement*. Remember what I said about the hinges. We'll be right back, there is no need to get up or cry out!

• • •

Ah, the expectant father, pacing out his worry in the hushed confines of the hospital waiting room, oblivious to all else, even the penicillin burns about his mouth. Permit me to introduce myself, I'm—aaaggh! *Monsieur!* I must ask you to—please stop! Of course I have never met you before! I am merely a newly minted father, much like yourself. May I suggest that it is merely *déjà vu*? It happens to me all the time. I have that kind of face, one devoid of character which acts much like a vessel into which others

"Overruled."

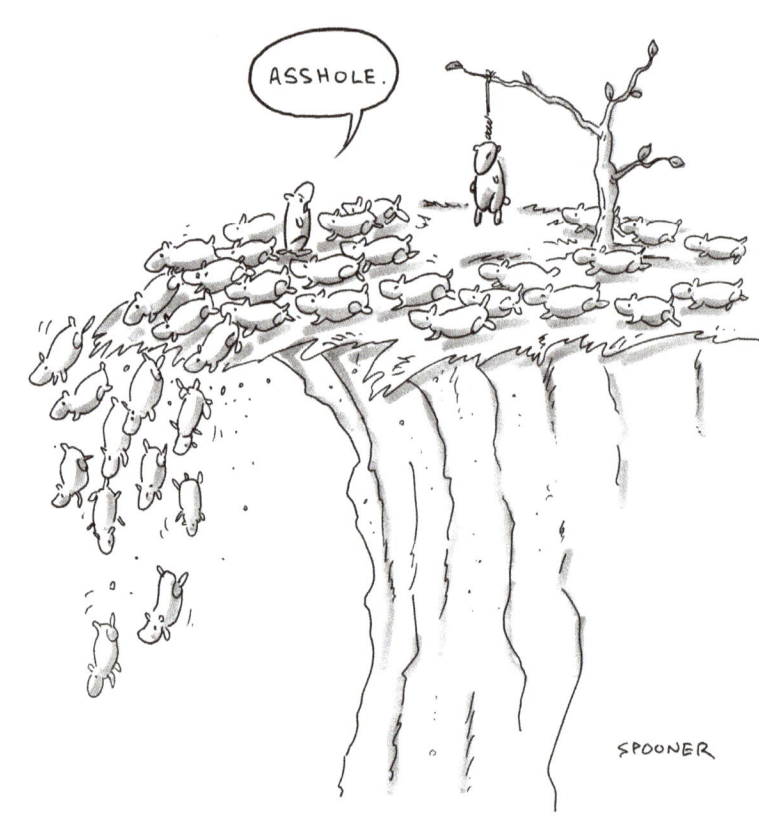

may pour their expectations, concerns and hopes. I understand how you might have mistaken me for another individual who wronged you thrice over. No, I insist we shake hands. May I ask what type of watch that is? I want to know because I collect vintage watches, but you don't have to tell me, of course you do not. My baby? Already born. A boy named…Henrietta? I know, odd, but is a family tradition. Do you not see it—er, him—swaddled in that chair in the corner, in the same blue and white swaddling blanket used in hospitals the world over? You know, I really like you and want our children to be as fast a pair of friends as we're clearly becoming. Look—they're bringing out a baby in one of those Plexiglas cribs. It's yours, isn't it? I'm going to put mine next to yours so they can begin to get acquainted. No? Are you sure? Well, I'm disappointed, but don't wish to impose. I'll just bend over and take my child back and leave yours where I found him. What? Handcuffs?!? Your baby just—ah, I see. It's no baby at all, but rather the cleverly disguised form of Officer Arthur MacDouglas, my oldest nemesis and tiniest police officer on the force. *Le poulets*, Henri! Run!

—*David Etkin*

TELEGRAMS FROM A CAVEMAN.

NOAA
NATIONAL WEATHER SERVICE
SILVER SPRING MD

WHY GIANT GLOWING ORB IN SKY DIP BELOW HORIZON QUERY EACH NIGHT CAVEMAN FEAR ORB NOT RETURN STOP SOMETIME THROW SPEAR AT SMALLER ORB THAT CHASE BIG ONE AWAY STOP NEVER HIT IT BUT SOMETIME IT HIDE STOP WHEN BIG YELLOW ORB RETURN EACH A M CAVEMAN REJOICE STOP EMOTIONAL ROLLER COASTER STOP APPRECIATE ANY ANSWERS FROM WIZARD THANKS
TOG COMMA HUNTER OF BRONTOSAURUS

OFFICE OF PARKING CLERK
BOSTON CITY HALL
BOSTON MA

DEAR SIR COMMA RECENTLY CAVEMAN MAKE TRIP INTO BIG VILLAGE FOR SUPPLIES STOP ROLL LARGE STONE WHEEL ALONG STOP GRANTED CAVEMAN STILL NOT SURE HOW THIS HELP CARRY SUPPLIES BUT GUESS IT WORK IN PROGRESS STOP POINT IS CAVEMAN LEAVE WHEEL BY SIDE OF ROAD WHILE GO INTO KITCHEN SUPPLY STORE TO GET SPEAR SHARPENED STOP COME OUT TO FIND SMALL ORANGE SLICE OF TREE ON WHEEL STOP NUMBERS ON TREE SLICE SAY CAVEMAN OWE BIG VILLAGE MANY GREEN TREE SLICES STOP TURN OUT PLACE WHERE CAVEMAN LEAVE WHEEL SPECIAL PLACE WHERE NO MACHINE MAY PARK COMMA AND WHEEL A SIMPLE MACHINE SO CLOSE ENOUGH STOP MAKE SOME SENSE BUT HOW CAVEMAN SUPPOSED TO KNOW WHAT SIGN MEAN QUERY LINE THROUGH LETTER P STOP HONESTLY THOUGHT MEANT NO PTERODACTYLS AROUND COMMA WAS RELIEVED STOP EASY MISTAKE TO MAKE PLEASE SEE WAY TO WAIVING FINE THANKS
TOG COMMA HUNTER OF BRONTOSAURUS

DUG
CORNELL UNIVERSITY
COLLEGE OF AGRICULTURE AND LIFE SCIENCES
ITHACA NY

DEAR SON COMMA YOUR FATHER PROUD OF YOU STOP LEARN HOW CAPTURE BEASTS COMMA LIVE WITH THEM LIKE FAMILY STOP VERY FORWARD LOOKING STOP TODAY MAN BRING FATHER TALKING LEAF FROM SON COMMA ASKING FOR MORE GREEN TREE SLICES STOP SON WANT TAKE WOMAN TO FANCY CAVE WHERE FOOD AND MAGIC DRINK SERVED STOP BUT FATHER NOT MADE OF GREEN TREE SLICES BANG HUNTING BRONTOSAURUS NOT AS LUCRATIVE AS ONCE WAS STOP MANY PEOPLE WANT FATHER QUIT HUNT ALTOGETHER COMMA GET JOB IN OFFICE OR SOMETHING STOP MANY OTHER NOT EVEN BELIEVE FATHER SELL REAL BRONTO MEAT STOP THINK ALLIGATOR OR SIMILAR COMMA WHICH SOMETIME TRUE STOP SOMETIME SQUIRREL STOP POINT IS MUST SAY NO COMMA SON MUST EARN GREEN TREE SLICES BY SELF STOP FATHER HAPPY TO SEND SQUIRREL THO STOP SQUIRREL ALWAYS WORKED FOR FATHER COMMA WINK HYPHEN WINK BANG
TOG COMMA HUNTER OF BRONTOSAURUS

—*Patrick Kennedy*

COMING SOON.

An unforgivable crime. A thirst for revenge. This time, a hero will take justice into his own hands. But here's the catch: he's 57 years old!

That's right, get ready for your new action thriller starring a middle-aged man. Except this time, it's grittier and realer than ever. So you can forget Liam Neeson, Bruce Willis, Nicolas Cage, Keanu Reeves, Jackie Chan, Kevin Costner, and any other aging action star who has been in a movie where they have to rescue and/or avenge the death of a family member. Say hello to Frank Biebelberg, the grittiest, realest middle-aged action star you've ever met.

Frank is just a normal dad living a quiet life in a suburban town, when tragedy suddenly strikes. His daughter is kidnapped. And then his wife is kidnapped. And then his brother is kidnapped. And then his car is keyed. "Mondays," he mutters to himself, because that's what a gritty middle-aged guy says in a situation like this.

Who's fault is it? The Albanian mafia's. Why did they do it? He was unwittingly working as their accountant, and he's bad at math. He didn't carry a zero, and the Albanian mafia is angry.

But Frank will take matters into his own hands, even more so than one of those younger action stars, or even a similarly aged action star. Hold tight onto your popcorn as Frank gets into his Volvo, turns the keys, and drives straight to the police station. His car might be under the speed limit, but he's over the hill, which is what we think audiences want in movies like this. A normal guy in extraordinary circumstances. With a paunch.

And you better believe the camera is going to be shaky.

Are the police going to help? Of course not. But they're going to assure Frank Biebelberg that they'll handle everything, and at first he's going to believe them, because as a middle-aged man he has developed a sense of trust in authority figures. You'll watch with bated breath as he gradually grows more frustrated with the bureaucracy. He's going to ask to speak to their supervisor, and then he's going to angrily throw his cell phone against a wall because he doesn't know how to use an app and his daughter, who would normally explain it to him, is still kidnapped by the Albanian mafia. That's the kind of intensity you're gonna get in the most realistic middle-aged action flick ever made.

But guess what? Frank is going to take matters into his own hands again. He's going to meet up with old Army buddies and start training to become the world's ultimate killing machine and get his family back. He's going to show those younger, stronger mafia fighters who's boss.

And then he's going to quickly realize

let's learn ENGLISH

toadstool — toed-stool — towed stool — toad stool

DECONSTRUCTED ···· NYC ···· STREET FOODS

by Cerise Zelenets

Selection of warm nuts in pouch with addictive honey-roasted vapor.

Halal falafel gougére with 'white sauce' drizzle, topped with aged, translucent iceberg shreds.

Pepperoni 'sashimi,' frozen crust crouton. Served with spoon of mystery cheese bisque and rolled dollar bill straw.

OFF OFF OFF OFF BROADWAY

that this is a stupid idea. There's only so many quick cuts that a film editor can do to make it look like Frank is winning a martial arts battle with the Albanian mafia. Maybe he'll just focus on losing ten pounds instead.

Then Frank is really going to take matters into his own hands, so GET. READY. FOR. ACTION. First, he's going to lose those ten pounds, which is an awesome accomplishment, and then he's going to fight the Albanian mafia with his secret weapon. That's right—he's going to fight them with words.

So buckle up for the final showdown between a Baby Boomer and some younger, stronger bad guys! No spoilers, but Frank is going to say a lot of passive-aggressive remarks, and he's going to hurt some feelings! Because he's a middle-aged action star, and this time we're making him more realistic than ever.

—*Matthew Disler*

STORY STRUCTURE IS EASY!

Don't be intimidated by story structure. Why? Because you are a born storyteller. Why? Because you are human, and stories are humanity's first art form. The first one after cave painting, anyway. Also after inventing new positions for "doin' it." So, third art form—but third is still way up there on the list. Thus: you write good, already.

Sorry if that was confusing. Sometimes my natural storytelling, I don't know, browns out or something.

What I am trying to say is that good story structure is at the heart of everything you like. Everything. You know this intuitively. For example: the thing you like most is Star Wars. But without story structure, Star Wars would just be explosions. And action. And the most unforgettable characters ever written. I know that's starting to sound good, but, intuitively, you know it is not.

Pull out a blank piece of paper. The paper is your canvas! Now put that paper away because right now we're focused on theory. Story beats. Alright, enough theory; let's get into mega-theory.

Across the entire history of human culture, every hero follows one Heroic Path™. Think about it: it's true! It's even true in those experimental stories where the hero has text messaging, or is a girl.

If your hero's story's structure follows The Heroic Path™, audiences will "get it." But if your story does not follow it, audiences will have The Universal Negative Reaction To Bad Structure™. They will get bored, look at their phone, leave, take a Lyft to a sports match, get lite beer spilled on their good moccasins, and track beer stink into their mid-century bungalow over on North Pruitt Boulevard.

You know you've had this reaction to bad story structure!

Back to your paper. Write a large "1" in the corner. Now you have what we in the biz call "Page 1." That's where you'll write a great beginning. A great beginning is like a sunrise, probably—I am not up that early, unless I'm going to the airport. But your favorite novelist was up that early every day. Unless they were an alcoholic, in which case they preferred nights. And are very likely dead. Sorry. Anyway a great beginning is like a sunrise. And great endings are literal sunsets, because that feels "cinematic" (Latin for "Hollywood-y").

Hot tip: you can borrow your story structure from other stories. Because hot fact: great artists steal! Hot proof: all of Pablo Picasso's masterpieces are ripped off from the Sistine Chapel. What makes them masterpieces? He gave them his own spin. His spin was a big "© PABLO PICASSO" next to that one angel.

Great news: if you followed this Universal Story Structure Structure™, you now have a beginning, an ending, and the stolen-hit middle of *Star Wars 2*. Wasn't that easy? It was! Best of luck with the remaining details. If someone buys your story, my name goes next to yours in the "Written By" part. And as they say in Le Movies, "Fín"!

—*Alex Schmidt*

MY NAME IS SCZÖGLJÅTCH.

Hello! My name is Sczögljåtch, your tour guide. You can call me Shuggie, for sure.

Do you know my country? Look on your map. Some people say my country looks like a foot, with the heel pressing down on our neighbors to the south, but their wells were poisoned in Roman times, and they have been simple-minded ever since.

Look out the window on your left. You see a huge, grand statue of Our Leader, all in ivory, but elephants are dead already, so no problem. He is so good, Our Leader. You say we have no rights, but we have. We don't always choose to use them. My dear guests, please do not say anything bad about Our Leader, even in your hotel room or on Internet or email or text. Thank you.

I am so surprised to learn your Presidents owned slaves—Washington, Jefferson, all of them! Except your President Kennedy. He had no slaves. But he had a mulatto, I believe that.

Now please look out the right window and see our mercury extraction factory.

"My security system sucks."

Liquid soft pretzel ravioli, yellow mustard pearls, served under crumpled **Time Out** *under kosher salt block.*

Sous vide hot dog round, dehydrated generic bun dust, sweet relish foam, ketchup tuile.

$1.00 ice cold water sphere with chili powder drenched mango puree spaghetti straw handle.

Assortment of stale pastry "petit fours" with instant coffee sorbet.

Mercury is our leading export, mostly for use in rectal thermometers. We have a saying that maybe you don't know us, but we know you. Ha-ha.

I will tell you our history, okay? So we began as peasants, like everyone. Then Alexander the Great marched through here with his Greek army. One of his lieutenants asked him, "Why not take this land and have intermarriage with the women?" But he said, "Why bother?" So that's where comes from our motto "Why bother?" When you ask someone from here a question, they always answer, "Why bother?"

Ottomans conquered us next, but we didn't mind because even to us Ottomans seemed exotic. Have you been to Ottomania? I hope to go someday, if I pass all my exams. Next came the Habsburg family. They ruled us for almost 326 years. No one knows much about this period. World War I we lost, also World War II, but it was good, too, because we found nationalism. A hero arose from our people named Jozep Krzysztp. You know him? He raised an army of rag-tags, but in the end he was defeated. The Dog-Faced Woman betrayed him.

So now we are up to modern days. We are still mostly peasants because history is a circle, I believe that.

In remote parts of my country you will still find some of the original people. They are like your red Indians. We don't have cowboys of course, but I wish we did. They could fight each other and we could watch.

Interesting fact: we have more doctors than patients. Can U.S.A. say that?

We are now crossing the longest, highest bridge in my country. No guard rails because company that built it is bankrupt. Can Chinese help us? Who knows.

We are very family-oriented. For example, on your left on top of big cliff is new nuclear power plant—the good kind of nukes. It is owned by Our Leader's brother. The company shoring up cliff is owned by his brother's wife. When nuclear plant is turned on, all of houses in the valley will glow. So nice!

We will take a rest stop here by beautiful Lake Drêd. Oh, wait, soldiers are pushing something into the water. We will have the rest stop later. You can wait, yes?

The white cloud we are coming to is from our concrete factory, owned by Our Leader's eldest son, just 16 years old but so smart. You will stop coughing soon.

Nothing to see in the building we passed, just a supermarket. People are lined up because there's a rumor about potatoes inside.

Thus ends our brief tour. Please spend your leisure time as we do, walking in the public square with our heads bowed humbly, looking straight down. You can watch the military parade later if you choose, but no photos, and erase from your memory the faces of our courageous soldiers. We also have coffee shops for idlers. By the end of the day you will be exhausted, for sure.

I will now leave you at the checkpoint. I have enjoyed this tour as much as you have. Good-bye to you!

—*Phil Witte*

AFGHANISTANDARD.

After almost two decades at war in Afghanistan, newspaper and magazine stories have become increasingly… routine. To save everyone time and energy, compiled below are the headlines for the next 20 years. While some headlines might not fit exactly, they'll all end up finding a home, just as sure as the Pentagon will promise that 'the war will be over next year.'

2019: War grinds on in Afghanistan
2020: No end in sight for US troops in Afghanistan
2021: 20 years in Afghanistan: a retrospective
2022: General asks: "What next?" for America's longest war
2023: War in Afghanistan continues, participants say
2024: Generals confident new "counterinsurgency" strategy will deliver long-awaited win
2025: Afghans, US brace for Spring Offensive
2026: 25 years in Afghanistan: A look back
2027: War should end "soon," Generals say
2028: Imagining a world where the United States is not at war in Afghanistan
2029: Taliban offers possibility of truce with the United States on Afghan question
2030: In Afghanistan war, war grinds on
2031: Can you believe it's been 30 years? The U.S. in Afghanistan
2032: New strategy proposed by Generals: Truce with Taliban
2033: Inside the longest war since some Roman shit
2034: Children of the heroes of the war in Afghanistan—what they're doing now
2035: No end in sight for Afghan, U.S. troops (in Afghanistan)
2036: Spring offensive looms for allied troops
2037: Promising gains made in Afghani-

"Sorry. That may have been the booze lashing out."

stan, some suggest
2038: Grinding, war, Afghanistan, troops, etc.
2039: TALIBAN SEIZE WASHINGTON / President missing / Monument in flames / Allah Akbar!, say citizen converts to sharia law.
—*Adrian Bonenberger*

AN AFTERNOON IN PORTLAND.

You're walking around town one beautiful afternoon when it hits you: I could really use a cup of coffee. Fortunately, you find yourself in Portland, Oregon, so getting coffee is about as difficult as locating the back of your eyelids. You cross the street and into The Beard & Bean.

"What can I do you for?" asks a mustache attached to a human face.

"One coffee, please."

"Would you like to try our new brew? The beans have passed through three generations of wild mountain goats, and were hand-roasted at 2,000 feet below sea level."

"I suppose I should," you say. It seems rude to say no, given all the effort.

After placing a down payment on your eight-ounce beverage, the iPad shows three tip options:
1. Hand over your watch.
2. (Paid sponsorship with Wells Fargo) Take out a $15,000 business loan on behalf of your barista.
3. Designate your barista as the primary beneficiary of your living will.

You fork over your $200 watch, then climb into a cryogenic freezing chamber.

One lunar cycle later, your beverage is ready. At this point, you've missed three of your daughter's soccer games, not to mention your flight home. Of course, you've been fired, and most people back home think you're dead. But this is a special brew. You thank the barista, with whom you feel a closer connection, now that you've grown a full beard.

"Enjoy, man," he says. You plan to. You walk your coffee outside and over to the edge of the Willamette River before taking your first sip. It's a rare sunny day in Portland, and not too hot. Despite all the angry—then concerned—then despairing—texts, life is good.

"Lick. Lick. Lick. Lick. Lick. Lick. Lick. Lick. Lick. Lick. Lick. Lick. Lick. Lick. Lick. Lick. Then I thought, why not just take a real bath?"

At first, you are physically shaken by the coffee's acidity. Fighting the full-body pucker, you squint down at the tan line where your watch used to be; surely it's an acquired taste.

You choke down sip after sip of sour bean water as colorful fixed-gear bikes and ludicrously high-end strollers pass you by. Just as you begin to lose yourself in the spectacle of wheels, a green, yellow and black hacky sack ricochets off the side of your head.

A man—either a member of the homeless community or an A-list celebrity—emerges from behind a nearby oak.

"Hey man, you got our sack?" You toss him the pouch. "You wanna get in?" he asks.

"I'm good." You've still got $14,500 of coffee left.

"Come ooon, man, don't be sackreligious!"

"Alright fine," you say, putting the coffee in the lee of the oak, so it won't get kicked over. "Hack me in."

"First you gotta hit this," he says, producing a joint from behind his ear. Before you can ask whether it too was grown 2,000 feet below sea level, two more homeless/celebrities pop out from behind the same tree, wrestle you to the ground, and force the joint upon you. It contains far more than just marijuana; as you fade into a Lewis Carrollesque delirium, every iota of regret you've ever experienced floods into your consciousness, compressed into a single unbearable moment. At the climax of your emotional agony, you lock eyes with the owner of the hacky sack and realize it's none other than Shia Labeouf. You feel as though you've known him—truly known him—for a thousand lifetimes. Your anxiety lifts.

Shia convinces you to stay in Portland another week to help him develop his latest experimental performance piece. He thinks it could be the big break that gets his career back on track, and you believe in him more than you've ever believed in yourself. And you've already lost your job, so…

As the sun sets upon the Willamette, the two of you make long, passionate love on the boulevard overlooking the water. After, you finish the coffee. Shia compares it favorably to ayahuasca.

Portland, you think to yourself. *What a town.*

—*Thatcher Jensen*

HOW TO CLEAN YOUR APARTMENT.

1. Look at the dust, debris and grime. Stare at your sink drain until you envision the germs at hundreds of times their size. Hear their command: "Give up."

"On cleaning?"

"For starters."

2. Worry about how this all looks. Your parents would be ashamed. They

always thought you were bright, handsome, promising. You're 35 and there's a dish in your sink that's been so soiled, for so long, that you're probably just going to throw it away.

3. Feel like you can't control any aspect of your life.
Others are exercising, excelling in their careers, and enjoying loving relationships. You can't even clean weekly so it doesn't look like you live in a meth den (minus the mood-enhancing benefits of meth).

4. Hide beneath the covers.
It's dark and warm in there. Safe. You needn't buy gloves, sponges, and spray, clean the vacuum filter, charge the vacuum battery, and empty the vacuum canister before you even start cleaning. Go back to sleep.

5. Panic about what this filth does to your health.
You can't sleep. You see the color of the windowsill. Car exhaust, asbestos particles, and whatever is rising off of the canal seep through the tiny gaps between your window and your wall second by second, and then into your lungs.

6. Try for one minute to clean the bathtub and then realize it's never going to look white.
Go to the store. Buy spray, gloves, and a sponge. Bring them into the bathroom. Put on the gloves. Spray the spray. Scrub. It still looks kind of brown. Scrub again. Still brown. That's what you get for trying.

7. Hire a maid and feel guilty about asking someone to clean for you.
Feel like a privileged monster as you watch her unpack her supplies. You can't order another human being to tidy up your mess. Pay 20 percent more than the agreed-upon fee; frantically tell her this was all a mistake and she must leave.

8. Wait 80 years. Die. Someone will clean your home before the next person moves in.
From dust you came, to dust you will return, and in dust you lived. Your apartment will be cleaned, one way or another.

9. Wait 7.6 billion years for the Sun to expand into a red giant and swallow the Earth.
All the dust on your floor, soap scum in your bathroom, and food particles in the crack between your stove and the wall have disappeared because the Sun swallowed the Earth and incinerated everything.

10. Wait 10,000,000,000,000,000,000,000,000,000,000,000,000,000,000,000,000,000,000,000,000,000,000,000,000,000,000,000,000,000,000,000 more years for the heat death of the universe.
The universe has expanded so much that it's reached thermodynamic equilibrium and is too cold to move ever again. Every molecule is still, in place, incapable of becoming disorganized. Your apartment is absolutely, irreversibly, finally clean.
—*Jonathan Zeller*

GO-SHICHI-GO.
*One has to assume
that haiku must be awesome
when in Japanese.*
—*David Chelsea*

FROM FANTAGRAPHICS UNDERGROUND

A Fistful of Drawings
A Graphic Journal by Joe Ciardiello

A paean to Hollywood, a love letter to the Western, and a tribute to its Italian influences.

In this gorgeous graphic memoir, Joe Ciardiello gracefully weaves together his Italian family history and the mythology of the American West while paying homage to the classic movie and TV Westerns of the '50s and '60s. Featuring Ciardiello's signature sinuous ink line and vivid watercolors, *A Fistful of Drawings* illuminates the oversized characters that dominated the cinematic American West—Clint Eastwood, John Ford, John Wayne, Claudia Cardinale, Sophia Loren, and many more.

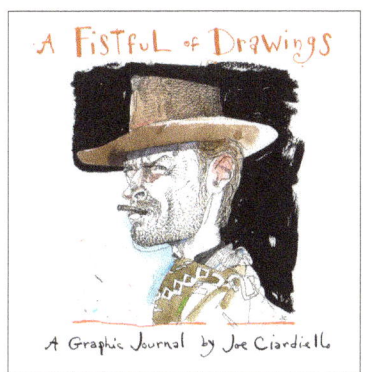

"Joe Ciardiello has been one of America's finest artists for the last generation. Here we finally have his magnum opus: a project that brilliantly blends mid-century culture, the Italian-American experience, and his own personal story into something rare in form, unique in content, and startlingly deep in every nuance. It is a work of genius."

—Steve Brodner
Illustrator/political satirist

AVAILABLE FEBRUARY 2019. PREORDER NOW AT FANTAGRAPHICS.COM

SPRINGFIELD CONFIDENTIAL

JOKES, SECRETS, AND OUTRIGHT LIES FROM A LIFETIME WRITING FOR The Simpsons

"A truly great comic is rare. Mike Reiss, by definition, is a rarity." —CONAN O'BRIEN

In celebration of *The Simpsons* 30th anniversary, the show's longest-serving writer and producer shares stories, scandals, and gossip about working with AMERICA'S MOST ICONIC CARTOON FAMILY.

Featuring interviews with JUDD APATOW, CONAN O'BRIEN, and *Simpsons* legends AL JEAN, NANCY CARTWRIGHT, DAN CASTELLANETA, and more!

ON SALE NOW

DEY ST.

www.hc.com

AFFIRMATION
BY ALICIA KRAFT

I BELIEVE IN YOU

Be strong—Ramón at the carving station will understand

Okay, Joey, today is the day. No more excuses. In fifteen minutes' time, when you find yourself in line at Old Country Buffet, you are going to help yourself to a variety of wholesome, tasty dishes—and at least one of those items is not going to be ham.

Make no mistake: ham will probably make an appearance, and a generous one at that. But when you carry your tray back to the table where your family is enjoying their Sunday dinner, today that tray will not be an unbroken mountain of pink, salted pork. You will not eat until you are full, only to find that you have eaten nothing but ham. You will not feel ill at the sight of any pieces of uneaten ham left on your plate, vowing to never eat ham again, all the while knowing that you will do it again next time. That all-or-nothing mentality has no place at your table today.

No, Joey. Today, when you see the spread of delightful side dishes, pastas, and non-ham meats that Old Country Buffet offers its diners, you will stop walking and you will scoop one of them onto your plate. They might have that baked mostaccioli that your daughter was enjoying two weeks ago, and today you can share that experience with her. Some spicy chicken wings might just hit the spot. Maybe even some sauteed spinach will find its way into your spread.

Heck, if things go well, who's to say you couldn't sample all three?

Do not, even for one second, let yourself think that Ramón at the meat carving station will take offense when you approach him with a plate that has other food items already on it. You do not need to leave your non-ham plate at the table so you can approach him unencumbered. Ramón is a true professional. He can easily place heaping portions of thick, sweet ham onto one side of a plate without disrupting its other contents. You've seen him do it with other people all the time.

Sure, Ramón may take genuine pleasure in making small talk about the 49ers while he slices hearty chunks of cured meat just for you, but it doesn't necessarily follow that he will feel pain if your conversation takes a few seconds less than usual. In all honesty, he would probably not even be upset if you skipped the carving station altogether today. Ramón respects the sanctity of his customers' free will, even when it means a slower day at work.

But your choices today are not for Ramón. They are for Joey and Joey alone. And this time, Joey, you are not going to make your blood pressure spike with the sudden influx of sodium that only a tray piled exclusively with ham can provide. If your blood pressure spikes today, it will be from the salt in all of the other delicious foods that you eat at Old Country Buffet—in addition to a still-ample serving of steaming, fresh ham.

You can do it, Joey; if only just for this week.

ALICIA KRAFT
(@theAliciaKraft) *is a comedy writer from Chicago who contributes to* **The Onion** *and would die for any cat. She asks for nothing but your effusive praise and money.*

SEASONS' GREETINGS FROM THE STEINBECK FAMILY

BY RIANE KONC

Dear friends and family,
Merry Christmas and Happy Holidays! It has been another dry and brutal year in the Salinas Valley. In case you do not have our previous holiday letters on hand, I will remind you that the Salinas Valley is a lush depression winding through the mountains west of the San Joaquin Valley. There is enough sunlight and enough rain in the Salinas that just about any crop a man plants should grow and flourish. A man could live off the land, if he put his mind to it. He could sell enough beans or corn or, hell, oranges even, that he could keep his belly tight and his flask full, and he could put a roof over his head, and once in a while, if he got the urge to, he could even go into town and lie with a woman. Of course I (John) am only joking about that last part!! As many of you know, Elaine and I will be celebrating 30 years of marriage this year!! We are Truly Blessed.

Elaine and I celebrated our anniversary the way we do every year: shivering outside by a dying fire. Our friends tried to throw us a surprise party, but there are no surprises in this world: only choices a man makes and things a man does. So we sat next to each other on a log, huddled together for warmth, our faces drawn and serious. We passed a whiskey bottle back 'n forth between us, taking long pulls from it, and in this way we passed the time. We knew that in a few hours, all of the men in the Salinas Valley would rise and would look for work, but they would find no work. The women would rise and look for their men, but they would find no men, only animals–for that is what being without work does to a man. But until that time, we would stoke the fire and we would take pulls from our whiskey and we would delight in each other's bodies. We also exchanged gifts! The 30-year gift is traditionally pearl, but, well, you know, so I gave Elaine what I give her most years: something fashioned from a corn husk. She in turn gave me what every man desires from his wife: a personalized flask with a moustache on it. When I drink from it, it appears as though I have a moustache, which brings me endless delight, and even Elaine, whose body has borne many children and has known unspeakable suffering, when she sees me drink from it, considers me as a man and desires me.

Our youngest, John Jr., is an exceptional student and was given responsibility for the class pet, a turtle. We were not surprised when it died, for the crops were bad that year. John's teacher took pity upon us, and trusted us to care for the class mouse, which died, then a bunny, which died, then a bitch pup, which died, then a shoat pig, which died, and then finally, a beautiful chestnut mare, who gave birth to a foal late one winter night, and then died before the foal could suckle from its teat. It was a slow and anguished death and brought no pleasure to the world. I watched as John Jr. pulled the foal from the mare's steaming belly, and saw that it was barely bigger'n him. Its ears were slick and wet and its legs wobbled when it stood. In the morning, John Jr. and I took this pony out behind the barn and let it lower its head into the feed bin, and while it ate I put the muzzle of my gun to its head and I pulled the trigger. I am not ashamed to tell you that I cried when the body fell to the unforgiving earth, for the death of a horse is one of the times in a man's life when he will want to cry, and should. I buried the foal beneath the magnolia tree and then I returned to work. When my son asked me why I shot the class pet, I told him the truth, which is that the Salinas Valley is no place for children.

RIANE KONC (@theillustrious) *writes for* **The New Yorker, The New York Times,** *and many other venues. Her interests include short lists, Oxford commas, and self-referential jokes. She peaked in 4th grade.*

STEPHEN KRONINGER

Tom, our oldest, has become engaged to a plain woman with sturdy hands. She puts a light in him in the way only a woman can. Several things imitate this light: a belly full of whiskey, maybe, or the way a man feels when he's built something with his own hands. Hell, a man walking in his fields may consider the dirt under his feet and feel something swell up inside him like creation. But these lights are all imitation when held up to the great sun of a woman's love. That love can bring a man back to life. Why, a good woman might do more for a man's resurrection than any preacher. Also Tom and Diane are registered at Crate and Barrel. They would be humbled to own either.

There's a lot to say about this year that hasn't been said, and maybe a lot that's been said that shouldn't've in the first place. Elaine and I finally took our dream vacation, which was a grueling eight-month trek west in search of fertile soil. We did not find it, nor did we expect to. Elaine and I also have begun several new hobbies this year, among them Bikram yoga. There is a saying I found on a Pinterest board regarding Bikram yoga, and it is this: "Sweat is the most honest thing to leave a man's body, not takin' into account blood, or piss, or bile. Of course most bile does not come from the liver, as some suppose, but rather from the mouth of a man who's been made to feel that he's nothin.' A man like that is dangerous'n any snake." What was delightful about this quote is that it was typed upon a postcard where two young women appeared to be whispering this very thought to each other while drinking milkshakes. This juxtaposition brought me a quiet pleasure, and it is the sort of pleasure I shall live off of for several months.

That's all until next year. In the hustle'n the bustle of the holiday season, don't forget to focus on what truly matters this Christmas: defending the migrant worker and doing honest labor with your hands.

This is the only thing a man can do, and it is enough.

— *The Steinbecks*

HEALTH FOOD HELL

BY DAVE HANSON

Come with us, won't you, back to Thanksgiving 1971...

My mother believed that a single slice of American cheese would cause cancer, that white flour was as toxic as enriched uranium, that just a nibble of bacon would strangle your arteries. When I was a child, we'd drive 45 minutes to pay top dollar for apple juice with extra sludge. She mailed away to an organic farm in Pennsylvania for unsulphured apricots as tough and sinewy as the dehydrated pig's ears they sell at Petco for your dog.

Mom wasn't just passionate about healthy food, she actually felt venomous toward any other kind. She pronounced "cookie" with the same contempt Himmler must've reserved for the word "Jew." And so for years, kale and whole grains were stuffed down my throat like I was a goose having its liver larded for the world's healthiest *foie gras*.

But in this long, nauseating childhood, one afternoon stands out: Thanksgiving 1971.

I was 12. Around 3:00 my mother called me inside for the holiday feast. "It's delicious and nutritious!" she trilled as I entered the house—but the odor said she was lying. "This food cuts out the middle man," I said, wrinkling my nose. "It already smells like it's been farted."

Seated at the table, the four of us looked like some kind of *Whole Earth Catalog* version of "The Munsters." Our hair had been left greasy by organic phosphorus-free shampoo and we wore hippie clothes that befitted down-on-their-luck lesbians. My mother was 5'1" and 99 pounds of soy-burning energy who could easily hoist a 50 pound bag of brown rice over her shoulder; my stepfather had a wildly unkempt beard that nowadays would get him a cavity search at any U.S. airport. My sister sat in her high chair, her face radiating an otherworldly orange glow, the result of being pumped full of carrot juice. And me? What a hunk. 90 pounds of scowl with black-framed eyeglasses held together with masking tape, my hair long and oily and styled with the same scissors Mom uses to cut burrs from the dog's ass-hair.

My mother had spent the whole day cooking—which is to say she'd taken a wad of bulgur, lentils, and diced tofu and smooshed it into the shape of a turkey. Side dishes included steamed parsnips, mustard greens in a foamy turbid broth, a grain dish made from seaweed and groats, and a gravy made from whole wheat flour, soy sauce, and apple cider.

My sister and I realized that Mom was trying to show her love for us, but I was kind of wishing she'd do it with hugs.

The mashed potatoes were the only thing that looked edible; I put a pile on my plate but before I could take a bite my mother had dumped a watery ladleful of beets beside it. I zeroed in on the unstained center of the potatoes, where they hadn't yet leeched up the soil-scented juice. But when the spuds hit my tongue, the bitterness made me squawk.

"Mom, there's something wrong with these potatoes—"

"I know!" she said. "They have no fiber or nourishment! So I added raw wheat germ."

"Joey's mom puts sour cream, bacon, and cheddar cheese in potatoes..."

"...and Joey's grandmother died of kidney failure at 61," my mother chirped victoriously. I was bracing for a detailed lecture on the many virtues of raw wheat germ, when I was saved by a loud crash from the living room. I forgot to mention something: this was the year we raised baby goats in the house.

The last few weeks, all family activity had been set against a backdrop of five cartwheeling, headbutting, hopping, flipping, flopping, clopping, crashing, twirling, absolutely maniacal baby goats. Why? Because Mom had read that goat's milk was healthier than cow's milk. Back then there was no Trader Joe's, so "teat-to-table" was the only option.

We scoured the *Pennysaver*'s "Goats For Sale" section—remember, this was 1971— and soon a nanny named Josephine was nestled in the back seat of our Volkswagen. My parents discretely pimped her out, and five months later, Josephine delivered a flock of baby goats — who I promptly named after members of the Yankees'. They were born during a cold snap so my mother decreed they would be living indoors, with us. She installed safety gates in the living room doorways, and we spread a few hundred pounds of newspaper on the floor.

Where you find baby goats, you'll also find a vigorously lactating mother. What did this mean for us? Homemade goat yogurt, goat ricotta, and goat butter, all of which, naturally, smelled like a goat.

We all leapt from the table and ran to the living room: Stottlemyre, Blomberg and Swoboda had pulled down Mom's gargantuan copy of *The Encyclopedia Of Organic Gardening*; Thurman Munson was now eating its cover. Like she had done with my hopes for a normal childhood, Mom put the encyclopedia out of reach and then returned to the dinner table, leaving the goats to frolic and pee in the next room.

I trudged through the awful meal like a prisoner—which, in some sense, I was. Even dessert was a gritty buzzkill, a shapeless mound of honey, grains and carob. My mother had spent all of my twelve years arguing that carob "tastes just like chocolate," but it was pointless.

DAVE HANSON *has written for Letterman,* **National Lampoon** *and* **The New Yorker***. He's wiling away the time before death writing an unpublishable novel he can adapt into an unproduceable screenplay.*

I'd resigned myself to flavorless misery—followed by hours of acrid, pasty reflux—when I saw a silver flash outside. Curious, Mom and I went to the window. A gleaming Mercedes was wobbling along our unpaved driveway. "It's Eddie!" I cried desperately. Eddie was my mother's cousin, a doctor from Manhattan who, and this is key, ate normally. Adrenaline coursed through me as we hurried out to greet him, his normal-eating wife Joyce, and their normal-eating kids Joan, Anne, and Will.

"We were driving upstate," Eddie said, "and I thought, let's stop and wish you guys a happy holiday."

I relished their visits; I loved the children, and Eddie and Joyce brought a rare soupçon of civilization to our hairshirt existence. Whenever they visited, they'd bring bags of delicious items from Zabar's, plus marzipan, chocolates, and desserts from New York's finest bakeries. Joyce reached into the trunk and began to pull out pastry boxes; I was transformed into a dog in heat. Practically feral from the smell of white flour and refined sugar, the flesh on my pleasure receptors was pulled tight. Joyce and Eddie's Mercedes was the relief plane delivering supplies to a remote earthquake-stricken community; they were missionaries bringing medicine to the forgotten leper colony; they were my Conjugal Visitor.

"Hello Uncle Eddie, hello Aunt Joyce," I stammered out, holding it together as best I could. "Great to see you." (Sugar and white flour had another effect on me—they made me polite and well-mannered.)

A few minutes later—after we'd explained the goats in the living room—we were settled inside over tea and an incredible assortment of desserts.

"Have you heard from Aunt Ingeborg?" asked Eddie.

"I got a letter last month," answered my mother, a hard eye following my hand as I plucked a glistening Napoleon from a plate. Joan, Anne and Will played nearby, mystified by my choice to sit with the grown-ups. They didn't understand; they never had to depend on my mother for a meal.

Eddie was telling a story but I didn't hear him; I was in a wild rapture as the sugar and butter delivered a skullbusting bolt of ecstasy. Out of the corner of one pleasure-glazed eye, I caught my mother staring daggers and I couldn't hide my sly smirk. Almost as delicious as the sugar rush was the visible frustration of my oppressor. Mom wanted to scream that this food was garbage, but with the generous benefactor standing by, her hands were tied. Shrugging off the weight of her glare, I stuffed myself silly. Some people like turkey or stuffing, but it was the taste of forbidden fruit filling that made this the best Thanksgiving ever.

My holiday table this year is replete with turkey, Stovetop stuffing, Ambrosia salad, and Hawaiian rolls—but it's been a long road. As an adult, there was a constant undertow of anxiety that everything I ate was killing me…until I found a cure: following Uncle Eddie on Facebook. In spite of all the raw wheat germ, liquid aminos and goat milk fresh from the teat, my mother died in 2011, a way-too-young victim of cancer. But Eddie, who was born six years before Mom? As I write this, he's on a cruise from Havana to Hawaii. His trophy wife just posted pictures of him posing in a pink '56 Chevy with a gaggle of assy Latinas. Yesterday I saw photos from a restaurant where they were knocking back mojitos and tearing into a platter of grilled meat. That's how I want to be when I grow up—even if that meat is goat. B

MODERN ROMANCE
BY RISA MICKENBERG

UNSUBSCRIBE ME
Let's not say anything we'll both regret

Do you really want to unsubscribe from this list? We hate to see you go. Did we do something wrong? We thought everything was going really well. This just kind of feels like it came out of nowhere.

You don't wish to receive emails in the future. The future?! That sounds like an awfully long time. :-) How about we give you some space and circle back when you're less cranky?

Was this a mistake? Did you forward one of our emails to a friend and they clicked the unsubscribe link, not realizing they were in fact unsubscribing you from this list—and now we have to go through this whole guessing game about our relationship status because of their carelessness?

Okay! We get it. "Unsubscribe me." Fine.

Please take a moment to tell us why you're choosing to unsubscribe. Check all that apply:
- ☐ *I never signed up for this mailing list.*
- ☐ *These emails are SPAM and should be reported.*
- ☐ *I'm just pre-menstrual and when I get this way I lash out at everyone close to me.*

We thought you liked all this attention. We had no idea it was bothering you until now—so how about this:

Manage the way you would like to receive correspondence from us in the future. Choose one:

Emotionally available, not afraid of intimacy. Yes! I appreciate a little attention once in a while! I want to be the first to know about special sales, new collections, private events, neat stuff that just inspires you. What I'm saying is, don't hold back whenever you're thinking about me throughout the day. *5-10 emails a day.*

I have other sources of emotional support but… I still want to enjoy exclusive savings and special offers. Please: I still want you in my life. *1-2 emails a week.*

Everything's cool. I'm seriously just really busy right now. I promise I'm not being weird. Yes I want to hear about great seasonal savings and everything. Don't be so paranoid. *Try to keep it to 2 emails a month but if you really need to get in touch, of course it's okay.*

Come ride my emotional rollercoaster. I run hot and cold and you're never going to know how I'm feeling. I'll be totally receptive and affectionate for a couple of days and then, for no apparent reason, I'll just need to be left alone. *Sporadic emails, sometimes 20 a day, then nothing for 2 months.*

Unsubscribe me, ha ha, just kidding. I want that thrilling, angry "rush" I get from unsubscribing but it's more of a gesture. *Wait 2 weeks, then 3 emails a week, ramping up to 2 emails a day and we'll take it from there.*

UNSUBCRIBE ME!!! UNSUBSCRIBE ME!!! UNSUBSCRIBE ME DAMMIT!!!!!!!! I'm 100% sure I want to be unsubscribed forever from this mailing list. Even if you're going out of business, I don't want to know about it and this is how I am: I just do whatever I want without stopping to think for a minute about what the other person needs or what my role was in this or what I could have done to change things.

Congratulations. You're only a few clicks away from seriously ending this but if you shop now, you'll enjoy free shipping on any purchase over $50 so…

One last question here. We think you owe us that. Don't you think you're being a little selfish? When all we're doing is letting you know great deals on things like women's cashmere sweaters in a variety of fall colors for only $32?

Remember when you bought those three mohair scarves? Then wrote that really beautiful four-star review on our site about how hard it is to shop for your mother but how this was the perfect thing and totally worth it for the price? Do you seriously want to unsubscribe after all that? *Seriously?*

Are you sure you wish to stop ALL emails? It's just that we have this huge friends and family sale coming up…

Fine!!! Although, frankly we don't see why you can't just leave your name on the list. It's just as easy to delete an email as it is to go through this whole rigmarole. Sorry, but this whole thing is ridiculous to us. Direct them to your SPAM folder—or just don't open them! *God!* They can't be so intolerable that you have to be so cold-blooded about it. "Unsubscribe me." We've been nothing but great to you for years, and then just "unsubscribe me." Seriously, *fuck you.*

Please enter the email address you wish to have removed. Please re-enter the email address.

You will receive an email confirming that you have successfully unsubscribed and we have to say, your timing is pretty crappy. You could have at least waited until after the holidays. This time of year is always difficult which is why we might have come across as a little needy. If you'd like to just wait till after the holidays and see how you feel, click here.

You may resubscribe at any time. We're not going to hold it against you. That was one of the things that was always true about our relationship—we never asked much of you at all. It was pretty one-sided and we were fine with that. Ironic how *you're* the one pulling away.

This will be your final correspondence from us. Thank you for giving us the opportunity to correspond with you, cruel mistress. Hope you die alone in a pool of your own urine. B

RISA MICKENBERG *(@taxidriverwisdm) is a writer, performer and flenser holding it down in New York City. Her feature film,* EGG, *a bleak comedy, will be in theaters January 18th.*

JONATHAN PLOTKIN

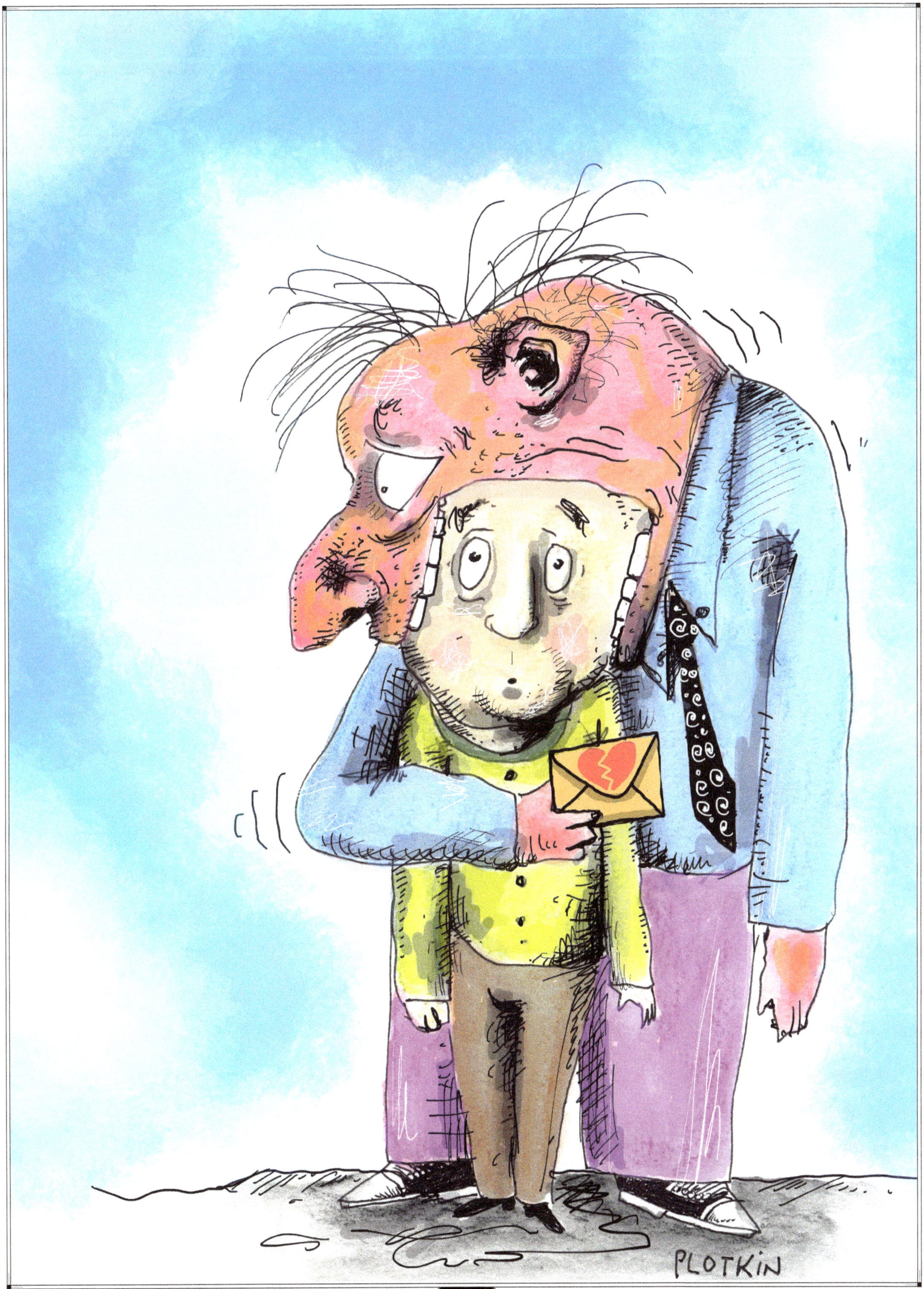
PLOTKIN

MERRY MITHRAS, ONE AND ALL

BY MIKE REISS

Happiness is…ritual sacrifice

It is the year 312 A.D., and Constantine the Great must choose a state religion to unify his sprawling empire. His choices: Christianity or Mithraism. The latter is a cruel Persian cult celebrating war, the king, and the ritual sacrifice of bulls.

On the eve of battle, Constantine receives a sign: the clouds have formed a cross. "Let the word go forth—the faith of this land shall be Christianity!" The winds shift slightly, and the cross becomes a pair of bull's horns. "Scratch that," says Constantine. "Let's go with the other one."

Western civilization is only slightly different under Mithraism: the world is a little bit colder, more violent, less civil. (France is virtually unchanged.) But the differences become more pronounced around the holiday season, as the old chestnuts—beloved books and movies—are dusted off.

A Mithras Carol tells the story of Ebenezer Scrooge, a man whose generosity and kind heart make him the laughingstock of London; it is only after the visit of three ghosts that Scrooge learns the true meaning of Mithras: screw the poor. Scrooge mends his ways and becomes ruthless and rich; Bob Cratchit gets fired, Tiny Tim dies, and all ends happily.

Dr. Seuss' *How the Grinch Stole Mithras* is an even darker tale of rejected redemption:

"…Though the Grinch brought back each bauble and present
The people of Whoville were rather unpleasant.
They twisted his tail and they tweaked his Grinch-nose
They tore off his twangler and stomped his Grinch-toes.
And Cindy Lou Who watched it all without flinching
She giggled and goggled all through the Grinch lynching."

But nothing captures the holiday spirit quite like the animated special *A Charlie Brown Mithras*. First broadcast in 1968, after *Perry Como's Holiday in Tehran*, the cartoon's conclusion still brings a lump to one's throat:

(The Peanuts gang is dancing as Charlie Brown returns from the stockyards.)

CHARLIE BROWN
Attention everyone. I have selected a bull for this year's ritual sacrifice.

(A sway-backed, bone-thin BULL enters. The gang LAUGHS DERISIVELY. The bull COUGHS CONVULSIVELY.)

VIOLET
Charlie Brown, you've been dumb before, but this time you really blew it.

SALLY
Blockhead!

LUCY
Christian!

CHARLIE BROWN
Everything I do turns into a disaster. Doesn't anyone know what Mithras is all about?

LINUS
I do, Charlie Brown. Lights, please?

(a SPOTLIGHT hits him)

"For lo, a raven came unto Mithra and told him to slay the bull. And Mithra was sore afraid. But when the bull died, his carcass became the moon. Its tail became grain and its blood became grape. And from its genitals came the seed that shaped every creature on earth."

(The Peanuts gang is visibly moved. Lucy pats the WHEEZING bull.)

LUCY
I never thought it was a bad little bull. Maybe all it needs is a little love.

(She sweetly plunges a dagger into the bull's throat. As it bleeds out, kicking and wailing, the children SING SWEETLY:)

PEANUTS GANG
Hark, the blood flows from the cattle
Soaking in our sacred soils
Mithra, guard our souls in battle
Smite our enemies with boils…

ANNOUNCER (V.O.)
"A Charlie Brown Mithras." Brought to you by Dolly Madison snack cakes. And Colt Firearms. Don't both belong in your child's lunch box?

MIKE REISS *has won four Emmys and a Peabody during his twenty-six years writing for* **The Simpsons**. *Reiss also co-created* **The Critic**, *and created Showtime's hit cartoon* **Queer Duck** *(about a gay duck).*

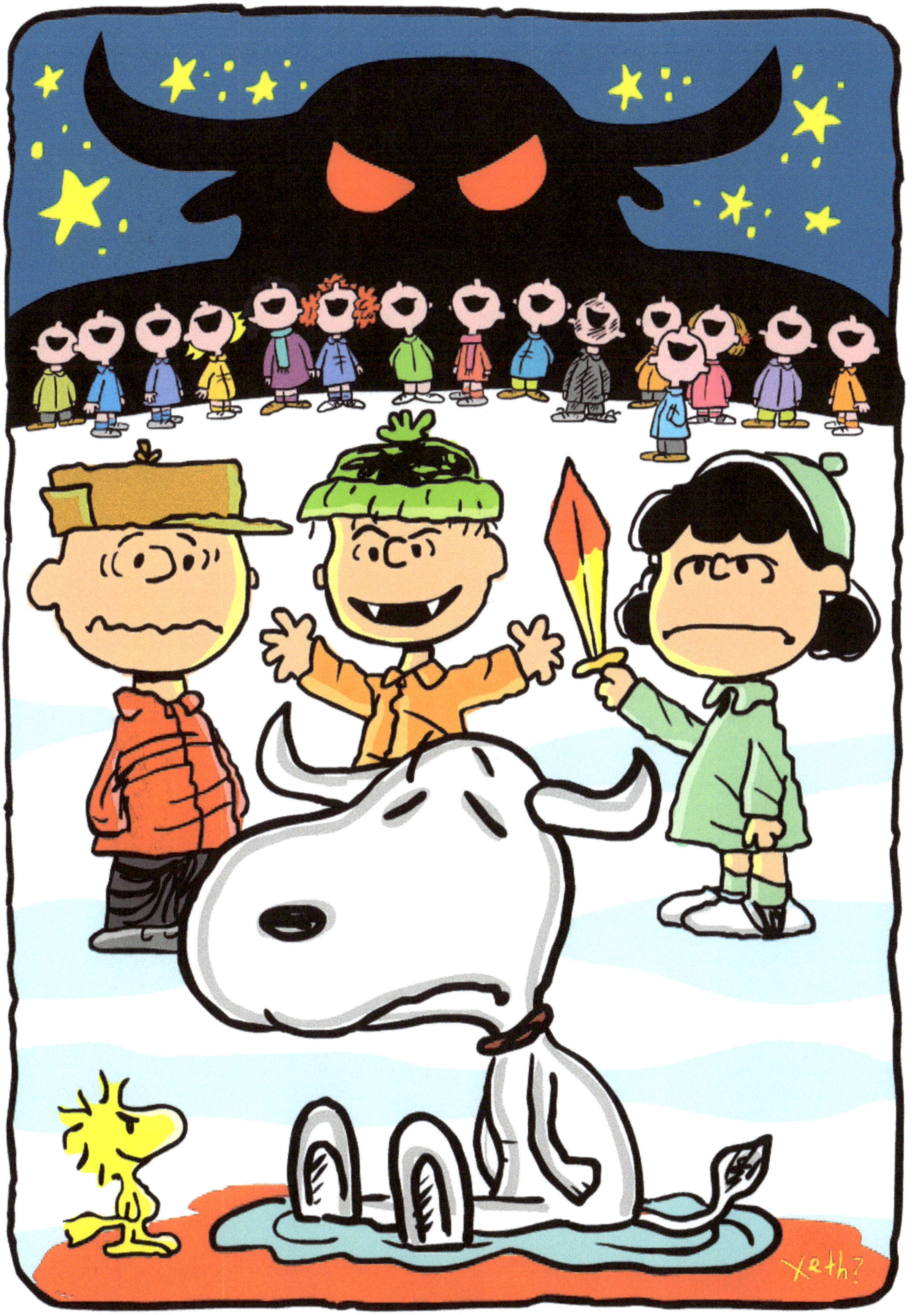
Xeth?

HOLIDAY 2018
BY TIM HARROD
NO, VIRGINIA
Inside the stocking there is only…emptiness

In 1897, *The New York Sun* published a letter by eight-year-old Virginia O'Hanlon and its response by Editor Francis Church, an exchange which would grow to be a perennial classic.

As Yuletide sentiment once more pervades the land, and seeing that *The Sun* has long since set from the journalistic landscape, we take great pride in reprinting the plaintive inquiry of a curious child and its wise response.

............◆............

Dear Editor: I am 8 years old. Some of my little friends say there is no Santa Claus. Papa says, "If you see it in The Sun *it's so." Please tell me the truth: Is there a Santa Claus?*
—Virginia O'Hanlon
115 West Ninety-Fifth Street

Virginia, you are eight years of age and you are asking whether a magical flying man visits multiplied-millions of homes in a single night? I suggest you listen to these "little friends" of yours. They sound pretty sharp, and if you and they are ever lost on a camping trip, I vehemently suggest putting them in charge. But let me approach your inquiry in this way: On Christmas Eve, do you leave some manner of food out for Santa, as many children customarily do? Now, having never met you and knowing nothing about the O'Hanlon family: it is a kind of food your Papa enjoys, isn't it? *Do you see where I am going with this?*

No, Virginia, there is no Santa Claus. Your home will not be surreptitiously invaded by a monumentally wealthy elf-man who rewards your fealty to his capricious moral code with trinkets and baubles; You get enough of that *ad hoc* moralizing, I am sure, from your parents, schoolmasters and clergy with their selfish and competing notions of how childhood "ought to" be.

Neither, Virginia, is there a Jesus Christ, nor a Jehovah, nor any force benevolent or malevolent which judgmentally supervises us from afar. Though you own the pleasure of total privacy in your personal affairs, know that this is neither gift nor privilege, but a happenstance artifact of how the universe has accreted, and the price of this liberty is a coldly indifferent cosmos which would not so much recover from your immediate death as fail to notice it, not for a thousandth of a second, nor one-tenth of one-ten-thousandth of a second.

You will one day grow to adulthood and become a parent yourself, and in that time, to your own little ones, you will perpetuate the endless lie of Santa Claus, the baroque charade of fearfully bartering obedience for material goods, a manipulative moral *non sequitur* that prepares children for a lifetime as dutiful consumers. And I can no more condemn an exercise that makes a meaningless life more bearable than I can condone it. But since my vocation is in the dissemination of facts, and since you in your precocity have thought to pose the question, duty compels me to disabuse you of this puerile myth. In a way, your childhood ends with you reading this response, young Virginia; I apologize to be the agent of your expulsion from the Paradise of ignorance into the bleak, grey corridor of adulthood that leads only to death. But I am shackled to my own conscience—rather than any concern for you, a total stranger—and must see to it that I sleep as easily as manageable to-night. May the Void embrace you with minimal sting.

— *The Editor.* B

TIM HARROD *(@quizmonster) has written for* **The Onion, Late Night with Conan O'Brien,** *and* **HQ Trivia***. So, you know, there's that.*

HI THERE READER!	THAT'S RIGHT, YOU!	THE ONE STARING DOWN AT ME RIGHT NOW!	WELL, I HAVE A LITTLE SECRET TO SHARE WITH YOU! 	JUST THE WAY YOU CAN SEE ME, I CAN SEE YOU! 	I MEAN, DID YOU REALLY THINK THIS COMICS THING WAS JUST ONE-WAY? 
I'LL TELL YOU SOMETHING ELSE, TOO!	WE DRAWINGS CAN BE VERY PERCEPTIVE!	AND AS LONG AS I'M SAFELY DOWN HERE WITH YOU UP THERE, I CAN BE TOTALLY HONEST! 	SURE, I KNOW THAT YOU CAN STOP READING THIS AT ANY TIME! 	YOU CAN CRUMPLE UP THIS PAGE UP OR EVEN BURN IT! 	BUT SOMEHOW, I'M BETTING THAT YOU WON'T!
BECAUSE IT'S HARD FOR YOU TO STOP READING SOMETHING RIGHT IN THE MIDDLE! 	AFTER ALL, YOU DO SEEM TO BE A BIT COMPULSIVE! 	I KNOW I MAY SOUND CRITICAL, BUT PLEASE REGARD ME AS A FRIEND! 	TO BE BLUNT ABOUT IT, YOU LOOK LIKE YOU COULD USE ONE RIGHT NOW! 	MAYBE IT'S THAT YOU FEEL A BIT DOWN BECAUSE YOU'RE GROWING OLDER!	AND YOU SENSE THAT LIFE IS STARTING TO PASS YOU BY?
MAYBE I COULD UNDERSTAND YOU BETTER WITH A LOOK AT WHAT'S AROUND YOU!	THAT IS, IF YOU DON'T MIND MOVING YOUR HEAD A BIT TO THE RIGHT!	GOSH, YOU SURE HAVE LET THE PLACE RUN DOWN! THAT'S NOT A GOOD SIGN! 	PLEASE REMEMBER THAT I'M ONLY SAYING THESE THINGS TO HELP! 	SOMETIMES EVEN A DRAWING HAS TO BE CRUEL TO BE KIND!	WHICH BRINGS US TO A TOPIC I KNOW WE'D BOTH RATHER AVOID! 
YOUR RELATIONSHIP! 	ARE YOU AFRAID YOUR PARTNER MIGHT AGREE WITH WHAT I'VE SAID? 	THEN, QUICK! TURN THE PAGE IF THEY START TO READ OVER YOUR SHOULDER! 	AFTER ALL, I'M THE LAST ONE TO WANT TO START A CONFRONTATION!	ACTUALLY, NONE OF YOUR FUTURE PROSPECTS LOOK VERY GOOD FROM DOWN HERE!	YOU SEE, I KNOW WHERE I BELONG IN MY FRAMES... 
BUT YOU LIVE IN A QUANTUM-MECHANICAL UNIVERSE BASED ON RANDOMNESS! 	I'LL TAKE MY TWO DIMENSIONS OVER YOUR THREE DIMENSIONS ANY DAY! 	YOU INVENT A GOD, BUT I REALLY DO HAVE AN ARTIST! 	AND THAT GIVES ME MEANING AND PURPOSE, TWO THINGS YOU FIND IT VERY HARD TO ACHIEVE!	TRUE, EVENTUALLY MY PAPER WILL YELLOW AND CRUMBLE!	BUT I CAN ALWAYS BE COPIED AND LIVE ON AND ON... 
WAY PAST YOUR SHORT SEVENTY OR SO YEARS!	WHY, WHO KNOWS? YOU MAY EVEN DECIDE TO MAKE A COPY OF ME YOURSELF!	YES, WE DRAWINGS HAVE SEEN SO MANY OF YOU READERS COME AND GO!	WE CAN LOOK INTO YOUR EYES AND SEE ALL THE THINGS YOU KEEP HIDDEN FROM YOURSELF! 	WE KNOW YOUR HEARTS, YOUR SOULS, AND MOST IMPORTANT OF ALL, YOUR FEARS! 	I WON'T EVEN MENTION WHAT I SEE WHEN YOU READ ME IN THE BEDROOM! 
OR WORSE, IN THE BATHROOM!	YOU'RE LOOKING A LITTLE TIRED NOW...HAS ALL THIS BEEN TOO MUCH FOR YOU?	THEN I GUESS IT'S TIME FOR ME TO SAY GOODBYE!	UNLESS, THAT IS, YOUR LIFE IS SO EMPTY THAT YOU COME BACK AND READ ME AGAIN! 	BUT BEFORE I GO, JUST ONE LITTLE REQUEST!	PLEASE DON'T ROLL THE MAGAZINE UP! IT GIVES ME SUCH A HEADACHE...

NEW FROM SIMON RICH

"One of the funniest writers in America."
—NPR

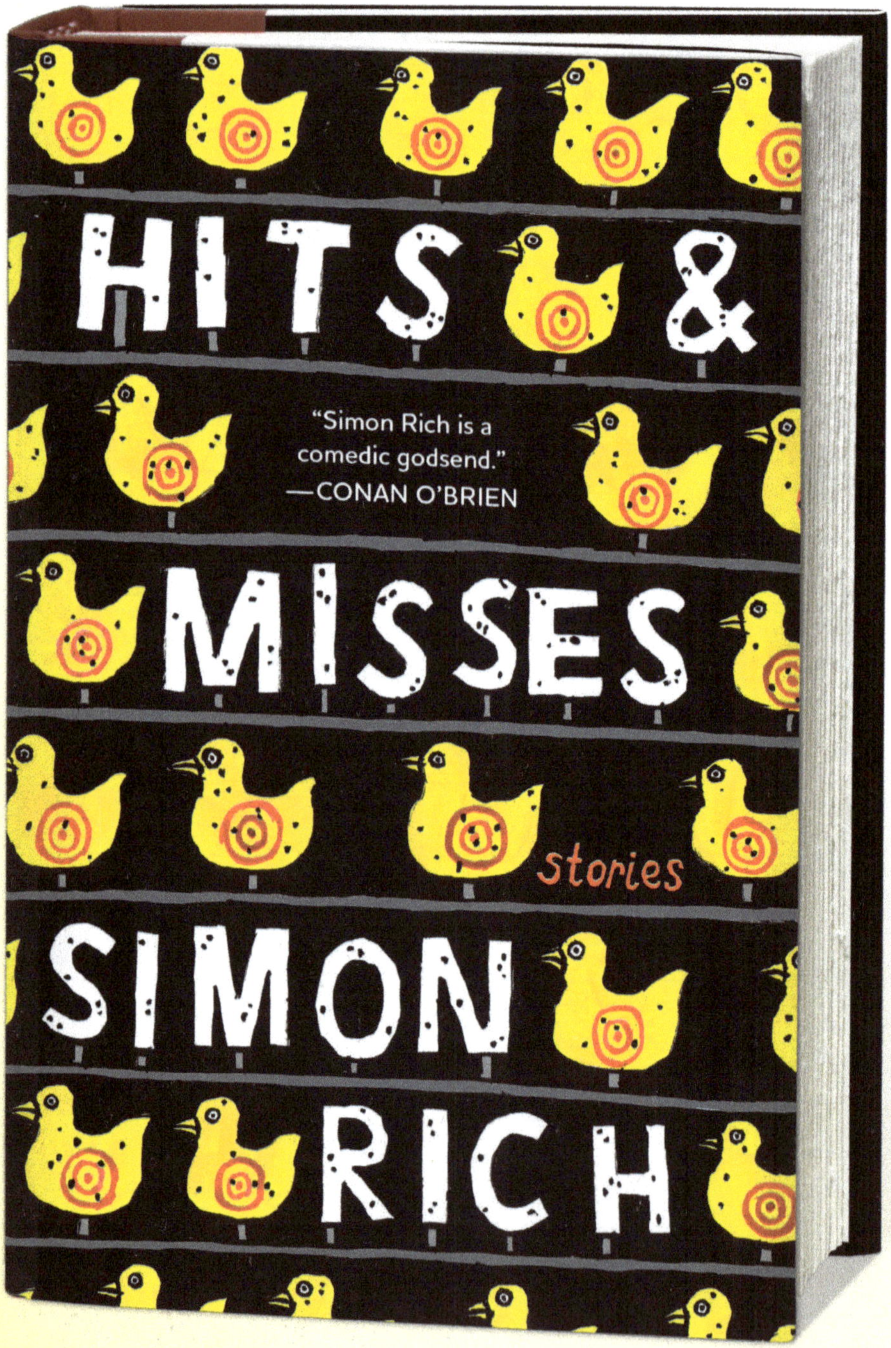

"A motherlode of silly, inventive, absurd brilliance."
—CONAN O'BRIEN

"First-rate comedy with a heartbeat.... One of my favorite authors."
—B.J. NOVAK

"The Stephen King of comedy writing.... HITS AND MISSES is his best collection of stories."
—JOHN MULANEY

ON SALE NOW
in hardcover, ebook, and audio
littlebrown.com

LITTLE, BROWN AND COMPANY
Hachette Book Group

JOE CIARDIELLO

Spaghetti Westerns

So Joe and I are sitting in the noisy, packed bar of New York's Society of Illustrators. Outside it's February-freezing, inside Joe's yelling into my left ear about his new project. "I'm exploring the connections between Italian culture and the American West!" I smile but don't follow, until Joe pulls out his phone...

Joe Ciardiello *is an illustrator whose work has appeared in many publications including* **The New Yorker, Rolling Stone, The Nation** *and* **The New York Times Book Review.** *He lives in western New Jersey.*

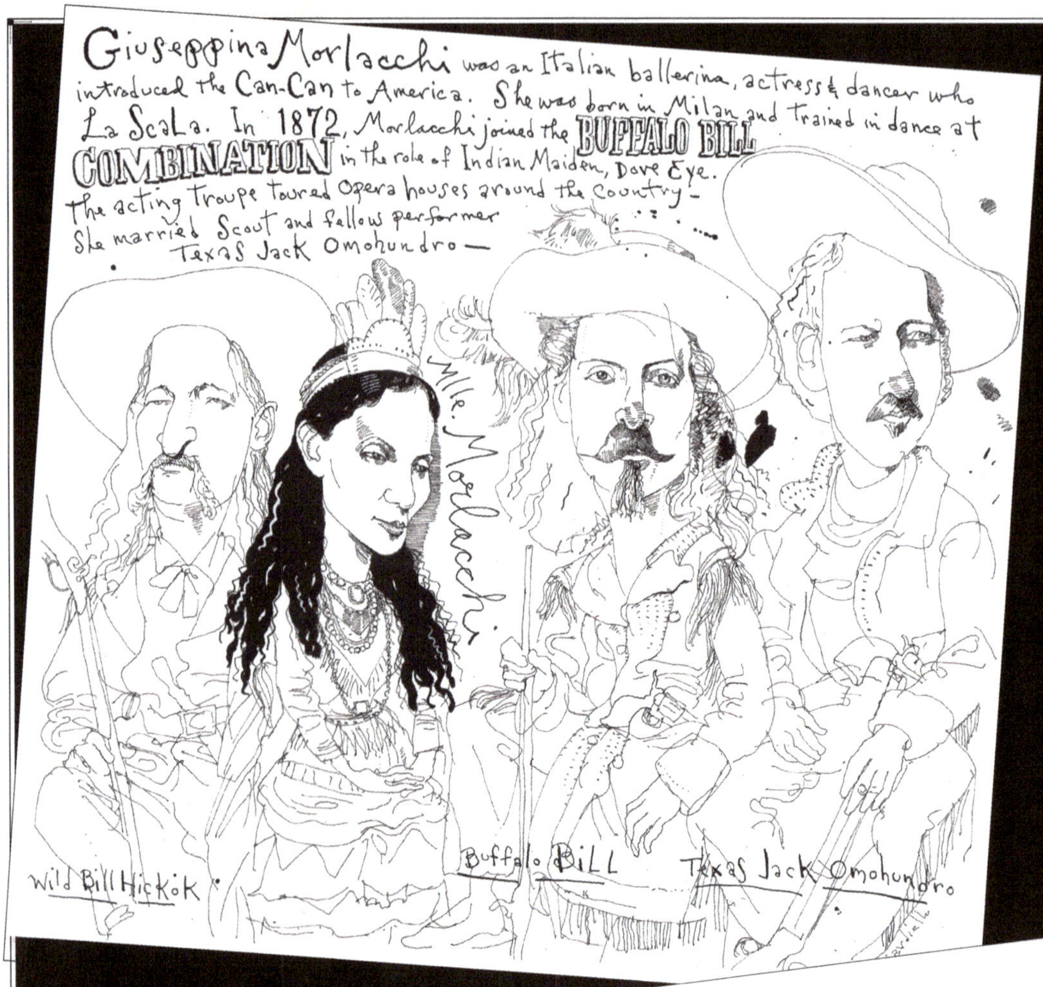
Giuseppina Morlacchi was an Italian ballerina, actress & dancer who
introduced the Can-Can to America. She was born in Milan and trained in dance at
La Scala. In 1872, Morlacchi joined the BUFFALO BILL
COMBINATION in the role of Indian Maiden, Dove Eye.
The acting troupe toured Opera houses around the country –
She married Scout and fellow performer
Texas Jack Omohundro –
Mlle. Morlacchi
Wild Bill Hickok
Buffalo Bill
Texas Jack Omohundro

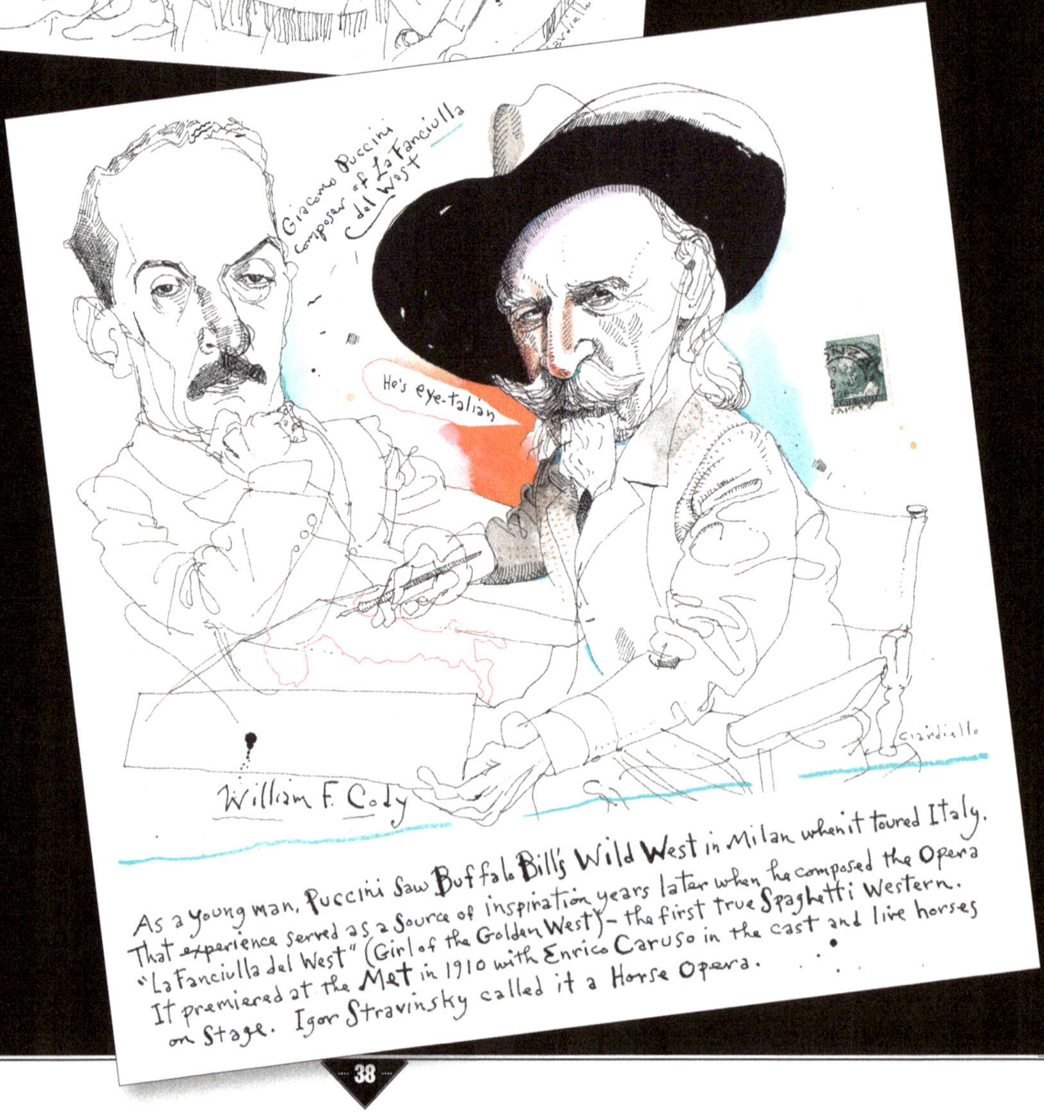
Giacomo Puccini
composer of La Fanciulla del West
He's eye-talian
William F. Cody
Giardiello
As a young man, Puccini saw Buffalo Bill's Wild West in Milan when it toured Italy.
That experience served as a source of inspiration years later when he composed the Opera
"La Fanciulla del West" (Girl of the Golden West) – the first true Spaghetti Western.
It premiered at the Met in 1910 with Enrico Caruso in the cast and live horses
on stage. Igor Stravinsky called it a Horse Opera.

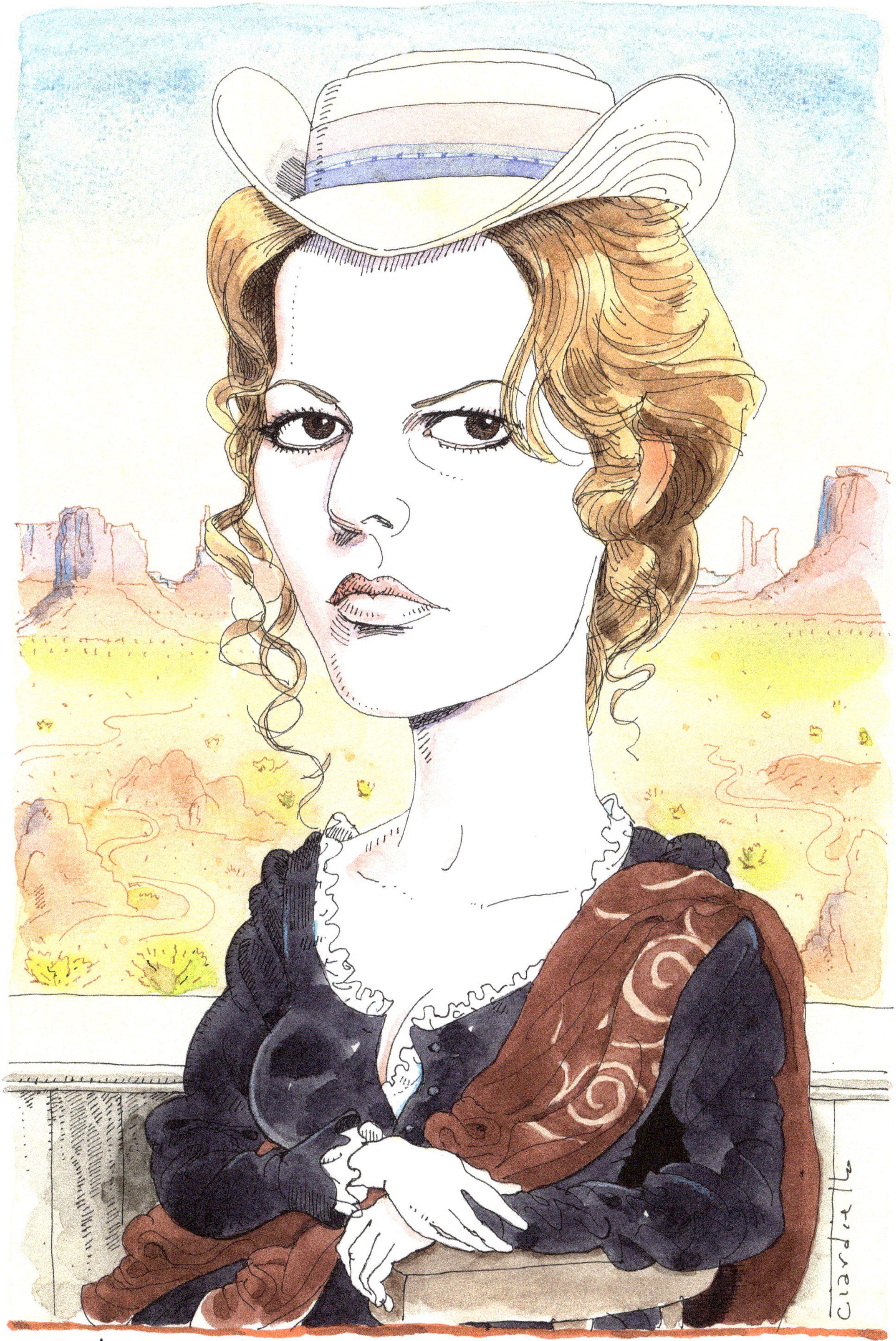

Claudia Cardinale

John Ford.

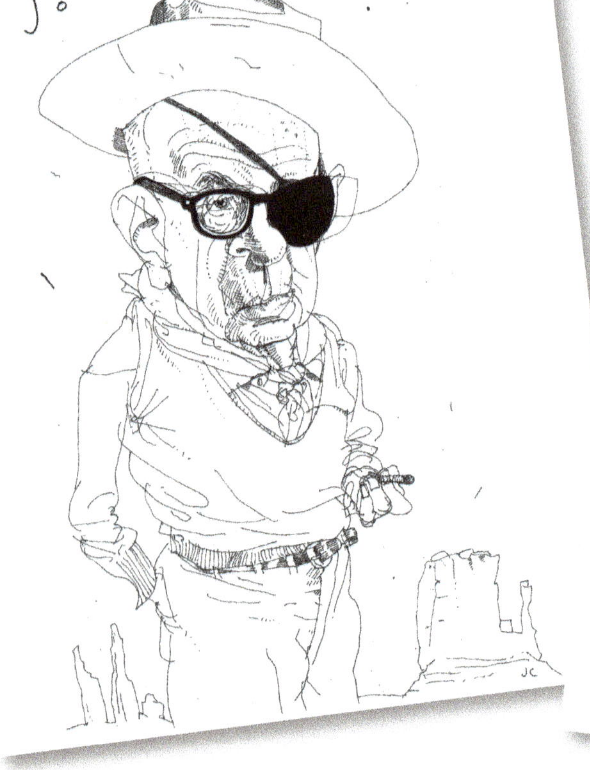

Sergio Leone has said, "John Ford is a filmmaker whose work I admired enormously, more than any other director of Westerns."

"Ford was full of optimism, whereas I on the contrary am full of pessimism."

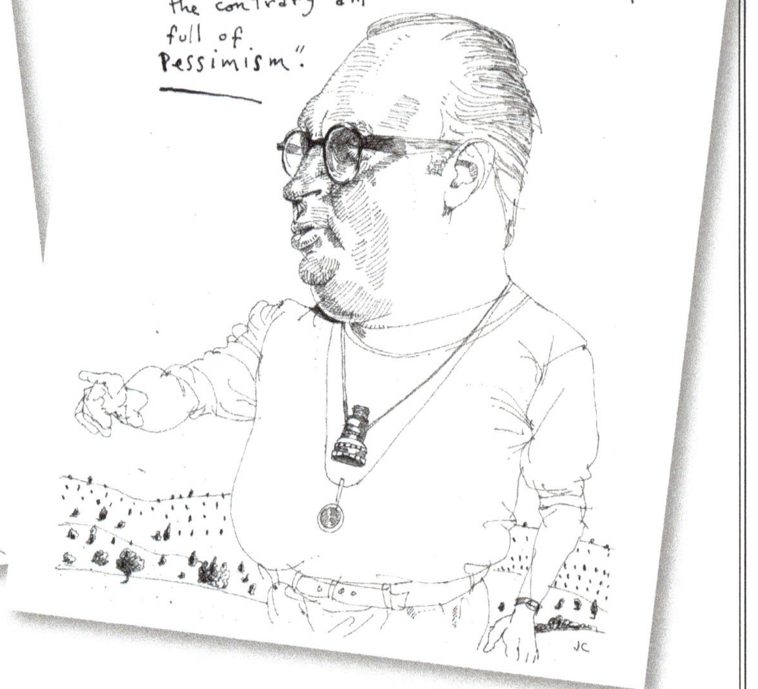

IL BUTTERO - the Italian Cowboy ...

Highly skilled **horsemen** of the **Maremma Region** in Southern **Tuscany** - Experts in Riding, roping & harding, they've been around for a few centuries.

When **Buffalo Bill** took his Wild West to Italy in 1890, the butteri challenged his cowboys to a contest of skill. Italian Legend has it that the butteri outskilled the American Cowboys - However, Buffalo Bill's account differs. Who knows for sure?

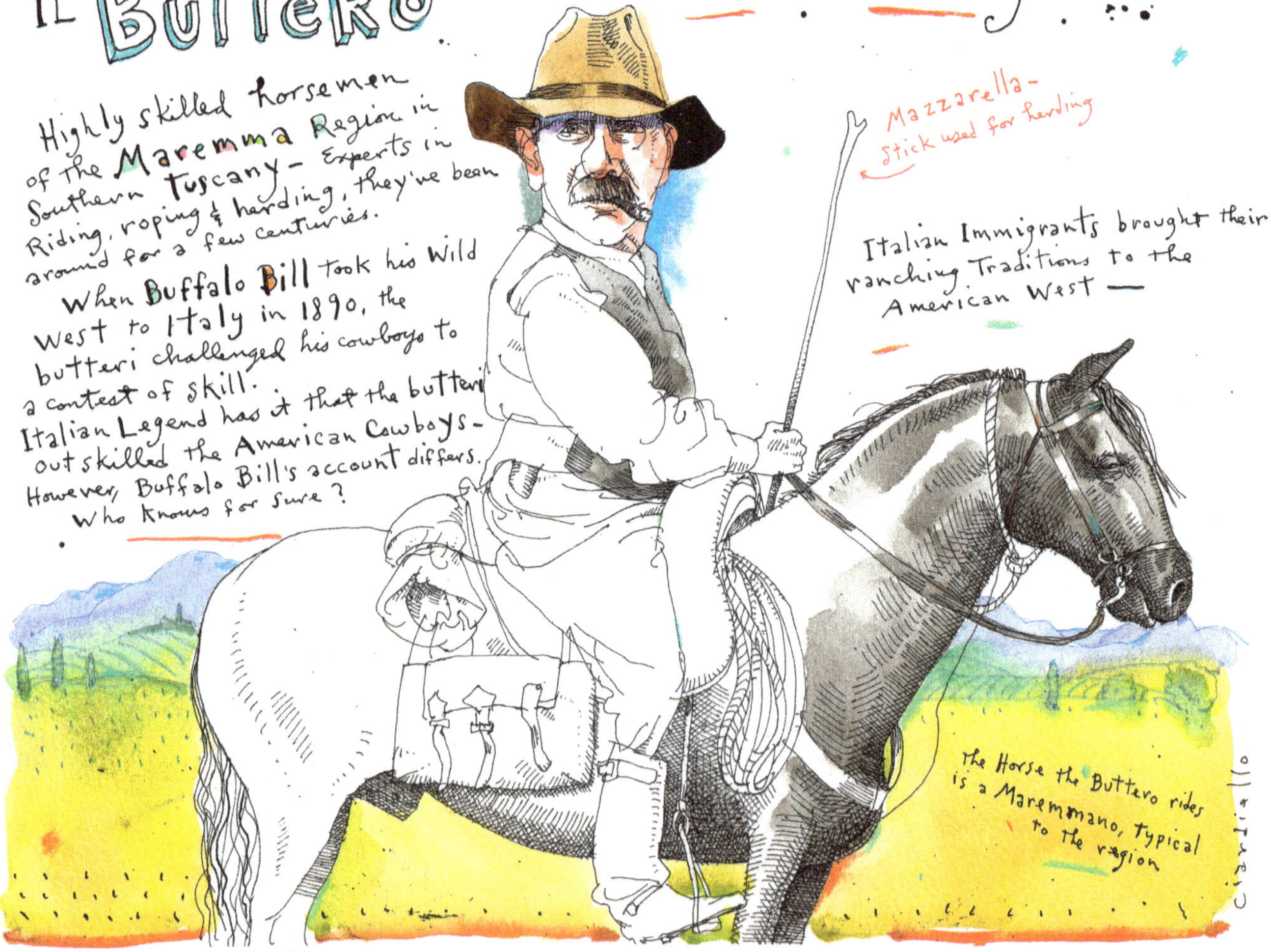

Mazzarella - Stick used for harding

Italian Immigrants brought their ranching Traditions to the American West —

The Horse the Buttero rides is a Maremmano, typical to the region

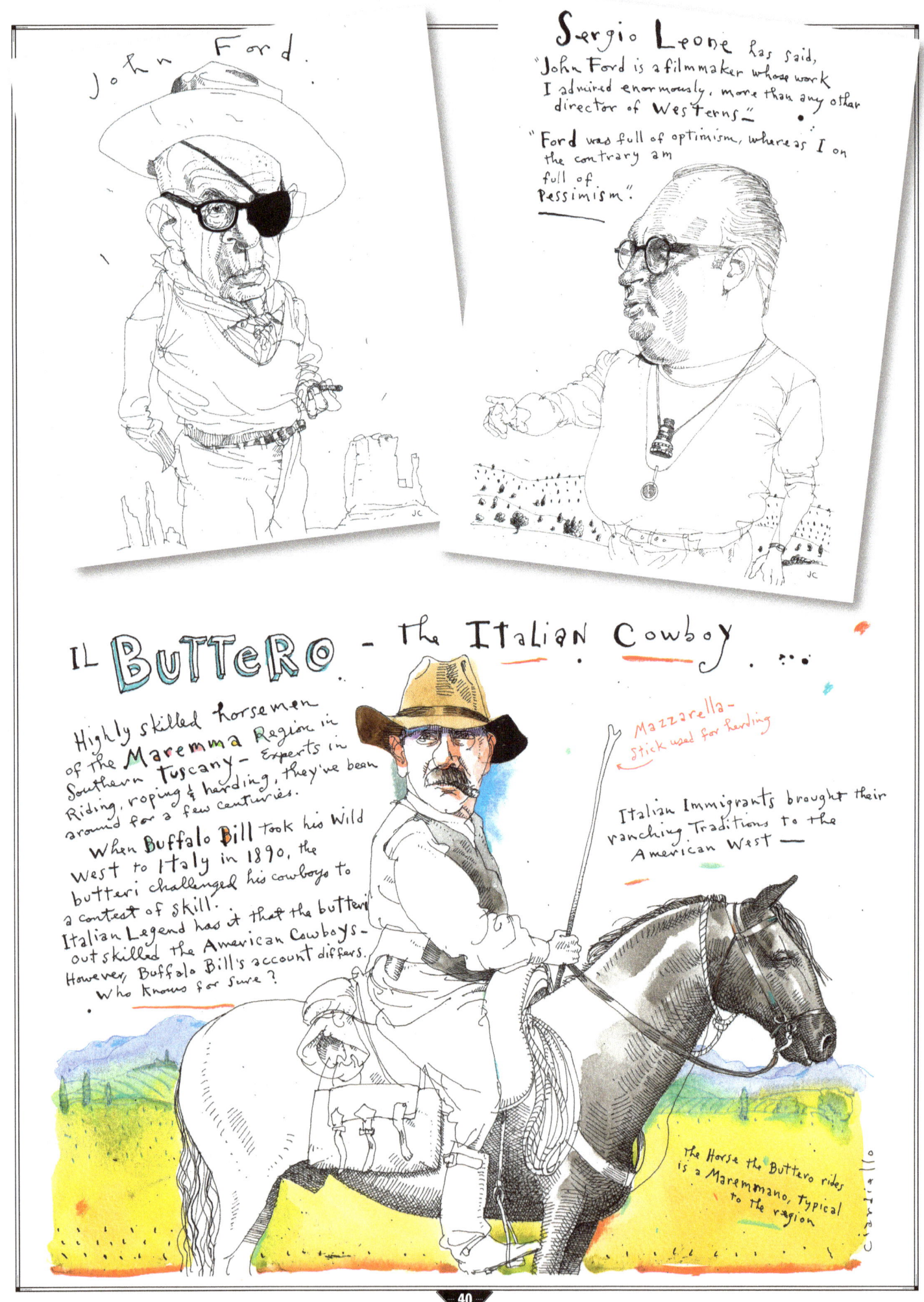

At a Rome Cinema in 1963, Sergio Leone watched Akira Kurosawa's Yojimbo and thought it would make a great Western.
Kurosawa's Seven Samurai had already been adapted as a western, The Magnificent Seven, by director John Sturges a few years earlier.
Yojimbo was inspired by Dashiell Hammett's novel Red Harvest and also by Hollywood Westerns.
So, in 1964 the western genre was reinvented in Italy as a low budget film originally called Il Magnifico Straniero - The Magnificent Stranger. The title was changed to A Fistful of Dollars. It was a huge success in Italy and made a star of Clint Eastwood. It also established the prototype for the cynical, ultra-cool, anti-hero of so many films to follow.

Due to a copyright lawsuit brought by Kurosawa, the film wasn't released in the US until 1967.

According to Leone, Kurosawa earned more $ from Fistful than from all his own films combined.

Enormous Blonde Herring-scented Nauseatingly Fair-minded Nymphomaniacs in Clogs

When I lived in Paris, nobody said "Paris? Why Paris?" Now they say, "Sweden? But...*why*?" I must defend the Swedes. Here goes.

If you're from Indianapolis, you can go to Chicago. If you're from Chicago, you can go to New York. But if you're from Manhattan, where can you go? By the time I was 30, I had to go to Sweden, just to calm down.

These are not a fondue people. Their trains are often late, their mountains are... meh, and their chocolate is ...adequate. No. These are the people who brought you The Nobel Prize, full frontal nudity, and suicide. Also your Ypperlig table and your H&M hoodie. These are the blondes. Enormous Blonde Herring-scented Nauseatingly Fair-minded Nymphomaniacs in Clogs.

But why love *Gothenburg*? It's not even Stockholm! Maybe because nobody there has anything better to do than to chat with me! My Stockholm friends are rolling their eyes (*which are mostly blue, but not always*). To them, it sounds like I'm saying "Behold, Trenton! Glorious epicenter of culture, romance and sophistication!"

New Yorkers make dates weeks ahead and cancel. Everyone's "crazed" all the time. Crazed! Please. Don't e-mail. Don't text. Say, "Hey, didja eat yet?" And even if I did, I'll *still* go with you.

I'm an artist. There, I said it. New York is for showin' it, but Gothenburg is for makin' it! Volvos, Hasselblads, ball bearings...paintings, stories.

Respect the Cheese Form!

I do not actually keep a diary, but since 1981 have felt guilty about it, which is almost as good.

Gothenburg, 2004: I share a studio with seven people, most of whom are called Lena. All Swedish women are named Lena, and all Swedish men are named Stefan. At break time, Lena, Lina, Helena, and Lene start yelling, "Laurie's been in the cheese again! It looks like a ski slope!" All Swedes use the *osthyvel*—the slotted cheese slicer—to level out the cheese surface every time. I suspect they keep a spirit level in the kitchen.

Allow Me to Translate Your Chair

Lagom means "Not too much, not too little. Just right." The Middle Road. Social Democracy. Fairness. Evenness. The three bears! Show-offs are not to be tolerated. Unsurprisingly, *lagom* can also be expressed in...cheese.

Generally speaking, Swedish is a word poor language, but they have some gems we don't. The crime of washing dishes in a sloppy, superficial way? *Fuskdiska!* "Fakedisher!" *Hjärnsläpp*, or "brain drop," means "senior moment." An onomatopoetic word for a hippie-dippy type? *Flummig*. If you're boring, you're a *torrboll*—a "dust bunny."

Invective's adorably tame. *Dra dit pepparn växer!* means, "Go where the hot peppers grow...like South America!" This is Swedish for "Go fuck yourself, and do it as far away from me as possible!"

Undulaut seems like punctuation, but actually means parakeet. Genitalia? *Underlivet*—"the underlife"! Camel toe? *Mummelbyxa*—"mumble pants." *Förnuftig* means "clever," and seems to me like something the Swedish Chef says. (Incidentally, my favorite word in French is *pneu*. Tire.) And before every toddler hugged one, Swedes called cell phones *juppinallar*, or "Yuppie Teddy Bears."

Laurie Rosenwald (@rosenwald). Principal, rosenwald.com & Iron Chef of Encaustic. Author, **All the Wrong People Have Self Esteem**. Speaks Swedish like a Native New Yorker.

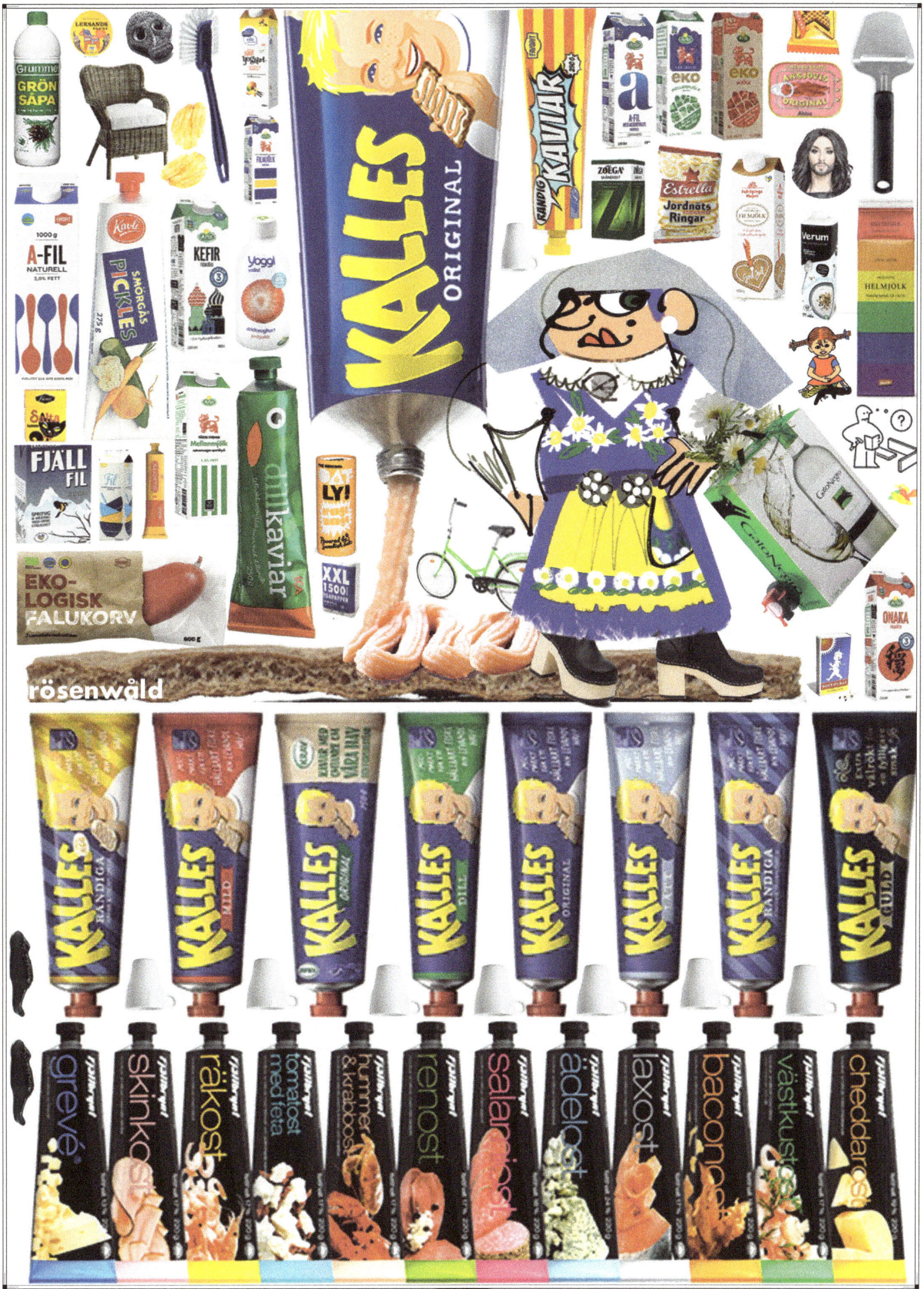
KALLES
ORIGINAL
rösenwåld
Grumme
GRÖN
SÅPA
A-FIL
NATURELL
SMÖRGÅS
PICKLES
KEFIR
Yoggi
FJÄLL
FIL
EKO-
LOGISK
FALUKORV
dillkaviar
KAVIAR
Estrella
Jordnöts
Ringar
HELMJÖLK
Verum
ZOEGA
XXL
KALLES
MILD
KALLES
ORIGINAL
KALLES
DILL
KALLES
ORIGINAL
KALLES
KALLES
KALLES
GULD
grevé
räkost
tomatost
med feta
hummer
& krabbost
renost
ädelost
laxost

Contrary to a cruel myth founded on corporate envy, IKEA does not mean "wobbly." Wobbly is *ostadig*. IKEA is an acronym for *Ingvar Kamprad Elmtaryd Agunnaryd*. Aren't you glad you asked? Kamprad, Ikea's founder, admitted his youthful affiliation with the Nazi movement was "the greatest mistake of my life," but in my opinion that honor should go to the ineluctably hideous *Byholma Marieberg* armchair. (See page 43.)

When that catalogue arrives, if I'm in the mood, I have the chops to decipher your *Möckelby*, your *Klaviatur*, and your extremely *ostadig Fjällbo*. Unfortunately, I am never in the mood. It's better for you not to know. Yes, *prick* means "dot" in Swedish. And, yes, the small, round bathmats were renamed. But not in a timely manner.

Rebels! Misfits! Horse Lifters! Girls!

Sweden's produced two of literature's most heretical heroines. Lisbeth Salander, inky protagonist of the "Millenium" trilogy, was meant to be a postmodern apparition of the brazen outlier—and early adopter of the "home alone" lifestyle—Pippi Longstocking.

Sadly, these radical gals must be entirely fictional. Because whether you're a freckle-faced, vermillion-pigtailed orphan living in Villa Villekulla with a monkey in a green sailor suit and a polka-dotted horse, and having "the strength of ten policemen," or a pierced and tattooed bisexual master hacker with a mohawk living in Södermalm, there's one Swedish tradition that supersedes all others: *Jantelagen*. "Conform or die." Even firebrand Lisbeth Salander eats Billy's Pan Pizza.

Flat-pack Your Ego, Darling. You're Nothing Special!

In Sweden, being ordinary rules. Or, as Swedes might express it, you are: *Inte mycket att hänga i julgranen!* "Nothing to hang on the Christmas tree!"

Patience. Sweden has been expressly designed just to help me learn this overrated virtue. At restaurants, salad, bread, and water are on the sideboard. Help yourself. I'm thinking, "No. Help me." Customers are lucky to receive service at all. Tipping's not expected. You'll never hear, "*Hej!* I'm Pernilla! How're you folks doin'?" Never.

Liquor is sold in state-run stores, closing weekdays at 6 P.M., 2 P.M. Saturdays and Sundays. Saturday at 13:45, take number 239 from the TurnoMatic, and wait your turn to purchase a desperately rowdy weekend. Enterprising drunks outside might sell you a low number tag for ten kronor.

"One question: Do the windows open?"

Otherwise, bring literature—this may take awhile.

Cinnamon Buns in the News!

In addition to baking, sewing, and indoor hockey, Sweden has an extremely active yogurt culture. Almost frantic. There's Japanese, Russian, Farmer, Icelandic, Vegan and Oatly styles, and no-fat to "call your cardiologist" versions as well as *filmjölk*, which is yogurt, but somehow not really. Also, along with the soy, oat, hemp and almond, you can now buy gay milk. Do I have to draw you a picture? Well, I did. (See page 43.)

Finally, Reindeer in a Tube

Swedes squeeze food out of tubes. The infamous *Kalles Kaviar* (bleak roe) is squirted, wantonly, everywhere. Ham, shrimp and reindeer can also be squeezed and squirted, as well as liquid pickles. At hot dog stands there's a lineup of condiments, each in foot-long, squeezable, rubber...udders. Toilet paper is packaged in gigantic 28 roll bales, with a handle. Swedes run around in public with these. *Have these people no shame?*

TV news sets feature flowered curtains, birch wood furniture, and homey throw pillows. Pastry is served. "Nightline," take note. Wouldn't Cory Booker enjoy a macaroon? Maybe *klädkaka* for Christiane Amanpour? Coffee is non-negotiable. I found this out the hard way.

Stefan called.

"You want to go for a coffee?"

"Sure," I answered, and jumped onto Jopo, my adorable Finnish bike.

Yes, I'm a bikesexual.

At Café Hängmattan, Stefan ordered a latte and asked what I'd like.

"Nothing," I said.

"You can't have a "nothing."

"Yes, I can!"

"But you said you wanted to meet for a coffee."

"No, *you* said that!"

"And you agreed! So you have to have *something*."

"No, I don't! I just had a coffee. 'Let's meet for coffee' means, 'I like you. I want to see you!'"

"No! It means 'Let's meet for coffee!' *Coffee!*"

Stefan stormed out, un-Swedishly banging the door.

The second he'd gone, I got up and ordered a cappuccino.

Whatever their sex life may include, Swedes sleep in single beds. And they all travel with sheets and towels. You can say, "You don't need to bring your towels from Malmö to Manhattan! I have everything here!" but they cannot be stopped. Also, if you go on a vacation with one, watch out, because when exposed to direct sunlight, they generally burst into flame.

Visine is illegal. Crazy glue is illegal. You can buy herring in any gas station. Swedes don't talk, except at the movies.

Hair *salonger* have terrifying English names, like "Klipper Krazy," "Cut & Blow," "Bazaar Movement," "HeadWig," and "Cut the Crap."

"Where is my Puppy," "Futurniture," "Spinach," "Canadian Taxi," "Brainforest," "Dogwash" and "Hey, it's Enrico Pallazzo," are all hipster ad agencies. (Here in Manhattan, there's a "Dogwash" on 6th Avenue, but I think they wash dogs in there.)

In the pre-Tinder days of personal ads, I posted this in the daily, *Göteborgs Posten*:

"Tired of Beautiful Blondes?
Try a Dumpy New York Jew!"
Turns out they weren't, so they didn't. But my masterpiece was:

"Desperate Woman Seeks
Man with Similar Interests."
I got several earnest replies to this, asking me to kindly list said interests and sympathetically asking me why I was so desperate. They're fluent in English, but not in sarcasm.

Is happiness our birthright? Our Constitution instructs us to pursue it. But to Swedes, this is simply asking for *trubbel*! Here's a Lagerkvist poem that says it all:

Ångest, ångest är min arvedel,
min strupes sår,
mitt hjärtas skri i världen.

"Angst! Angst is my heritage!
My throat's wound,
My heart's shriek in the night."
Isn't that cute?

Swedes don't need yoga. They find inner peace through home economics. How many men do you know who make their own pants? How many bachelors, of any sexual proclivity, who bake fresh bread every Wednesday?

And the following scenario would never have played out Stateside: I visited Lene's apartment one Sunday. Here was a vibrant 31-year-old woman, serenely occupied with some task. "What are you doing?" I asked. "I am making washcloths," she replied. Hmm. There is a scene in Fellini's *Juliet of the Spirits* where a neurotic neighbor visits Juliet's backyard. "What are you doing?" the neighbor inquires. "Stringing peppers," replies Juliet. "Ah!" cries the neighbor, "If I could string peppers, I would be saved!" *I get her.*

Lördagsgodis, "Saturday's candy," is the designated day for sweets distribution to children. Sold by the kilo, try Mixed Sour Lips, Body Parts, Salted Herring, Fried Eggs, Gummy Frogs, Mushroom Marshmallows, Peppered Skeletons, Termites, Red Ammo, and Sega Rats. Salt Licorice is its own food group.

You Don't Think Abba Just *Happened*, Do You?

Fredagsmys means "Cosy Fridays," where one eats even more chips and watches even more TV than usual. Bag-in-Box, a/k/a "housewife's temptation" comes in a 4-liter box with handle and spigot. I've got a brand new Bag-in-Box Chardonnay, salty *jordnötsringar*, and no place to be.

Now please be quiet. It's the Eurovision Song Contest and Conchita Wurst's crushing it for Austria. She has a full beard and moustache. Cool.

The city of Gothenburg was built on highly absorbent clay. Legend has it that this makes one sink in and stay. There might be something to that because while you are reading this, I've either just returned, or I'm on my way.

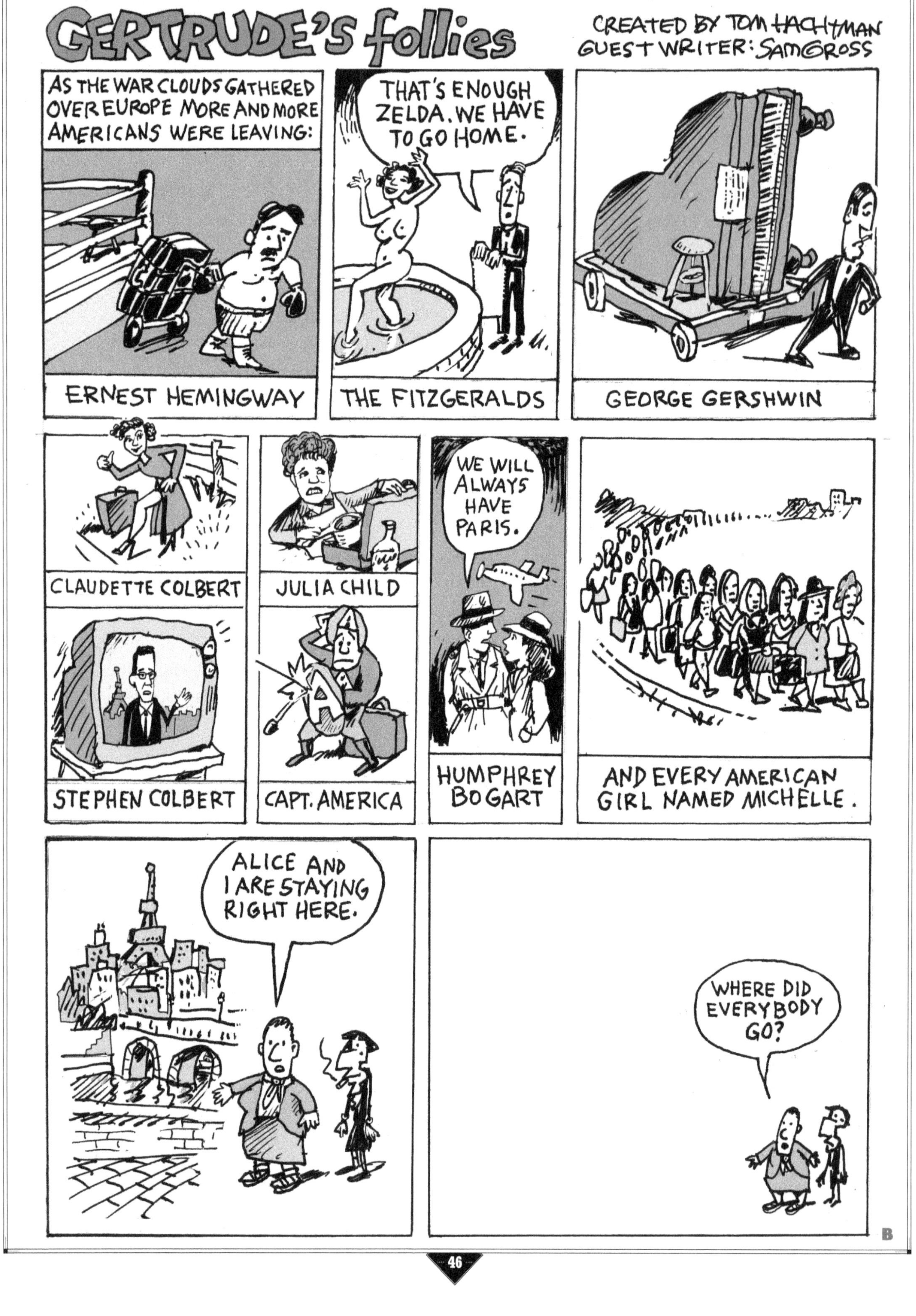
GERTRUDE'S follies
CREATED BY TOM HACHTMAN
GUEST WRITER: SAM GROSS
AS THE WAR CLOUDS GATHERED OVER EUROPE MORE AND MORE AMERICANS WERE LEAVING:
ERNEST HEMINGWAY
THAT'S ENOUGH ZELDA. WE HAVE TO GO HOME.
THE FITZGERALDS
GEORGE GERSHWIN
CLAUDETTE COLBERT
JULIA CHILD
WE WILL ALWAYS HAVE PARIS.
AND EVERY AMERICAN GIRL NAMED MICHELLE.
STEPHEN COLBERT
CAPT. AMERICA
HUMPHREY BOGART
ALICE AND I ARE STAYING RIGHT HERE.
WHERE DID EVERYBODY GO?

A Turkey for Lewis

A Very Special Holiday Tale for Dogs.

Once upon a time, in a town called North Hollywood, there was a 95-pound black dog named Lewis who lived with a woman who only fed him twice a day. Ever since an evil veterinarian cast a spell to make the woman think Lewis needed to lose a few pounds, the poor dog watched helplessly as all his meals grew smaller.

Lewis knew there were many delicious things to eat hidden throughout the house. The cabinets were full of cans he could see and smell but not open. Occasionally, he caught a glimpse inside the cold metal box where the woman stored amazing delicacies. "Damn," he could hear a dark voice bubbling up from deep inside of him as his eyes feasted on shelves full of glistening meats, and fragrant cheeses, tubs full of buttery sauces and plates of gooey pastries. "Go on, Lewis!" the voice urged him. "Jam your upper body into that box and start chewing, NOW!" But by then, the door on the metal box had slammed shut, leaving Lewis frustrated, grouchy and even hungrier than before. So every night, as he stretched out his big inadequately nourished body in the center of the woman's bed, taking up as much space as he possibly could, he prayed to the God of All Dogs to deliver unto him an endless dinner.

And then one wintry day, something unusual happened.

After the woman put on her jacket and got into her car to go wherever it was that she always went without him, Lewis became aware of a tantalizing new smell. "What is that?" he wondered, as long rubbery strands of saliva spilled out of his mouth and hung from the bottom of his lips like tetherballs. Now Lewis found himself pulled through the house by a scent so thick he could almost gnaw on it like a steak.

Slowly he searched through each room in the house, looking for the origin of the mesmerizing new smell. "Nope, nothing in here except this tiny bit of spilled soup," said Lewis, after he finished licking his way across the whole living room floor. "And nothing in here except this hardened smear of peanut butter and a microscopic trace of icing," he said as he licked his way all across the dining room, making sure to also carefully check the table top and every inch of the lower third of the walls.

This brought Lewis into the kitchen.

"Bingo!" he said as soon as he entered. "There's something in the far corner of that counter." He was startled by how his nose had located his quarry way ahead his eyes.

The next thing he did was bounce himself up onto his hind legs and plop his front paws onto the countertop.

Instantly, time stood still.

As soon as he saw it, his head was filled with the sounds of a heavenly choir of wolves baying in the Arctic night! There, pushed up against the wall...waiting for him and him alone... defining the word "destiny"...was a frozen 25-pound Butterball turkey. Lewis craned his neck toward the bird, stuck out his tongue and tried to reach it with his teeth. "It's not that far away," Lewis thought, "I should be able to grab it." So he heaved his body as high as he could, thrusting it forward, lunging again and again. But relentless though he was, the turkey remained unreachable.

"You're making me drool so hard the kitchen floor is getting slippery," Lewis yowled at the bird, as he twisted, he heaved, and he lunged repeatedly. "God damn you, you miserable turkey on your very own styrofoam tray!" he yelled. "My back is sore, my legs are sore and I am STARVING."

By 3 P.M., Lewis collapsed onto his side, defeated and panting from exhaustion. "I just can't do it," Lewis whined, humiliated and ready to give up.

And then he heard it again: that low growling voice that came from the depth of his being. And this time when it spoke, it spoke to him even more clearly. "Lewis, this is Tomarctus, your ancient ancestor from 30 million years ago," it said. "I am shocked and dismayed at your attitude." Lewis froze. "You, who are descended not only from wolves but from bears and hyenas...You, whose great-grandparents tracked and outran deer and squirrels and musk ox, are now outmaneuvered by a deceased turkey? Are you a hunter and a predator, Lewis? Or some adorable little rent-boy parakeet?"

Lewis sat straight up as the hackles on his neck stiffened, surprised at the way his spirit had been revived.

"I am a hunter and a predator!" he cried, resuming

Merrill Markoe *has published eight books and written for a long list of television shows and publications, including the one you are holding.*

his jumping and thrusting with new vigor, "Dammit! That turkey will be mine!" And less than a minute later, something wonderful happened: he hit the front of the unthawed turkey with the nails of his left foot, causing it to slide just far enough forward that he could grab a piece of its icy packaging in his teeth. And this time when he gave the turkey a tug it was almost as though the turkey itself sensed that their two destinies were meant to be entwined. The turkey came sliding toward him on a cushion of water, skidding toward the edge of the counter until it was airborne, then sailed like a missile aimed straight at his head.

Lewis tucked his tail between his legs, closed his eyes and scampered away before—boom!—the icy carcass hit the floor with a crash so thunderous it caused the dishes on the counter to bounce. A box of cinnamon fell off the spice shelf. A fork fell on to the floor.

And when Lewis looked up, he again heard that familiar choir of joyously baying wolves and saw that a celestial light was beaming down from the window toward the kitchen floor. And there, in the center of its rays, was the turkey, directly across from him.

Lewis was almost too excited to move. Cautiously he approached the turkey, sniffing its earthy bouquet, savoring the smoky notes, not too tannic or woody. "I know I should just leave it alone," thought Lewis. "That turkey isn't mine. I'm a 'bad dog.'"

"Excuse me?" growled Uncle Tomarctus, "I did *not* just hear what I think I heard. If any of your relatives thought like that, do you think your species would have survived for 30 million years? You won that turkey fair and square, Lewis. It is yours."

"Mine! Mine! Mine!" howled Lewis, as he ran to his turkey with the passion of a lover reunited after being separated by war. And he bit into the turkey flesh, again and again. And he ate and ate until he realized he was experiencing a brand new sensation: For the first time, maybe ever, Lewis was no longer hungry.

After he had eaten about half the turkey, Lewis noticed that the sun was now low in the sky. Soon the woman would return from wherever she was and try to steal away his prize forever.

Difficult though it was for Lewis to walk, so full of raw frozen turkey was he, Lewis grabbed the plastic styrofoam tray to which the turkey was still partially bound by plastic wrap and dragged his turkey over to the screen he had dislodged to gain access to the back yard. Once outside, he knew he must hide his treasure from the rats and the crows and the woman herself. But where oh where would he hide it? And that is when a true holiday miracle occurred.

Because when Lewis began to dig, he discovered that the usually hard-packed surface of the earth had become nice and soft from a recent rain. In practically no time at all, he was able to dig a big enough hole to bury the entire turkey and also cover it back up with the loosened dirt.

His timing was impeccable.

As he was kicking the last dirt over the turkey's new grave, he heard the woman

rattling around at the front door. He heard her shoes clomp-clomp-clomping as she walked into the kitchen. Then he heard her gasp, and cry out "Oh my God!" followed by "Shit!" when she saw the mess and that the corner of her counter was empty. So preoccupied was she as she attempted to piece together what had happened that she barely noticed Lewis's bloated torso or dirty feet as he waddled past her, lapping up all the turkey juice that was smeared on the floor. "I don't get it. Nothing outside the kitchen seems to have been touched," the woman was shouting into the phone as Lewis lumbered off to a couch in the next room to enjoy a long peaceful nap.

And the next day was Christmas Day—a day as perfect as any day could be. Somehow the woman had found and cooked another turkey. She had decorated the house and set the table in time to greet her guests. Yet, though she spent the day making all kinds of special foods, it appeared that she had no plans to prepare anything special for Lewis. She'd fed him his usual meal at the usual time. And as always it was far too small, far too bland and much too crunchy. Yes, Lewis had eaten the meal anyway, without a complaint, as he always did. But as he ate, he was concocting a special plan. So after the guests were seated at the table, and the turkey was about to be carved, while Lewis sat drooling from the irresistible smells that were filling the room, he found himself inspired by the spirit of the holiday. Or maybe it was his new and deeper ancestral bonds. Whatever it was, Lewis felt himself pulled out to the backyard. He moved so quietly that no one even noticed when he left the room.

But they sure as hell all noticed when he returned.

Because when Lewis came back, he was dragging his very own special turkey, now a little muddier but none the worse for wear. "It's even better the next day," thought Lewis, as he relished the delicate flavor of the wet soil marinade on his tongue, pleased that he could detect a faint sprinkling of fertilizer and a hint of ants. "Its moist but gritty," said Lewis, enjoying each mouthful as everyone stared. "I ate most of it yesterday, but there's plenty left. *MMM*—just the way I like it. Merry Christmas everyone!!!"

And so, for this one bright shining moment, as Lewis bit into his turkey, nothing that happened could possibly mar his good mood: not even the shrieking guests or the angry woman as she chased him around the room, trying to grab both Lewis and his turkey. "Oh I get it," said Lewis, "You get all of your turkey, plus as much as you want of mine. Well, watch me swallow it all and make this the very best Christmas ever!" And Lewis bit off at least a half of the the remaining turkey carcass in one mighty bite, putting as much of it as he could fit in to his mouth at the same time. And then he took a deep breath and he swallowed it, bones and all. "Merry Christmas one and all," said Lewis. "Let's do this every year!" B

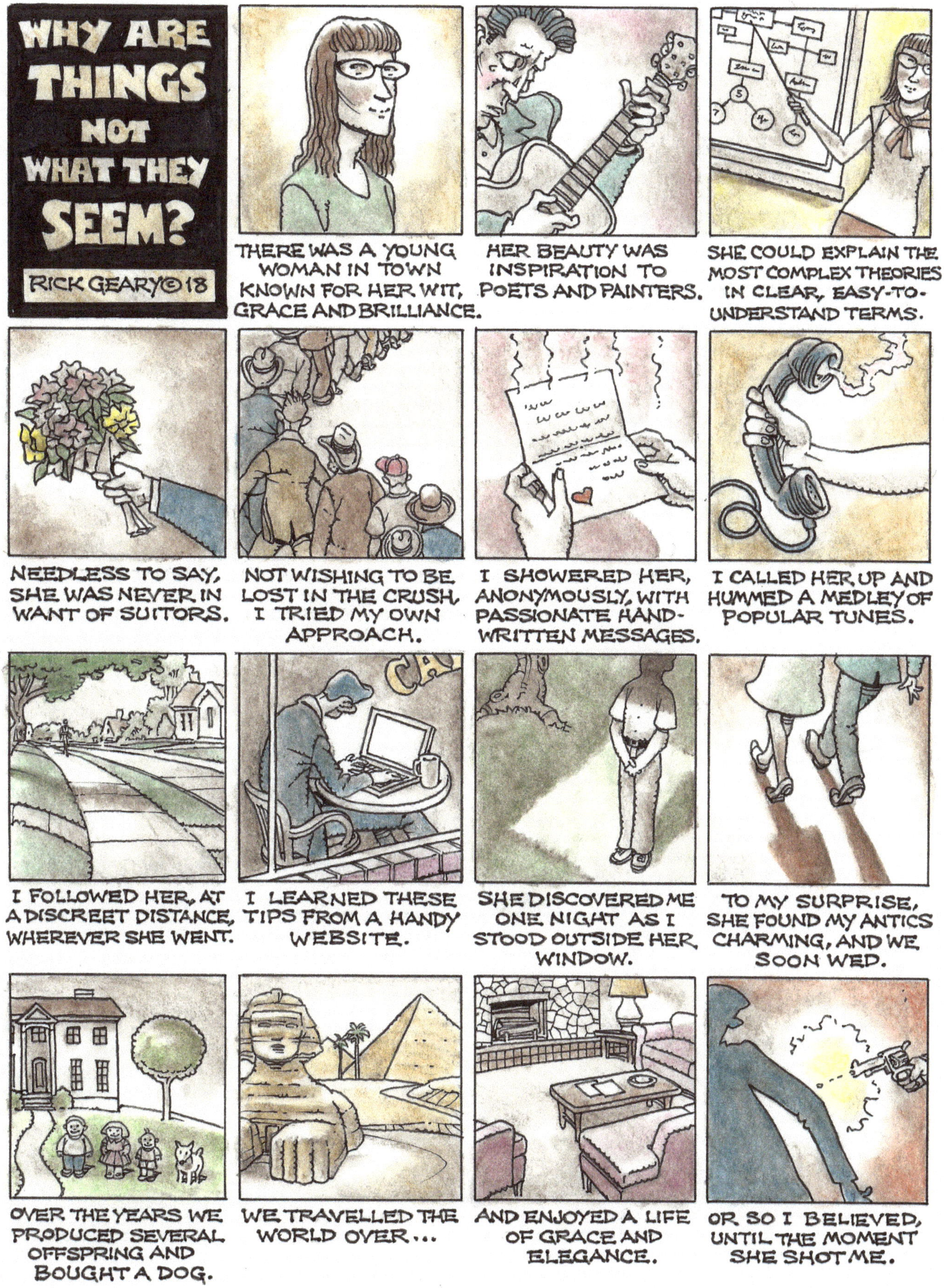
WHY ARE THINGS NOT WHAT THEY SEEM?
RICK GEARY©18
THERE WAS A YOUNG WOMAN IN TOWN KNOWN FOR HER WIT, GRACE AND BRILLIANCE.
HER BEAUTY WAS INSPIRATION TO POETS AND PAINTERS.
SHE COULD EXPLAIN THE MOST COMPLEX THEORIES IN CLEAR, EASY-TO-UNDERSTAND TERMS.
NEEDLESS TO SAY, SHE WAS NEVER IN WANT OF SUITORS.
NOT WISHING TO BE LOST IN THE CRUSH, I TRIED MY OWN APPROACH.
I SHOWERED HER, ANONYMOUSLY, WITH PASSIONATE HAND-WRITTEN MESSAGES.
I CALLED HER UP AND HUMMED A MEDLEY OF POPULAR TUNES.
I FOLLOWED HER, AT A DISCREET DISTANCE, WHEREVER SHE WENT.
I LEARNED THESE TIPS FROM A HANDY WEBSITE.
SHE DISCOVERED ME ONE NIGHT AS I STOOD OUTSIDE HER WINDOW.
TO MY SURPRISE, SHE FOUND MY ANTICS CHARMING, AND WE SOON WED.
OVER THE YEARS WE PRODUCED SEVERAL OFFSPRING AND BOUGHT A DOG.
WE TRAVELLED THE WORLD OVER...
AND ENJOYED A LIFE OF GRACE AND ELEGANCE.
OR SO I BELIEVED, UNTIL THE MOMENT SHE SHOT ME.

A Christmas Peril

...But what happened the next Christmas Eve?

I. SCREW-AGE.

Upon the existence of ghosts, reasonable people may differ; and in the matter of Ebenezer Scrooge they certainly did. One clique of disbelievers was certain he had suffered a minor stroke, while another faction pointed to the mind-altering properties of some of the food additives found in your less-reputable taverns. But on one point there was no disagreement: Scrooge was a changed man.

Overnight, the miser had become a firehose of generosity, spraying good works and good fellowship forcefully in every direction. No one could escape his hoarse shouts of "Merry Christmas!" which lasted until March (and began again in October), nor could they ignore the rictus-like smile which hung across his features like so much brittle and decaying holiday garland. "Merry Christmas! Happy Easter! Good Kissing Friday! I'm sending you a turkey whether you want one or not!"

No one was safe from this relentless two-legged cornucopia: In the daytime, Scrooge doled out large sums at his counting-house, and in the nights, he walked London's neighborhoods, flinging coin like a farmer broadcasts seed. Were there injuries? To be sure—but Scrooge kept up his manic charity. After all, didn't his very soul depend upon it?

Decent people avoided the new Scrooge. They believed in the wisdom of our ancestors regarding leopards and spots. What good was it for the new Scrooge to gift them a pound, if the old Scrooge demanded it back—with interest? Surely Scrooge's old ways would return. Surely the old miser-mind still crouched in Scrooge's brainpan, waiting to ooze forth at the moment of maximum injury!

But it did not. By the next Christmas Eve, the sacred, crazy spark inside Scrooge burned more brightly than ever. This was excellent news for London's baser sort, who circled the old man like sharks, drawn by the penetrating scent of free money.

No mountebank collecting funds for a fake orphanage, no gambler swaddling his losses in a tale of blameless woe, no "widow" with malnutrition makeup and a rented child neglected to pay a visit to Ebenezer Scrooge. Once there, no gambit was too brazen for them, secure in the knowledge that their payday had been vouchsafed by a collection of bullying spirits. For while Scrooge had changed, the world around him had not; and the dark impulses that impel the wicked to prey upon the good remained as strong as ever.

Scrooge knew this, but tried not to let it bother him overmuch. He embraced his new profession with the same single-mindedness that had once made him pinch every penny until the copper smudged his fingers. Where Scrooge had once accumulated, he now disbursed. And he was good at it, too—he even advertised.

"Short of Cash? Money Troubles Making Life
Too Much to Bear?
Come See EBENEZER SCROOGE,
Benefactor to the World!
No Want Too Small! <u>No One</u> Turned Down!
Scrooge & Cratchit (Formerly Scrooge & Marley)
Near the Stock Exchange
Don't Wait! Apply Today!"

Scrooge had put into practice every lesson the spirits had imparted. The only trouble was that one side of the ledger held all the world's misery, while the other side contained only Scrooge, and no man, no matter how well-intentioned, could reconcile that account.

And so, at the twelve-month anniversary of his transformation, Ebenezer Scrooge was exhausted. His features were drawn, his wrinkles deeper. His eyes were bloodshot, his tongue was coated, and his hair was falling out. If Scrooge's circulation was bad—and it was!—his digestion was even worse; most foodstuffs transited his quailing system practically whole. Scrooge's movements were slow and clumsy; his thinking, muddy and erratic. And to top it all off, Scrooge took even less care with his appearance now than before—moments spent combing his hair or blinking or using a handkerchief were moments lost to his greater goal. ☛

Michael Gerber *edits this magazine. On Christmas Eve 1975, his mother read him* **A Christmas Carol***, and it blew his tiny mind.*

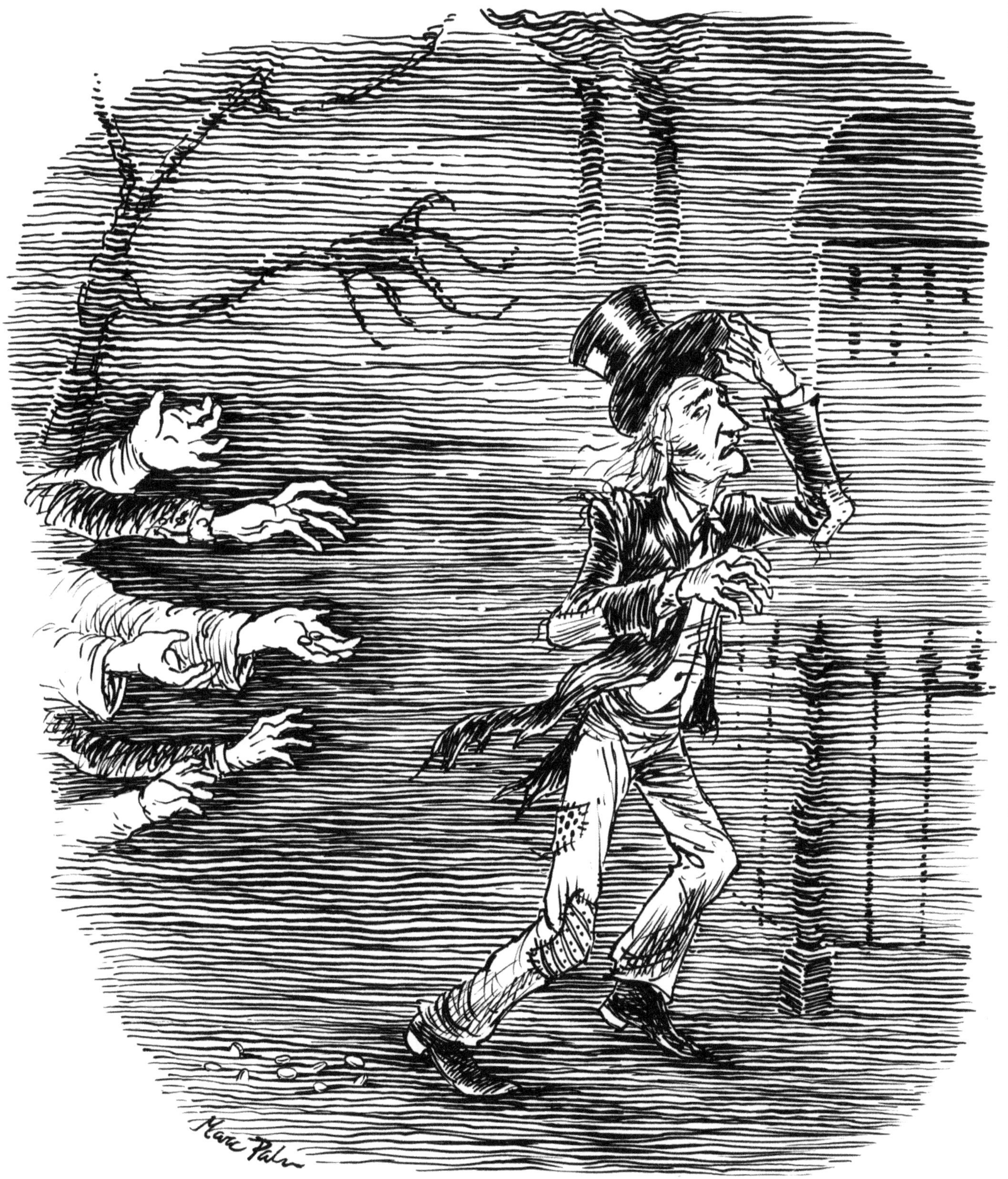
Marc Palm

The goal was great, there was no doubt about that—just ask the supplicants jammed into Scrooge's counting house! In a small waiting room outside Scrooge's office, a mass of humanity clamored and writhed, wreathed in wretchedness, profanity, and stink. They jostled against Scrooge's door, pounding on it when he took too long, kicking it when they were angry. There was no getting past the grasping, chanting, many-armed mass—they'd frequently lift Scrooge up and rifle his pockets, providing the reason for the old man's "charity" only after they'd taken the coins. Scrooge had to climb out of the window just to get his lunch.

Today he was unlucky; Scrooge had slipped on the sill and toppled into a snowbank below. No one had bothered to help—last-minute shoppers scurried oblivious through the midday murk, and even the children, whom one might expect to be slightly more sensible to the sentiments of the season, had merely pointed and laughed. One, a pug-nosed urchin with a prominent wen, had tossed a stone at him. It was standard treatment; kids teased Scrooge all the time, following him in a pack demanding money, and swearing at him when he ran out.

Now, four hours later, Scrooge rubbed the knee he'd wrenched. The old man tried to concentrate on the deranged charwoman babbling out her dreams in front of him.

"I aim to dust the entire world," the woman said in a sing-song particular to the mentally ill. Not that Scrooge needed the extra clue; she was as smudgy as a chimney sweep, and as she talked, she danced an unspeakably grimy duster over Scrooge's desk and environs.

"Go on." Scrooge tried to listen, really he did, but after a while all the stories sounded the same. His mind wandered… Perhaps the spirits would visit the pug-nosed boy tonight…Let's see him chuck a rock at the Ghost of Christmas to Come! The old man chuckled to himself at the thought of it.

"Is there something funny about dusting the entire world?" the charwoman demanded.

"No, no, Mrs. Speckle," Scrooge lied. "It was a hiccup."

"Well," she said prickily, "don't interrupt. It's rude."

"I'm sorry," Scrooge said. "Please continue."

"What did I just say about interrupting?" She flicked her duster at him.

Scrooge smiled silently, hoping Mrs. Speckle wouldn't become violent. It happened frequently, and was no wonder; in a society were money is the only measure, it is only natural that the needy resent their benefactors most of all. Scrooge knew this, and tried to forbear, but did not relish the prospect of another pocketbook across the face. If it came to that, there was really no place to escape—Mrs. Speckle sat between him and the window.

The offices, always cramped, now held three chambers instead of two; and since it seemed wrong to inconvenience Mr. Cratchit, the waiting room had come out of Scrooge's portion. Now he did not have an office as much as a closet. Small as it was, this little room saw exceedingly heavy traffic: one hundred visitors a day was usual, and two hundred was not unheard of. On this day—Christmas Eve, as I have said—the flow of customers had become a torrent. Some were feeling the pinch incurred by that most expensive of holidays, while others were convinced the anniversary would make Scrooge even more generous than usual.

"I want five pounds," the hard-faced Mrs. Speckle said, naming the highest figure she could conceive. They all did.

Scrooge felt a pang. Five pounds could buy enough rotgut to float a ship of the line. If this was simply a gambit to enrich a local pub, the poor sot would be frozen stiff in Regent's Park within the week. Still, the spirits had tasked him to serve, not to judge…

"Very reasonable indeed," Scrooge lied, unlocking his desk and extracting some coins. "After all, it is the entire world."

Mrs. Speckle didn't answer, busy counting her windfall. Then the greed lighting her broad, grimy features dimmed with concern. "What if I need more?" she croaked.

"Just come back," Scrooge said, sure he would never see her again. In the unlikely event that her ambitions were genuine, her days were just as numbered. As a rule, dear reader, the world's wild animals do not wish to be dusted, and respond intemperately towards anyone who attempts to do so.

"No need to thank me, Mrs. Speckle," Scrooge said, guiding the calico-covered maniac towards the door. "It is my belief we were put on this earth to help one another."

"You don't have to get all high and mighty about it," Mrs. Speckle said, flicking her duster at him.

Hand on the doorknob, Scrooge felt a particle crater into his right eyeball. Shutting his eye tightly against the searing pain, Scrooge opened his heart even wider. He knew Mrs. Speckle's condition wasn't her fault, any more than his miserdom had been. Who knew what malign Fate had forged the freak waddling beside him? "All I ask, Mrs. Speckle, is this: if you ever have an op-

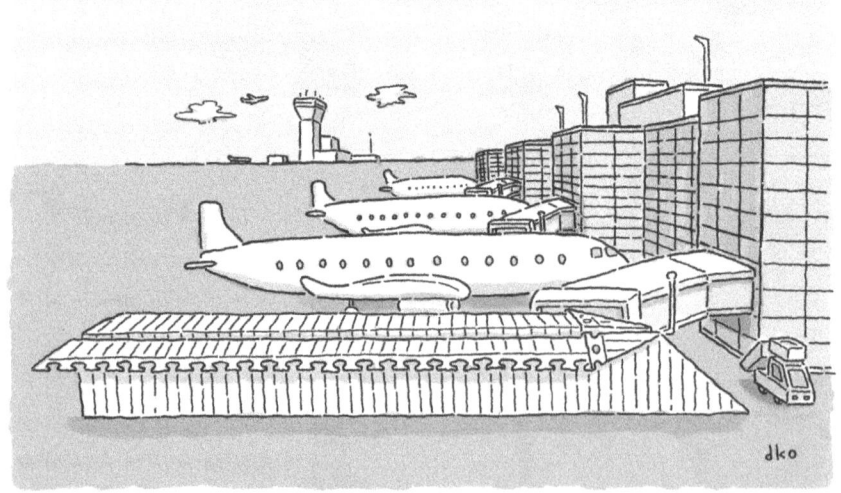

"Flight time is approximately 3 seconds and—I won't lie to you folks—it's a bit choppy up there."

portunity to help someone else…"

"Someone else?" the smudgy dynamo suddenly screeched. "There's someone else aiming to dust the entire world?"

"No, no, no, most assuredly not." Scrooge spoke in soothing tones, but edged towards the window just in case.

"Tell me who it is! I'll kill her!"

"Calm down, Mrs. Speckle. Deep breaths." Scrooge knew that flattery was the Achilles heel of the monomaniac, and poured it on. "I only meant, if you meet someone doing something else equally worthy—as if such an activity could possibly exist—consider helping them as I have helped you. Now, go: fulfill your great destiny."

As soon as Scrooge opened the door, a mass of bodies heaved forward. People began to shout.

"I'm next, Mr. Scrooge!"

"Don't listen to her, Scroogie—I'm next!"

"You godd—d son of a w—e, give me some money or I'll gut you!"

Scrooge smiled—things always got a little hostile near closing time. "Last of the day!" he called out mildly. These words were the signal for a vast brawl.

This, too, was usual. Scrooge closed the door. He looked out of the window as he waited patiently for the violence to take its course. As something heavy thunked against the door—almost certainly a skull—Scrooge noticed it was snowing again.

When the cries and tumult died down, Scrooge stepped back to the door and opened it. A bloodied pair of victors waded out of the tangle of broken humanity: a clergyman and his African ward.

"They cut in line!" someone yelled weakly.

"Good afternoon, gentlemen," Scrooge said, offering them each a handkerchief to staunch their various wounds. Then Scrooge extended his hand in friendship and welcome.

"Chief Oobu-Joobu don't shake. 'e thinks it steals 'is soul," the clergyman said, shaking Scrooge's hand. "Kype's the name. Reverend Phineas Kype." Kype chewed a toothpick as he talked, and his eight knuckles bore the words "Love" and "'ate" tattooed on them, one letter each. He turned to the Chief. "SCROOGE," Kype said loudly, jabbing a sausage-like finger at the ex-miser. "'IM GOOD MAN."

"MONEY ME!" the Chief said, thumping his chest.

"In a moment, Chief." Greed truly knew no nationality. Scrooge turned back to the man of God. "So you're some sort of…?"

"Bloke what goes an' 'elps out…You know, in darkest Africa."

"I see," Scrooge said, inwardly impressed with the creativity. He decided to have a little fun. "I've never been to darkest Africa. What's it like?"

"Erm…well…" The clergyman began to perspire. Several seconds ticked by.

"Dark, perhaps?"

Kype seized upon this with gratitude. "Oh, yeh! Very dark."

"Incredibly dark," the Chief chimed in.

"So he knows English?" Scrooge asked.

"A few key phrases," Kype said sweatily.

"You got lucky," the Chief said.

"That one, too," Kype said, striking his companion lightly on the back of the noggin. "Anyway, Africa's so dark, you can 'ardly see your 'and in fronta your face."

"Really?" Scrooge said. If these people would put one-tenth the effort into

"Mother? You might want to rethink posting #Momswhoread."

actual jobs…

"Oh, yeh! The natives there aren't black—they're bruised. From bumpin' inna things."

The Chief mimed bumping into something comically, then smiled broadly.

Scrooge smiled back. "Tell me," he asked, "did you see the Eiffel Tower when you were there?"

Kype drew another blank.

"Come, now," Scrooge said. "Surely you saw it. It's world-famous."

"Oh, that Eiffel Tower," Kype said. "I thought you were talkin' about the other one. 'Course we did." Kype jabbed a thumb towards the Chief. "'e practically lives in it."

"Does he? That's very interesting, since"—Scrooge applied the cat's paw—"the Eiffel Tower isn't in Africa. It is in Paris, France!"

There was another embarrassed silence.

Finally, Chief Oobu-Joobu spoke. "But gov—it's only 1844. The Eiffel Tower won't be built for another forty years."

"Don't try to change the subject," Scrooge said. "Reverend Kype, I know you're not a real missionary. In fact, I'd wager you've never traveled farther south than Croydon."

"Not even," the Chief said with a

SELF-PORTRAIT AS THE BIG TOE

chuckle, but Kype feigned indignation. "'ow dare you, Mr. Scrooge! Insultin' a man of the cloth!"

"A man made from whole-cloth, perhaps...Since when does the C of E tattoo 'Born to Raise 'ell' upon people's necks?" Scrooge reached over and dabbed at the Chief's cheek, then presented his blackened fingertip. "Boot blacking," he said. "And 'Oobu-Joobu'? That's just silly. Come on, fellows—even a life of crime requires a modicum of effort."

"'e made it up, I swear!" the Chief said, pointing to Kype. "Don't turn us in, gov—I've got a wife and two babes."

"I highly doubt it," Scrooge said. "But I am not here to judge. Judging's for a higher authority." He opened the desk, then tossed them each a coin. "Here's a guinea. Merry Christmas."

Their eyes lit up with the myriad perversions that could be inaugurated for such a princely sum. "Thanks!"

"Now go and sin no more," Scrooge said.

"We won't," they lied.

"I believe you," Scrooge lied back.

The waiting room was empty now, save for some sticks of broken furniture, and the bodies of the injured. Scrooge sighed—what a sight for Christmas Eve. But then again, it was Christmas Eve, and nothing could be wholly bad on that day. This brightened Scrooge considerably, and he whistled as he hauled the ruined chairs and tables out into the snow.

He was endeavoring to revive the sundry unconscious (after, of course, slipping tuppence into their unknowing pockets) when the front door burst open. Scrooge grabbed a weapon, fearing that Speckle had returned—but it was only Fred, Scrooge's nephew.

"Merry Christmas, Uncle!" he boomed. Never did these words exit his lips without rattling windows.

Scrooge straightened—at his age, not a painless process—and returned Fred's salutation. In Scrooge's estimation, Fred seemed half in the bag. And so he was; in those difficult times, dear reader, ones so much less diverting than our own, it was the custom to walk around in a constant state of semi-inebriation. This is an essential fact, and nothing in the story that I am about to relate makes much sense at all unless you believe it. Who sees ghosts? Who is prone to sudden, violent shifts of behavior? In this story, as in the first one, the wise reader must assume that every character is more or less drunk.

At the moment, however, Scrooge was basically sober. "Would you give me an early present and help me get this gentleman up and about?" It was well past dark, and Scrooge wanted to eat and get to bed, as well as remedy that sobriety I just mentioned.

Unfortunately, in addition to being the family's original Christmas freak, Fred had been born with a deep and abiding horror of gainful employ. He considered any form of purposeful activity as the first step down a slippery slope. So he demurred.

"Gee, Uncle, I'd love to," Fred said, "but I've got this dreadful frayed cuticle…"

"Right," Scrooge sighed. Since he had opened his coffers, his nephew had become even lazier than before; and that wife of Fred's was no better—she had just hired a servant to breathe for her. "Then can I prevail upon you, Fred, to go outside and get me a handful of snow? It might numb your injury."

Fred assumed an expression of pained remorse. "Normally I would, but—"

"Forget it! Forget it!" Scrooge said, exasperated. He dashed outside—it was bitter cold—and scooped up a handful of the soot-streaked snow. Back in the waiting room, he pressed it against the faces of the unconscious people, to wake them up. Then Scrooge fished a gold sovereign out of his pocket, and showed it around. "Attention, everyone! I'm going to throw this outside, and whoever finds it first, gets to keep it."

"Excellent!" Fred said. As lazy as he was, free money always invigorated him. Limbering up, he looked around at the injured. "You blighters are going down!"

"Not you, Fred." Scrooge opened the door, and tossed out the coin. The waiting room emptied like a shot. "The lame walk," Scrooge said. "It's a miracle."

"A Christmas miracle," Fred said. "Anyway, I was in the neighborhood, Uncle, picking up a thing or seven for the wife, and—"

"—you needed a little extra money?"

"Now that you mention it," Fred said good-humoredly. "Trust me, Uncle: you did right not to marry. It's ruinously expensive!"

Especially with your wife, Scrooge thought, imagining that dimple-creased, bow-bedecked monster with an involuntary shudder. Our virtues and faults, dear reader, often issue from the same sources, and Fred's partner was no exception. Scrooge's niece-by-marriage was an attractive woman, some might say too much so; and while that made her unquestionably delightful to look at, it also made her a perfect hell to live with. For as surely as she turned gentlemen's heads, Fred's wife carried the curse of her sort: vanity. Everything she owned had to be as pleasing and rare as her many suitors said she was; only then could Fred's wife be momentarily content. And valuable things were necessary, too, to cushion the day when her beauty was gone. Her looks were all she had—there never walked a woman less equipped to exist upon her virtues, nor less willing to try.

Fred's wife knew this, and the thought of a penniless future filled her with dread. She was preparing to abandon Fred for a man of better prospects (or possibly just a Bank) when Scrooge's metamorphosis took place. The softening of Scrooge's heart filled her own breast with hope—hope of prying as much money out of her husband's Uncle as possible.

At first she tried the direct approach, but the old man proved uninterested in the pleasures of the flesh. Her present tactic—making Fred wheedle for cash—was a temporary measure, as she weighed various options up to and including murder. To give her husband's wheedling maximum urgency, Fred's wife had instituted monthly target amounts, and drove her mate ruthlessly. There was even a thermometer illustration in their kitchen, which Mrs. Fred colored in whenever her husband brought home more of Scrooge's money.

With a supreme effort, Scrooge drove the nasty Mrs. Fred from his mind. He slid open his desk drawer and asked his nephew, "How much do you need?"

"Oh...not much," Fred said, then with a studied casualness named a figure that made Scrooge briefly lose consciousness.

Fred saw the flutter. "Uncle Scrooge! Are you all right?" he asked, instantly calculating the bequest.

"Yes, yes," Scrooge said, rummaging through the coins. "Only I don't think I have that much on-hand."

"Whatever you've got is close enough," Fred said. He'd become much more brazen of late; Fred's wife had announced that there would be no physical affection between them until her Draconian targets had been met.

"Open your pocket," Scrooge said, then filled the right one until it bulged like a tumor.

"Top it off, top it off. It can take more."

As he filled the other, Scrooge said, "Fred, I can't keep doing this. I must help those in need."

"I am in need," Fred said, hopping up and down so more coins could fit. "I'm desperate." His lonely groin throbbed in silent agreement.

"No, you don't want to get a job," Scrooge said. "There's a difference."

Fred scowled. "Out of all London," he complained, "should I alone be unable to call on your generosity simply because I'm your flesh and blood? Forgive me for saying so, dear Uncle," Fred said, "but that is f—d up. Our relation should give me more claim, not less. And I alone have shown affection for you regardless of your generosity. Remember how nice I was to you last year, when you were still despised by all?"

"I wasn't despised," Scrooge said. "Disliked, perhaps, misunderstood—"

"Pish and tosh!" Fred said. "People were burning you in effigy, and on the hottest days of the year! Yet I wished you 'Merry Christmas.' I even invited you to dinner!"

"I remember—you make sure I do," Scrooge said. "Still, it is true you have been kind to me and I appreciate it. But even you must admit that your wife cannot say the same."

"Oh, Uncle, you'll like her better in time," Fred lied. He certainly hadn't. In fact, the money in his pocket was going towards an Escape Fund. When Fred reached a certain plateau, he planned to hop a ship for Italy and never return. Let her shift for herself, the rouge-caked trollop. "My wife merely hides her affections—as you used to, Uncle."

Scrooge grunted.

Fred swallowed nervously. Grunting was uncomfortably close to Scrooge's old manner; could he be slipping back? Fred wondered. He changed the subject. "Tell me, Uncle: how many of God's creatures did you help today?"

"Let's see," Scrooge said, beginning to dress for the cold walk home. "Someone trying to start a fake orphanage, three widows with rented children, a raft of girls about to give birth to pillows, some gamblers, some degenerates..."

"Stop, stop! Before my view of humanity darkens to blindness!"

"Welcome to my world," Scrooge said, with a wan smile. "The spirits didn't tell me about the crooks. Or the crazies."

"Of course they didn't. They probably work on commission."

Scrooge had finished putting on his coat. Next to the coat tree sat a large parcel wrapped in brown paper. "Oh, I also got a bronze bust from the Prince of Wales."

"Uncle! We must celebrate!" Fred exclaimed, angling for a better dinner than he would get at home. (His wife's legions of servants, though full of boy-toys and gossip-buddies, did not include one decent cook.) "Let us toast the royal gift!"

Scrooge deflected this suggestion, wishing to eat alone and turn in early. "I'm not sure it was meant in esteem," he said. "They gave it to me as a bribe. Apparently I've given so much money, inflation is skyrocketing throughout the Empire."

"Well," Fred said, "that s—ks, if you don't mind my saying so." He looked at the object. "It is the very image of you."

"Looks rather crosseyed to me...Fred, could you help—"

Fred had a special horror of anything heavy. "Oh, my lord, no!" he exclaimed with a laugh. "Uncle, are you mad?"

"Thought not. Just being optimistic, since it's Christmas..." Scrooge leaned

55

down and picked up the package, feeling several essential internal structures give way. "I was just hoping…after I gave you all that money…"

"Uncle, it's precisely that money which prevents me from helping," Fred said, patting his distended thighs. "I'm loaded to the gunwales as it is. Any more effort, and I might swamp. Anyway, I'm the one doing you a favor. You had to give me that money, otherwise"—Fred wiggled his fingers—"'crackle, crackle, crackle!'"

Scrooge was annoyed. "Everybody knows I have to give them money. And yet they have to give me nothing in return! No matter how much I give, it's never enough!" he muttered.

Fred, naturally, saw none of his own behavior in this remark, only an opportunity to enrich himself further. "Uncle, you know I support your new generosity. But you are being used by all these strangers. What about spreading joy and affection within one's family? For one thing, there are fewer of us, so it's bound to be cheaper!"

"Doesn't seem very cheap."

Fred slapped Scrooge on the back jovially, nearly toppling him. "Better hope the spirits aren't listening, you old grouch!" he teased, silently heaping another blessing on those spectral bullies. "Have you done any shopping? What will you do for Christmas? Will you come over for dinner again? We so enjoyed your company last year—especially the wife." This was a lie; Fred's wife had ritualistically destroyed everything Scrooge had touched, eaten from, or sat on.

"There's no time," Scrooge said. "Tomorrow is a 'wandering day.'" This was Scrooge's term for treading the streets of London, forcing money on anything vaguely sentient. "I would dine with you, Fred, but I must think of my immortal soul. I have so many years to make up for, so much meanness to expunge."

"Easy, Uncle." Fred oozed faux-concern. "You'll blow a boiler. One man can only hold so much grace…Ready for the deep-freeze?"

Fred's hand was on the knob, but Scrooge bade him stop. The ex-miser rested the bust on a splintered end-table, then commenced digging through his coat pockets. "Must leave a few farthings for the mice—"

"Oh, Uncle," Fred said, "rodents don't even use money."

"These ones do."

"Then you've spoiled them," Fred said sternly. "Uncle, you must measure your charity, giving where it makes the most good. It's not enough to give—one must give wisely."

"The spirits didn't say anything about that," Scrooge said.

"It was implied," Fred said. "Go home. Rest. Then come over for dinner."

"The last time I did, your wife's cooking made me violently ill. I think she was trying to poison me."

She probably was, Fred thought. "So bring your own food."

Bob Cratchit leaned out of his office, a wave of delicious heat rolling forth. "Mr. Scrooge," he said, fixing his employer with a gaze slightly unfocused by strong drink, "I wonder if I might have a word with you?"

"Of course, Bob. I see you've started celebrating early." Scrooge pointed to the umbrella-bedecked tiki mug in Bob's right hand.

Cratchit was shirtless, and his skin bore the reddish hue that comes from prolonged exposure to a roaring blaze. He noticed Scrooge was not alone.

"Fred," he said icily.

"Bob," Fred answered, the smallish syllable packed with hate.

Ever since Scrooge's transformation, the two men had fought for control of the old man's affections, like dogs tussling over a beefsteak. It was an even fight: While the former was a blood relation, Cratchit was now Scrooge's partner in the counting house, and tended to all the business that Scrooge, preoccupied as he was with matters of income redistribution, could not.

"Any new business today, Bob?" Scrooge asked.

"No, sir," Cratchit said. There hadn't been any for months. Vastly immature, Cratchit had always been much more interested in play than work. At first, he contented himself with long lunches, then extended vacations, which he filled playing blind-man's-buff and other insipid contests. But eventually the local urchins had tired of the man-child's company, and barred him from their games. Forced to stay at work, an angry Cratchit had embarked on a campaign to alienate all of Scrooge's old clients, as well as discourage any new ones; happily, this gambit was totally successful.

Now with his days blessedly free and Scrooge a ridiculously easy touch, the ex-wretch had turned his formerly bone-chilling office into a Caribbean fantasia, complete with palm trees and a sand floor. Maintaining a constant temperature of 85 degrees Fahrenheit took so much coal that the plume stretched into the ionosphere. It had become a London

"Aim for your party."

landmark. On a clear day, you could see it from Belgium.

"I'd like to hire a steel band," Cratchit said.

Scrooge looked at Fred, who looked cross. "Uncle, charity begins at home," he whisper-snarled.

"Erm, perhaps after Christmas, Bob," Scrooge said. "Surely we can get them cheaper then?"

Cratchit wasn't ready to give up yet. "But it would spread so much joy!"

A vein had emerged from Fred's temple. He grabbed the thing nearest to hand—a piece of that afternoon's mail—and began mauling it with great thoroughness.

Scrooge got the message. "I don't think so, Bob..."

Cratchit wheeled out his big gun. "But Mr. Scrooge, my son Tim specifically asked for it...You remember Tim? The..."—Cratchit paused for effect—"The cripple?"

"Oh, dirty pool!" Fred exclaimed.

Cratchit ignored him. "It was to be Tim's only present. You know how he never thinks of himself, only of others."

Right on cue, Scrooge began to trickle.

"I know it's a lot, but it would mean so much...to Tim." Cratchit poured it on. "After all, we don't know how many more Christmases he'll have..."

Scrooge burst into tears. The bust hit the floor with a clang. "What is the admiration of the Prince of Wales," he exclaimed, "compared to the love of one little boy?" He hugged Cratchit, getting suntan lotion all over the front of his coat. "Forgive me, Bob—what was I thinking? Hire the musicians immediately. And tell Tim they're from me."

Fred threw down his handfuls of half-shredded mail in disgust. Everyone but Scrooge knew that Tiny Tim, a/k/a "Master T.," was now the head of one of London's top criminal gangs—and that Scrooge's sentimental largesse formed the very foundation of his unholy empire.

"I shall." Mid-hug, Cratchit looked over Scrooge's shoulder and stuck his tongue out. This was too much for Scrooge's nephew to bear. "Uncle, Mr. Cratchit is taking advantage of you."

"Oh, Fred, you believe everyone is taking advantage of me," Scrooge said, still speaking into Cratchit's sunburned pectorals.

Cratchit pulled away from his boss. "Fred, I can't believe you would say such a thing."

"The state of your office alone suggests that I must," Fred said. "My God, man—is that a pelican?"

"Which I am nursing back to health! For the London Zoo!" Cratchit said indignantly. He turned to his employer. "The poor animal was—those of us without money must tend to our immortal souls in other ways."

"Good, Bob," Scrooge said. "The spirits would be proud of you."

"Oh, sod the spirits!" Fred said.

"Fred!" Scrooge was appalled; Cratchit was delighted. To impugn the spirits—this had to spell the end of Fred as a rival. But before Scrooge could lay into his nephew, a lithe woman with Asian features and a coconut-shell bra leaned out of the doorway.

"The coconut oil is warmed, Mister Robert. It is time for your rubdown..."

"In a moment," Cratchit said quickly, then saw the look Fred was giving him. "She's my sister," he explained.

"B—s," Fred mumbled.

"FRED!" Scrooge said angrily. "If you do not show Mr. Cratchit a little Christmas cheer, I swear by every spirit, I'll cut your hourly allowance in half!"

"What do the spirits say about employees with two sacks of unanswered correspondence under their back porches?"

"That's a total lie," Cratchit said, truthfully. There were actually four sacks.

"Fred, I am ashamed of you! You're asking for a visit tonight, truly you are," Scrooge said. "We'll discuss it later."

"Yes, Uncle," Fred said, "we most assuredly will." Fred jammed his hat onto his head, yanked open the front door, and stomped out into the swirling snow.

"See you tomorrow for dinner! I'll bring the turkey!"

Fred turned. "Merry Christmas!" he shouted with maximum irony. As he did so, Fred was nearly run down by Tiny Tim's massive, pimped-out omnibus.

"Get outta the road, yeh freak!" Master T's driver Crippen yelled.

Scrooge picked up the bust once again.

"What's in there?" Cratchit asked. "A present?"

"Of sorts," Scrooge said. "The Prince of Wales gave it to me, in hopes of keeping me from donating to anything in the coming year. Apparently it demoralizes the other donors."

"You must be proud," Cratchit said.

"Sure. But it won't stop me," Scrooge said, smiling. "The spirits made it clear: I have a job to do, Bob, and I can't stop until either everyone is happy or all my money's gone."

"That's the spirit!" Cratchit said, delighted. Then the clerk added in his most honeyed voice, "You know, we meant to get you a present, Mr. Scrooge..."

"Don't worry about it, Bob. That's not what Christmas is about."

"I know," Cratchit said. "You of all people have proven that. It's just that a groat doesn't go as far as it used to. There's all the kids...And Tim's artificial spleen. It's made of Sumatran manganese..."

"I wanted to ask how that worked out," Mr. Scrooge said. "I apologize for being so callous."

"It's functioning perfectly, Mr. Scrooge. Though it may need some expensive new

"They're friendly, but they're also carnivorous, so remember that when you're called on to beg and roll over."

parts in the coming year."

"I stand at the ready, Bob. Well," Scrooge said, stepping outside, "a very Merry Christmas to you, and to all the other Cratchits. The turkey is from me, of course—and whatever else you require. I've opened accounts in your name at every grocer in Camden Town, so don't be stingy with yourself, Bob!"

"Thank you, Mr. Scrooge! Merry Christmas!" Still bare-chested, Cratchit closed the door quickly. His smile faded the moment the door closed, and was replaced by a worried expression which did not fade. Fred had threatened his gravy train before, but this time it was more serious. He'd have to keep a very close eye on that fellow—

"Mister Robert?" the voluptuous native-girl called from inside his office. "Aren't you coming for your 'happy ending'?"

—but first, Bob needed a massage!

INTO THE SOUP.

By a quirk of London's topography, the region which contained Scrooge's office—as well as his chambers, some distance away—was a natural bowl, so that all the smoke and fog in the city collected there. This made getting around difficult, somewhat like swimming through gruel. On particularly bad evenings, when the atmosphere was positively viscous, the inhabitants were wont to employ small, hand-sized shovels to speed their progress by digging a sort of passage, or channel, through the air as they walked. This night was particularly difficult going, with Nature adding her own frosty ingredients to the particulated stew.

Scrooge didn't mind this inconvenience a bit, as it ensured that this neighborhood was the cheapest in London. Frugality was still a watchword for him: before his skirmish with the spirits, Scrooge insisted his money stay securely in the bank. After, he tried to keep his expenses to a minimum, to maximize his charity.

With the bust tucked under one arm and the scent of Bob Cratchit's suntan oil still wafting from his overcoat, Scrooge trudged through the sooty snow. He shoveled with his right hand, but it did no good. The air was especially hefty this evening, and while that meant slow going, it also made things distinctly safer for the brittle-boned ex-miser; anyone who happened to slip on a patch of ice would fall quite gently, gravity being offset by the pudding-like quality of the vapors. On the way down, Scrooge had had enough time to wonder if other holidays boasted a contingent of spirits. Were excessively mild people visited on Halloween, and exhorted to be scarier? Were prudes rousted from their beds on St. Valentine's Day? And what was their lesson? Scrooge blushed to think of it.

It may surprise you, dear reader, to know that the reformed Scrooge took his evening meal in the same melancholy tavern as he had exactly twelve months before. First, it was close to his office, a signal virtue on a teeth-chattering night like this. Second, it was cheap—and we have already discussed Scrooge's views on that subject. And, third, habits of the stomach are even more difficult to change than habits of the heart—even if, as in this case, they put the bearer in quite a bit of danger.

Danger? Certainly. On Christmas Eve? That night above all others. Christmas can be a bitter experience, a time when what one lacks, or has lost, looms larger than any current blessing. There's a reason why the suicides go up.

As we have seen, Scrooge's activity had attracted a sizeable portion of the criminal element to the precincts of his office; and after such an influx, it was only natural that the shops and restaurants there would begin to cater to this roughest trade.

The aim of Scrooge's local, The Ball and Chain, was to put its customers in a spending mood by reminding them of home—"home" in this case being Newgate Prison. With depressing décor, an alarming clientele, and truly execrable food, The Ball and Chain did a brisk business…mostly due to the fact that there was a guy in it who constantly bought everybody free drinks.

Scrooge held criminals in no higher esteem than the rest of us do, but he could not afford to play favorites. The ex-miser assumed that any act of kindness was a point in the proper column, regardless of who the kindness aided, or whether they deserved it. Maybe this was incorrect, but the spirits hadn't left behind a rulebook; if they ever came back (and Scrooge sometimes hoped that they would), he could ask them. Until then, however, he had to play it safe: charity for all. From that day to this, Scrooge had not finished one evening's meal at The Ball and Chain without furnishing everyone's drinks, or meals, or both.

But this evening was different. He tipped well, as usual, but when the bill was presented, no free drinks were announced.

"What are you waiting for, Warden?" Scrooge said to the man behind the bar, who was also the owner. "My change, if you please."

The owner gave Scrooge a puzzled smile. "Aren't you…I just assumed…"

"Not tonight," Scrooge said, firmly. Fred's words had found their mark.

The Warden glanced around, then spoke to Scrooge in low tones. "Pardon me for saying so, sir, but I don't think that's a very good idea. It's meeting night for The Full-Loads, y'see. They'll be wanting their free drink."

The Full-Loads was the name of a local wheelbarrow gang. They terrorized the neighborhood, partying, getting into fights, moving stuff around randomly. They'd scoop up passer-by and refuse to let them out unless they paid a ransom. Up until now, Scrooge had been safe, thanks to his nightly generosity.

"It'd be a terrible shame if they 'took you for a ride,'" the Warden said. "A terrible shame." The Warden drew his finger across his throat, suggesting that such a ride might be Scrooge's last, but the ex-miser would not budge.

"You know how it is, Warden," Scrooge said. "Money's always tight around the holidays…It will do everyone good to skip an evening—it will make tomorrow's drink that much more appreciated."

Directly to Scrooge's left, a man resting his face on the bar—a habitual drinker by the name of Sozzle—took loud exception.

"No free drink tonight?" Sozzle cried, raising his head in unsteady indignation. "It's Christmas Eve, Mr. Scrooge! Think of your fellow man! What would Jesus have done?"

Sozzle's mate Sot awoke, and commenced a similar barrage from Scrooge's other side. "I'll tell you what He would've done," Sot said defiantly, "He would've turned the water into wine! Or beer! Or maybe even hard stuff!"

"Some people shouldn't be allowed to read the Bible," Scrooge grumbled, but Sot continued.

"This season is consecrated for the purpose of giving gifts," Sot said. "This is the one time of the year where one can look at his fellows not as competitors or impediments, but as friends."

"Well said, friend," Scrooge replied, leaning heavily on the last word. "While I have given you innumerable free drinks and meals, friend, I'd like to know: what gift have you ever given me?"

Looking down his scarred nose at Scrooge, Sot sniffed, "I never pick your pocket on Sundays. The other days, sure. But Sundays? Never."

Scrooge's face colored. "I wondered—you rascal—"

"No need to thank me," Sot said. "That's simply out of the goodness of me heart."

The rest of the patrons had developed an interest in the discussion, and had gathered behind Scrooge.

"He's got a point," someone said. "He could've robbed you blind."

"I would've," another person added. "If I'd only known Sundays were free…"

"Be quiet!" Scrooge demanded. "I weary of your twisted jailbird's logic!"

"Twisted?" "Jailbird?" "Logic?" Whispers circumnavigated the room. As Scrooge received his change, grumbles were building.

"I told you he was no good."

"Once a miser, allus a miser!"

"I'll use his guts for a Christmas stocking!"

Scrooge heard all this, and it made him even more resolved not to break down. After all the kindness he'd shown, this is what everyone thought of him? The old man turned, as to make for the door, but no one moved. He pulled out his miniature shovel and dug gently at the patrons massed between himself and the exit. The crowd of ruffians only wedged in tighter. Someone named Dogmeat wrenched the shovel away from him with a practiced swipe.

"Hallo, you seem to have taken my…" Scrooge went quiet, as Dogmeat snapped the shovel in two, then gave a menacing growl.

Beads of perspiration gathered at various points on Scrooge's person. He turned, and found himself face-to-sternum with the chieftain of the Full-Loads, a pocked and lumpy gentleman everyone called "Axle."

Axle pushed his way to the bar next to Scrooge, and bellowed out an order. "Warden, I'd like my free drink now. Put it on this gentleman's account."

"Yeah!" someone else shouted. "Me, too!" another added.

The Warden looked at Scrooge. "How about it?" he asked.

Now, Scrooge hadn't always been a perfect man, but he was always a brave one—after all, it had taken three full spirits, plus the ghost of his best friend, just to get him to quit being a git. He was equally feisty now. "I don't think so, Warden," Scrooge said. "What you're doing isn't charity. It's extortion."

The Warden saw the malign effect Scrooge's legalistic term had on the crowd, some of whom had spent considerable time in the stripy hole for that very offense. He saw a few removing the prison-themed "flair" from the walls, for use as weapons. Though the Warden placed no particular value on the hide of Ebenezer Scrooge, he had an establishment to protect, and could not afford the inevitable collateral damage. "If it's all the same to you, Mr. Scrooge, I suggest you leave," the Warden said.

"I don't want any trouble, especially not on Christmas Eve."

"This is preposterous!" Scrooge said. "I've bought food and drink for everyone in this wretched house!"

"But what have you done for us lately?" Axle snarled, to general approval.

"He's a fraud!" one ruffian said. "I say we throw him out!"

"But take his money first!" another added, slapping a well-used cosh against his palm.

Another whipped out his knife. "I'll make a belt out of his esophagus! A liver makes an excellent cravat!"

Axle turned to Mr. Knife. "Dude, please. I just ate."

"Sorry, Axle," Mr. Knife said. "I was just, you know, riffing."

"Well, it's gross. And where did you even learn a word like 'esophagus' anyway? You know what the mid-Victorian school system is like." Axle turned away, then turned back. "You always freakin' take it too far, you know? Sheesh!"

This internecine strife brought the proceedings down a fraction; looking back, it probably saved Scrooge's life. Still, Scrooge's person was far from secure: he was surrounded by inebriated ex-cons, people on the lam from the law, and punks with souped-up wheelbarrows and nothing to lose. As such, he felt it best to attempt another exit quickly, and with as little fanfare as possible.

Scrooge pushed his way through the crowd, which pushed back, hurling curses and spitting. At the door, a particularly large Full-Load blocked his way. This was Sparky, a Full-Load so untouched by civilization that his 'barrow didn't even have a front wheel. He just pushed it, scarring the ground, throwing sparks as he went. People had lost toes, dear reader, and those were the lucky ones!

"Where d'ya think you're goin'?" Sparky said, leering through rotting teeth.

Show no fear, Scrooge thought. They can smell fear. Unfortunately, they could also smell urine, which was collecting in a puddle at Scrooge's feet. "Please don't kill me," he mewled.

"Mebbe I will, and mebbe not," the hulk said. "Ya gotta pay the toll first."

"Oh?" Scrooge asked, his voice quivering. "How much?"

"I dunno—I can't count."

Sparky's horny, vise-like palm closed over the old man's collar. Scrooge's attempts to struggle free were no more than the twisting of a pennant in an ill wind. As the crowd shouted its savage encouragement, the brutal man-mountain roughly turned our hero upside down;

who ralphed in my Lambo?; Shake it like a Polaroid picture! Hey ya!!

Mohammad bin Salman bin Abdulaziz Al Saud

Riyadh 12911, Saudi Arabia

Varsity Yacht-Owning, 3, 4; Varsity Falconry, 3, 4; *Guys and Dolls*, "Miss Adelaide" (All-Male Production); Suppressing Debate Club, 1, 2, 3, 4; "You can't get a hangover from Johnnie Walker Black"; Self-Investigation Club (President); Voted Most Likely to Blockade Yemen; "He's reading *Game of Thrones* again…"; Devil's Triangle: You, Me & My Nigerian Bodyguard; "Yeah, I SAW him!"; Are you a Friend of FFFFFFFaisal?; Yodeling towards Mecca; Grandad was the George Washington of our country, in the sense that he founded it and also owned human beings; "Beach Week? We *invented* Beach Week"; Qadi — Have You Boofed Yet?; Riyadh Working Girls' Benevolent Association — Chair; Memories… getting deflowered by Dad's 4th favorite concubine… blaming the cocaine on my terrified Filipino servants… suffocating, omnipresent paranoia; Killing Dissidents (it's a drinking game); Exchange Student, Georgetown Prep.

129 The Minaret 2003

GERBER & SCHWARZ

then grasping Scrooge by the ankles, began to shake. Coins came tumbling out of Scrooge's pockets, and the crowd scrambled to retrieve them like chickens hard after seed.

The crowd's levity was infectious, and Sparky naturally caught it; when he was laughing too hard to continue his work, he dumped the dazed Scrooge onto the mud-streaked tavern floor. As Scrooge attempted to collect himself, someone reached down and stole the old man's spectacles. This was the signal to begin a spirited performance of "monkey in the middle," with Scrooge cast as the unfortunate banana-grabber.

"Hey! Stop fooling about, now! Those are mine!...All right, fine, I don't even want th—GIMME!"

It would've lasted longer, had it not been so easy; even society's dregs appreciate a challenge. Truthfully, once they were in possession of Scrooge's liquid assets, the old man ceased to interest any of them, and they went back to plotting various dark enterprises designed to take advantage of people's holiday goodwill.

"Here, Scroogie," one said, waving the eyeglasses. He opened the door, then tossed them outside. "Fetch!"

Scrooge was not even trusted to provide sufficient propulsion for his exit. Sparky's foot on Scrooge's backside ejected him with such force that he was plunged head and shoulders into a snowbank. After extricating himself, the old man spent a cold ten minutes looking for his glasses, as London's rapists, thieves, and murderers pointed and jeered at him through the tavern window.

"Nothing like this ever happened to me when I was a miser," Scrooge griped. "Only the good are so mistreated in this world!" His conscience burned at the injustice. "Just you wait!" he spat quietly at the warm shadows capering inside. "After I die, I'm going to haunt the s—t out of all of you!"

Seeing that Scrooge was saying something to them, the criminals laughed harder, and pounded on the glass until the Warden feared that it might give way. Then they pulled faces at the old man, and oh!—one showed Scrooge his b-m.

Sparky's rough treatment had not helped Scrooge's knee, which was now fairly yodeling for attention; and during the hunt for his glasses, Scrooge somehow succeeded in getting snow down both of his socks. This discomfort was not entirely bad, in that it (as small discomforts sometimes do) focused Scrooge's mind and stimulated an idea.

"Whoop! Hallo!" Scrooge clapped his hands and laughed aloud at the thought of his sparkling new plan. "They'll be f—g sorry they ever messed with 'The Scrooge'!"

Once he'd found his spectacles, the ex-miser walked—ever so casually, now—around the corner, to where all the Full-Load gang's wheelbarrows were propped up against the wall. Checking to see that nobody was watching, he took out his house key. Then, deliberately and with great relish, he scraped it against the garish custom paint-jobs of the 'barrows, marring them severely. On the last, Scrooge even wrote a profanity—then he ran for all he was worth!

The thick atmosphere, and his age, and his lack of a shovel, slowed Scrooge to a crawl; fortunately, everyone inside the bar was busy spending the money they'd liberated from his pockets. After two blocks of giddy flight, he looked behind and saw no one, so he slowed to a normal pace. Scrooge felt invigorated, like a child again. "Whoop!" he said to no one in particular. It echoed off the streets, and shook the snowy trees, and caused people to frown out of parlors that looked warm and inviting. "Merry Christmas, Full-Loads! I've got your present right here!" Scrooge clutched his organ of generation through his pants, and shook it. This was a childish act, there's no denying it. Yet sometimes it is good to be childish, and what time could be better for it than Christmas?

Unfortunately, Scrooge's braggadocio faded as quickly as it had come, and in its place a full measure of bully-dread set in. "What the f—k did I just do?" Scrooge mumbled, walking faster. "A tavern full of ruffians—they're going to beat the s—t out of me." Poor impulse control, a moment of elation, and then pants-pooping fear; yes, dear reader, it was exactly like being a child again.

Now, it may have been the dankness of the atmosphere, or the continuing snow (the flakes were still falling, but more slowly now, as the temperature dropped). It might have been his cracked and filthy glasses, or a trick of his memory, or hallucinations brought on by extremely cold feet. Whatever the cause, when Scrooge arrived at his

Future Superlatives

MOST LIKELY TO BE INTERNET FAMOUS

BEST BIONIC EYE

MOST LIKELY TO SUCCEED WHEN THE APOCALYPSE HITS

CLASS CLOWN

de Recat

"I'm transitioning."

door, the knocker was not a normal knocker. It was the spitting image of his old partner, Jacob Marley.

Scrooge spied the change from several houses away. "Oh, give me a break!" Mounting his steps, the old man looked skyward, assuming that was the right direction to address the spirits. "Not tonight, okay? I'm tired, and there's slush in my shoes."

As if on cue, the papier-mache face dropped to his doorstep with a clunk. "Damn kids," Scrooge grumbled, embarrassed at his credulity. He kicked the crude mask off his doorstep into the street, and went inside.

Thanks to the mixture of gelid mud and horse-excrement in which he had been drenched by Tiny Tim's omnibus, Fred trudged home from his Uncle's counting house bone-cold and powerfully rank. After a while, his nose became insensible to it; but Fred knew he stank by the way all the shoppers crossed the street to get out of range. But it was after he arrived at home that his discomfort really began.

As I have said, Fred's wife had never liked Scrooge. At first she refused to believe that the old miser had actually changed. Then, when it was clear that Scrooge's coffers had well and truly been blasted open by fear and remorse, she became determined to get their share of the booty.

Scrooge saw this, and forbore it as best he could. The old man politely declined the shady business deals, real estate scams, and chain-letter schemes she constantly dangled (to say nothing of the sexual favors), while at the same time providing funds for any legitimate need that arose. As long as Scrooge was alive, Fred and his wife need not worry about the wolf at the door.

Unfortunately, Scrooge's decency had only stoked Mrs. Fred's ravenous greed. If Scrooge had refused to help them at all, perhaps Mrs. Fred would've given up, moving on to her other dreams, such as becoming best friends with the Queen. But every little kindness they received reminded Mrs. Fred of the larger things they did not get; her resentment was now of sufficient heat and pressure to run Mr. Fulton's celebrated train. This anger was counterbalanced, and only just, by her fevered fantasies of what she could do with all that Scroogian lucre. These two thoughts became so inflated in her mind that there wasn't room for anything else, certainly not Christmas spirit.

The harridan met her husband at the threshold. "Well?" she demanded.

"Well, what?" Fred said.

"Did the old coot give you anything?" she barked. "You smell like horses—t."

Fred was in no mood. "Perhaps you could let me change clothes before..."

"I should've known! You didn't get a penny!" Mrs. Fred said angrily, cracking him on the head. (Mrs. Fred wore a thimble on her thumb for just this purpose, which she had nicknamed "The Persuader.")

"Ow! F—g h—l!" Fred said, feeling his head, then checking his fingertips for blood.

"Serves you right," a chambermaid offered.

"What's all that lot?" Fred pointed at the stack of boxes the chambermaid was carrying.

"New dresses," Mrs. Fred said defiantly. "Got a problem with that?"

As yet another means of encouraging Fred to french-press more money out of his uncle, his wife had begun systemically increasing their standard of living. First, she had upgraded her wardrobe—my God! no Sultana or courtesan had anything on Mrs. Fred. "Marie Antoinette had the right idea," she was fond of saying to her husband, "but she just didn't go far enough."

This was followed by the hiring of an army of servants, each of whom was more outlandish and unnecessary than the last. Though Mrs. Fred hadn't a scrap of civic spirit, her efforts in this area had made a measureable decrease in the unemployment rate of the district. Charity often works like that, dear reader, and its good shouldn't be discounted a jot for it. It's a rare donation that isn't made for selfish reasons, or to spite someone, or to demonstrate one's place atop the heap—but I digress.

"So did you get some more money, or not?" Mrs. Fred said, ready to dislodge it with another whack.

Fred scrambled away, covering his head. "I think you broke through to my brain!"

Mrs. Fred stopped; a dead husband was no good to her, not yet. "I'm sorry to have to thump you in front of the help."

"It's all right," Fred said. "They hate me anyway." And they did; Fred had retaliated against his wife's extravagance by "paying" the servants with banknotes he drew himself.

"We hate you, too!" chorused his wife's sisters, and that wretched demi-gigolo Topper, who was determined to sleep with all of them even though they thought he was a creep. All of them had moved in after the money had begun to flow.

"Oh, go home!" Fred said, dumping out the contents of his pockets, and coloring in the thermometer. "I'm quite close..." Fred said. His loins suddenly kindled.

"Might you give me a little something… on account?"

Mrs. Fred grabbed his roaming hand and twisted it painfully. "No way, buster. You know the rules."

Fred's pain turned to anger. "Listen, you! I'm your husband, and this is my house, and if you don't start showing me the proper respect, I'll…"

Mrs. Fred turned, all buttons and bows, her Medusa-like locks flouncing. "You'll what?"

"I'll—I'll—!" The fact is he would do nothing; Fred's wife had convinced her rather sheltered husband that she had invented the physical act of love, and was the only one of her gender who knew how to pull it off. So Fred backed down. "I'll—I'll thank you to remember that it's Christmas Eve!"

The mention of the holiday—another one, and here she was, not yet dining at Buckingham Palace—set Mrs. Fred into a fresh rage. "Bah, humbug!" she hollered, working her way about the room, clambering over servants and relatives, destroying expensive, hard-to-replace items at random. "I hate all my stuff!"

Fred watched this with familiar feelings of revulsion and horror. As with other great natural engines of destruction, flight was the only alternative. Unfortunately, the army of hangers-on had turned their once-comfortable home into a standing-room-only affair. Still, his stink was a powerful wedge, and Fred was able to push through the crowd halfway to the water closet.

"Don't you dare run away from me," Mrs. Fred yelled. "I sent you over there to get real money out of that stale old freak, and you come back with nothing!"

"Well," Fred said, "it was impossible. He was occupied."

"Giving money away! To other people!" Mrs. Fred saw every act of charity as theft from her pocket.

"But dear, those people are poor," Fred said. "They need it so much more than we do."

"But we're his flesh and blood!"

"Yeah!" bleated a maid sprawled across a nearby divan. She was having her nails done by another maid (who was receiving a pedicure).

"No, you're not!" Fred said. "By the way, that divan is new, isn't it?"

"And what if it is?" Mrs. Fred spat. "What's wrong with my wanting to have nice things? Don't I deserve it? My friend Vicky gets to have nice things and her husband isn't beastly to her!"

Fred grabbed his beard and pulled it in frustration. "First of all, she's not your friend—"

"She is too my friend!"

"No, she's not! She's the Queen, and you're a nutter!"

The room went utterly silent; Fred had said the unsayable.

"O-ho! Get ready, Mr. Bruised-Brain!" Eyes blazing, Mrs. Fred had gathered her skirts and was set to rush across the room to dispense some Victorian justice when a distinguished-looking man appeared in the doorway to the dining room. "Dinner is served."

"Thank God," Fred said. "I'm starving!" He walked full of purpose towards the waiting food, until he was stopped by his bride.

"Uh-uh," she said, stretching herself across the doorway.

"What do you mean, 'Uh-uh'?" Fred said, pushing at her slightly, and enjoying the physical contact.

"I mean, 'Uh-uh,'" Mrs. Fred said. "You're not eating. Not until you go back and get more money from your uncle. Some real money this time. The kind that folds."

"This is ridiculous! I won't be bossed around in my own house! Let me through!" Fred gave another push, harder this time, but his wife refused to move. She simply shook her head "no."

A beefy woman got up from the table and shambled over. "Is he bothering you, ma'am?" she rumbled.

Fred was incensed. "Who is that?" he said, pointing. "Who are you?"

"I'm the new governess," the woman said, daring him to do something about it. Other servants, his wife's private army, got up from the dining room table and massed behind her. Fred

calculated his odds. He was bigger and stronger than most of them, but there were loads—where did she find them all? Each one clutched a utensil, and wore a hard expression; knowing upon which side their bread was buttered, they relished the prospect of battle.

Fred gave up. "Fine!" he said, glowering. "I'll go back!" As yet another servant closed the door behind him he shouted, "A governess? We don't even have children!"

Fred pulled his beard and twirled his mustachios, a nervous habit. Scrooge's nephew had reacted to the sudden onset of prosperity in the time-honored fashion, by cultivating a luxurious set of facial hair. His beard and moustachios were so profuse and poke-y that they called to mind nothing so much as a cat's whiskers. And indeed they performed the same purpose, to prevent Fred's head from getting stuck in holes. A useful thing that, as Fred was tirelessly poking into every tiny facet of Scrooge's affairs, hoping to tease out any profit hidden within.

After his conversation with Scrooge earlier that day, Fred knew he had to come up with a plan. Simply asking wouldn't work. As I have said, Scrooge knew of Fred's wife's designs upon his fortune, and refused—out of principle as well as personal dislike—not to indulge her.

"D—n it," Fred said aloud. It was appreciably colder, and this, plus the closing of most of the stores, meant that the streets were deserted. "You know where there's no bloody snow? Italy, that's where!" He kicked a snowdrift in frustration—then found it hid a brickpile.

Fred's yell woke up some dogs, which in turn caused a few disapproving faces to appear. "Get inside, you drunk!" It only took him two fingers for Fred to respond.

Fred trudged along, limping badly and cursing his lot. The only people who went out on Christmas Eve were people that…had to work. Fred's gorge rose at the thought of it, and he was sick a little, in his mouth.

"This is the most horrible Christmas Eve imaginable! What did I ever do to deserve this?" How Fred longed to be on the other side of every lighted window he passed, warm and content in front of the crackling hearth. How he longed to kick his wife and her bloodsucking staff in some vital, sensitive portion of their anatomies! If only some spirits would visit him this night, and tell him it was okay to do just that!

"What I need," Fred mumbled to no one in particular, "are some spirits of my own." What Man needs, the Creator provides—though it must be said, not always in the expected form; and just as Fred spoke these words, he passed The Ball and Chain. With an unpleasant errand ahead, and nothing but snow and cold wind between himself and the completion of that task, Fred decided to pop in for a drink. A little Christmas drink—what could it hurt?

Fred found a space at the bar between Sozzle and Sot, and set to work. One drink led to two, as it often does; then, three and four. The spirits warmed his brain, and set it to working. By the sixth drink, Fred had birthed an idea on how to finagle his Uncle that he thought was foolproof. Simple, direct, even seasonally appropriate—splendid, if he did say it himself!

The Warden came, bottle in hand. "'Nother?"

"Nah," Fred said thickly. "How much you want for the chains? Up there, on the wall."

"Sorry," the Warden said, scratching his ample belly. A steady stream of freaks came in asking about the "flair." He'd loaned the whips and handcuffs out once, and they'd come back all sticky. "Those are my mum's chains from Bedlam. Not for sale."

"That's okay," Fred said. "I don't wanna buy 'em. I just need to borrow 'em. I wanna play a trick on my uncle."

"Who's your uncle?"

"Ebenezer Scrooge," Fred said. "Ex-miser. Now he walks around throwing money at people. Except for me, of course, because—"

The Warden cut him off. "You don't have to tell me who Ebenezer Scrooge is. Earlier tonight he nearly caused a riot."

Well, you could've knocked Fred over with a feather, dear reader. Perhaps his Uncle wasn't as boring as a box of dead moths after all.

"Couple of us have a bet," the Warden said. "Do you think he's a flamer?"

Fred shuddered; even inebriated, the thought of his uncle's sex life was too much to bear. Swallowing back, he said with some difficulty, "So, can I have the chains or not?"

The Warden thought.

Fred pushed the point, and thank goodness he did, for the plot of this story depends on it. "If things break right, he'll c—p his pants." Seeing the Warden wavering, Fred decided to sweeten the deal. "If it works, I'll come and buy everybody a drink."

The Warden got the chains down and handed them to Fred. "Here you go," he said.

"I'll bring 'em back before midnight," Fred said.

"You had better!" the Warden said. "Or else I'll have you back here in a wheelbarrow!"

After its bad beginning, Scrooge's evening had settled down considerably. All was silent; even the neighborhood, which was proudly squalorous, kept its peace on this, the holiest night of the year.

Scrooge had built an unusually large fire, splurging a bit after his cold walk home. Now, as its last embers clinked merrily in the grate, the old man snacked on a plate of gingerbread. Thanks to his change of heart, Scrooge's mania for charity occasionally extended even to himself.

It was amazing how good something as simple as a cookie could taste, after a lifetime of cold gruel. And this treat was doubly tasty, coming as it did from one of the few genuinely needy people to cross Scrooge's path. A few days after his transformation, before the criminals and con men and crooked corporations squeezed out all the decent folk, Scrooge gave some money to an actual widow. She and her non-rented children had moved back to the healthful countryside, where they had relations. Now, every so often, she sent him treats in the mail, out of gratitude. Scrooge thought of her happiness, and savored every bite.

Outside, the wind howled, making Scrooge appreciate his fire all the more—everyone should be safe and fed and warm, he thought, always. All it would take would be for us to decide to make it so; and yet we do not. Why is that? Scrooge dressed for bed, putting on his complimentary clothes; after his story had hit the newspapers, the old man became synonymous with nightshirts and sleeping caps, so a local manufacturer had given him a lifetime supply in exchange for an endorsement.

But even though he was warm, well-fed, and swaddled in swag, Scrooge was not quite content; it is a lamentable fact that worries and cares have a tendency to emerge just before bedtime, and Scrooge was not immune to this. Decapitating his last cookie, Scrooge pondered the events of the evening. It would've been so much simpler just to buy everyone drinks. But by not doing so he had discovered the truth: His charity was not making him loved. Most took

without a thought—and thoughtlessness was the best he could hope for! The rest actively despised Scrooge for a fool!

"The spirits made it seem so simple," Scrooge sighed. "Perhaps it is—on their plane. Here wickedness taints everything, even acts of goodness." Scrooge looked at the blue-painted tiles of his fireplace and focused on his favorite, one of Salome. This buxom cartoon was all that the old bachelor had in the way of female companionship, and he did with it what he could.

"I realize Fred squeezes me, down to the last vinegary dreg; I see Cratchit leveraging my sympathy into more trollops and coconut oil! But what can I do, Salome? What can anyone do?" Scrooge addressed these questions to the tile, his passion rising to its height. "For the sake of my soul, I must give. But how, without simply gilding the world's wickedness and misery?...I wish the spirits would come again tonight, not to tell me to give, but teach me how! Oh! Oh! OH!"

Scrooge's passion faded. "If only the world was the way it is in books," he sighed, spent. Perhaps tomorrow he would find the answer. If any day could show him the right kind of kindness, surely it would be Christmas?

Scrooge turned things over in his mind as he drifted off to sleep. Maybe charity does begin at home, as Fred said. But Fred's wife was such a harpy! Helping strangers was so much more appealing, because you didn't know what jerks they really were... Still working this puzzle, Scrooge fell into a deep and restful sleep.

As a result, the old man became aware of the noise outside only by small degrees. Someone was rummaging

around in the street below…kids, probably. No, it wasn't children, the steps were too heavy; it was a man. Was he drunk? In this neighborhood? Scrooge leaned over and stuck tuppence into the pipe by his bed—it snaked down and emptied out onto the sidewalk. Conscience salved, Scrooge decided that whoever it was, they would finish their business and go away…

But they didn't. Scrooge couldn't make out what was happening; it seemed like the man was attempting to open the door. This didn't alarm Scrooge—the door was heavy enough, and the lock secure—but it didn't let him fall back asleep, either. A scrape, a thump, a muffled curse—who was it? And what in blazes were they doing? Scratch, scratch, scratch…Just soft enough to be heard, too regular to be the wind; it was as if a drop of water was hitting Scrooge's forehead at irregular intervals, with each drop's impact nudging him infintesimally further from slumber.

Scrooge lay in bed between sleep and wakefulness for what seemed like an age—then, in a moment, his guts turned to ice! That was a moan, he knew that sound! And the rattle of a chain! Suddenly bolt upright, Scrooge pulled the covers to his chin. He waited, too frightened to move.

"Just a trick of the mind, that's all," Scrooge said in as firm a voice as he could manage. "Or a nightmare. I know I believe I'm awake, but some dreams are like that. Totally understandable on the one-year anniversary…" Speaking the circumstance aloud made him even more frightened, but this was nothing compared to how he felt when he heard another rattle.

"Ebenezer SCROOGE!" a voice called, the wind shifting between words so that the last name sounded louder, like an accusation.

"Oh!" Scrooge cried out. "Go away, spirits! I have done as you wished, why are you tormenting me? I don't want to see you again, I was only kidding!"

"Good, you're home," the voice noted matter-of-factly. Then the voice and the rattling became louder still. "EBENEZER SCROOGE!" the being commanded. "LET ME IN!"

Scrooge's fear dissolved for a moment—Let him in? Can't he walk through walls? They could last year. Scrooge cleared his throat, then addressed the spirit. "My slippers are all the way across the room. Why can't you just glide up here yourself?"

Scrooge heard swearing. Did the spirits swear last year?

"DON'T"—the wind shifted again— "argue!"

Leaving his warm bed unwillingly, Scrooge lit a candle, then padded to the top of the stairs. "Who is it?" he said.

"Jacob Marley's ghost."

"Oh, for God's—Jacob, why do you torment me? Everybody knows I learned my lesson. Don't they have newspapers where you are?"

"Uh…" Then the voice began again: "FOOLISH MORTAL! Do you dare question the wishes of the spirit world?"

"No-ooo," Scrooge equivocated, "but I was really hoping this wouldn't become an annual thing. Also, you sound drunk."

"And you sound just like my wife!"

"Since when are you married, you pederast?" Scrooge scratched his gut sleepily. "Listen, Jacob: the party's over. Go find a distant relative and crash on their couch—"

Downstairs on the stoop, Fred gave his chains an angry rattle. After a mournful moan, however, he went blank. What the hell do ghosts say? "Ebenezer Scrooge, you have more yet to learn…"

"Like what? Send me a letter."

"Cheeky b—d!" Fred said. "I'll tell you when you let me in!"

Marley was just as headstrong as ever, Scrooge thought; there was never a tougher man of business, nor a more difficult person to get rid of. For God's sake, the man had been dead for years, and here he was, still showing up at all hours!

"You better have a bottle of champagne, that's all I can say." Reluctantly, Scrooge padded down the stairs. It was freezing in the stairway. "I've given away a ton of money, Jacob," Scrooge said through the door. "If there was more to it than that, really, I think it's got to be on you guys."

"Do not argue!" Fred yelled, teeth chattering in the cold. "St-t-t-tubborn sh-sh—t!"

Hand on the lock, Scrooge paused. "I distinctly remember you walking through walls."

Fred was losing feeling in his extremities. "For God's sake, let me in! It's bloody freezing!"

"OI! SHADDUP!" somebody yelled. Several neighborhood dogs began to bark.

In the name of peace and quiet, Scrooge opened the door. There standing before him was his old partner Jacob

Marley. Well, sort of—Marley was taller than he remembered him, and thinner, and had more hair on his head than Scrooge remembered, too. Since when did Marley have a moustache? But Scrooge was an old man, with vision to match. And who else would be visiting him on this day, and this hour? It had to be Marley.

"Thank Christ!" Fred said, shuffling inside. "Take your sweet time, don't you?"

"Jacob, I ask again: why do you torment me?" Scrooge said, after he'd closed the door and locked it. "Can we make this brief? I've had a busy day—giving money to the needy, don't you know."

Fred hurried past and up the stairs. "I'll explain everything," he said, his chains jingling merrily as he walked. "Tell me you haven't let the fire go out. I can't feel my thighs."

Five minutes later, Scrooge and the spirit were sitting in front of a fire Scrooge had coaxed back to life. Fred was in Scrooge's favorite armchair, and the ersatz spirit had a hot toddy in his hand.

"Jacob, I thought you were insensible to heat and cold," Scrooge said rather snottily. Nobody sat in his favorite chair.

"Yes, well," Fred said between slurps, "when you've lived where I have for the last eight years, you get used to a certain level of warmth."

At the mention of eternal torment, Scrooge broke again; he instantly fell to his knees, and grasped the eerie visitor around the ankles. "Oh, Jacob!" he said. "I've done as you asked—as all the spirits asked! Save me from h—l!" Scrooge looked up, with tears in his eyes. "It was that thing with the wheelbarrows, wasn't it?" he said in a piteous voice. "I'll buy them all new ones, I promise."

"Why does everybody keep mentioning wheelbarrows?" Fred said. "I have no idea what you're talking about."

Scrooge's manner changed instantly. "Thank God! I mean, forget it," Scrooge said, straightening up. "But Jacob, haven't I done as you asked?" The old man tugged at the chains that wound around the ersatz spirit. "These are lighter, are they not?"

"Hey!" Fred said, "I have to return those. Get up off the floor."

"Okay," Scrooge said. This year's Marley seemed much less ominous—almost ridiculous, compared to last year's version. "Hey, spirit," the ex-miser said, "do your jaw thing again."

"What?"

"You know, the trick with your jaw—you untie it, and it falls to the floor," Scrooge said. "I loved that."

Scrooge hadn't been shy about revealing the details of his Christmas visit from the spirits, but there were certain aspects Fred couldn't approximate. For someone tipsy and in a hurry, Fred had done quite a good job. In addition to wrapping himself in light chain, Fred had put some cold porridge in his hair, and pulled it into a Satanic-looking mess before letting it dry. Then he wrapped a handkerchief around his jaws—which, obviously, did not detach.

"NO!" Fred boomed, spilling his drink. "I did not come all this way to perform parlor tricks, Ebenezer Scrooge! I must deliver a further message regarding your immortal soul."

"Do me a favor, and blot the chair first," Scrooge said. "You got toddy on it."

"Oh. Sorry." He untied his jaws, and blotted the liquor with the cloth. "Anyway, about your immortal soul—"

"I'm all ears," Scrooge said.

"What?"

"It means 'I'm listening,'" Scrooge said. Had Marley's ghost gotten stupider? Was that possible? Certainly he was a lot less terrifying than Scrooge remembered, though the old man couldn't put his finger on why. Maybe it was the fact that he had brought a page of notes, which he referred to as he spoke.

"Scrooge," Fred said, scanning the crumpled sheet in his hand, "you have misunderstood the visit from the spirits. You have been generous, it is true, and while that is part of our message, there is another part. It is not enough to give—you must give wisely!"

"Funny thing," Scrooge said, already wishing he were asleep, "I was just talking to my nephew Fred about that this afternoon."

"A wise man, that Fred."

"You know of him? In your world?"

"Most certainly," Fred said. "He is known as a noble, wise, and kind man. One of the sages of the Ages. In fact, in the opinion of all of us, you could do a lot worse than giving all your money to him."

Scrooge noticed that Marley wasn't as translucent this year. "You guys know about his wife, right?"

"Oh…sure…" Fred wasn't used to thinking on his feet, and the extra-ominous Marley voice was hurting his throat. He really wished he'd hired an actor. "She seems like a worthy woman."

"Not from down here, she doesn't," Scrooge snorted. "To us, she seems like a two-ton, nickel-plated, steam-powered b—h."

"Remember where I live, mortal," Fred said, backpedaling. "There are comparatively few females…down there."

"Well, make room for one more," Scrooge said.

"Look," Fred said impatiently, "I didn't schlep all the way here wrapped in bondage gear to argue with you about

67

AW, MAN –

by Lila Ash

"Shoulda brought the weed."

"Shoulda brought the weed."

whether Fred's wife is a b—h or not. This is about saving your immortal soul. And there is only one way you can do that: give money to Fred."

"I already give him a little," Scrooge said. "I bought him a nice corkscrew for his birthday."

"Oh, well, then!" Fred said sarcastically. He put down his drink, and gave the light chain an annoyed rattle. "Not enough! Not enough! Ebenezer Scrooge, you have a lifetime of wrongs to fix! You must act quickly, and with all your heart! For the sake of your immortal soul, funnel cash to your nephew tout suite!"

"All of it?" Scrooge asked, hoping the answer was no. He liked being Sir Gives-a-lot. For one thing, women occasionally kissed him.

"Ideally, yes," Fred said. "Or you can leave it to him after you're dead. For now, just give him a big old chunk. And more whenever he asks for it." Fred rattled his chains. "Or else you'll end up like me-e-e!" Fred tried to give a super-bloodcurdling moan, but his booze-roughened voice gave out. It was time for him to go. Coughing, he moved towards the door.

Scrooge pounded him on the back. "Jacob, were you always so…solid?"

"Yes," Fred croaked. "I just chose to be different this year, is that all right with you?"

"Sure, sure. But aren't you going to fly out the window? What's next, using public transportation?"

"Enough prattling, mortal! Do not bother me with trifling questions about things you cannot understand—just remember what I've said to you tonight!"

"That I should stop throwing money at everybody who asks, and give it to Fred instead?"

"Yes!" Fred turned to go. "Charity begins at home."

Scrooge grabbed the spirit's jacket, which seemed strangely sweaty. "What about Tiny Tim?"

"What about him?" Fred said.

"Surely I should still give money to him," Scrooge said. "Surely he—"

"No!" Fred said quickly. "That kid's a stone thug! Trust us, we know all, see all." Fred started down the stairs.

"But he's crippled…"

"Maybe he's faking," Fred shouted behind him. "Anyway, so what? Crippled people can be jerks, too."

Scrooge thought of something. "Jacob!" he cried from the top of the stairs. "Wait!"

Fred tripped on his chains and fell heavily against the door. "What, what, WHAT?"

"Is this the only visit tonight?" Scrooge asked. "Or will there be more spirits, as there were last time?"

"No, this is it." Fred opened the door and plunged out. "Farewell, Unc…" he caught himself. "…Ebenezer Scrooge!"

The blast of wind from the open door blew out Scrooge's candle. The old man took this as his cue to go back to bed.

"Only one this year," Scrooge said, pulling the covers to his chin, and nestling back in. "At least that's an improvement."

In his haste to leave, Fred opened Scrooge's door right into Tiny Tim's nasty, malevolent manservant. "Watch it!" growled the slight-but-menacing Crippen. He was checking the "FREE MONEY! TAKE SOME" bucket Scrooge kept on his front steps.

"Already checked it," Fred said. He had always loathed Crippen.

The feeling was mutual. "It's Christmas Eve, not Halloween," Crippen said, looking at Fred's costume.

Fred made a face. "Did the zoo let you out for the holiday?"

"Oh, good one." Both men were now crammed in Scrooge's doorway, and neither would back down or step aside. Fred put his left fist behind him, and began wrapping the light chain around it. Simultaneously, Crippen was sneaking his hand into the pocket of his overcoat, feeling for his trusty sand-filled sock. But before battle could commence, Tiny Tim stuck his head out of the pimped-out omnibus parked nearby. Four teams of horses idled in front of it—it was a hot-rod, faster than anything the cops had. "Anything in the bucket?" the hard-boiled runt asked.

"No, 'Master T,'" Crippen said.

"Well, then, let's move on," Tim said, in a high yet commanding voice. He looked at Fred. "What are you doing here, d—knose?"

Crippen's beating would have to wait. "The same thing you are. You'll be dismayed to know that I've derailed your little gravy train. Permanently!"

"Bah!" Crippen said, spitting into the

"Shoulda brought the weed."

"Shoulda brought the weed."

snow. "Should I thrash him?" he asked Tim.

Fred laughed, but there was no jolliness in it. "You? Thrash me?" For all his talk, Crippen was incredibly weak—they all were, thanks to rampant malnutrition and lungs filled with coal dust—but Crippen was particularly so. He looked like something you might find coiled at the bottom of a drain, only less cuddly.

"Enjoy the high life while you still can, w—kers," Fred said triumphantly. "Uncle's just had a visit from a new spirit. Can you guess what that new spirit said?" He looked at Crippen. "I'm asking Tim. I know you couldn't guess."

"That I'm going to kill you?" Crippen growled, fingering his sand-filled sock. (At least I think it was his sand-filled sock.)

Before Tim could give an answer, a feminine hand emerged from the inside of the omnibus and tousled his young locks. "Come back inside, Master T! Don't bother with those nasty men!"

"B—h!" Tim slapped blindly. "I'm working!"

All of it was just too sordid for Fred. "The spirit said to cut you off, Tim. Not another cent. And I think Scrooge believed him."

"You b—d," Tim piped, adding to the truly shameful number of swears in this story.

Fred began to walk away. "Someday you'll realize that the world is run on brains, not brawn," he told them. "Now, if you'll excuse me, I have a little celebration to attend."

Tim and Crippen watched Fred walk away. "Should I kill 'im now, boss?"

"No," Tim said, allowing his spoon-chested henchman to have his fantasies of lethality. "As much as I'd love that, we haven't bought enough policemen in this district, and you're too valuable to let you go to prison."

"Thanks, boss."

"It's nothing personal. HEY!"—Tim rounded on a hottie—"would you stop pinching my b—m?" Then he disappeared into the holly-bedecked booty caravan.

Ignoring the giggles, Crippen mounted the driver's perch. They had gone less than a block when Tim stuck his head out again. "I've just had an excellent idea. The Majestic Theater, Crippen, as fast as these nags can take us!"

As they passed Fred, Tim threw an empty champagne bottle at him. It missed Fred's noggin by inches.

"Missed!" Fred taunted. "Get ready for the workhouse, you scum!" He heaved a snowball with a large rock in its middle.

It cracked a window, but the conveyance drove on. Time was of the essence, and Tim's dark purposes would not wait.

A MEMORABLE PERFORMANCE.

Tiny Tim was not kind, or cheerful, or thoughtful, or concerned with others more than himself. He wasn't even (and this is strange to hear, I know) a cripple. What Tim was, dear reader, was a master of deceit, a perfect monster really, and the true facts of his existence are enough to make anyone ponder what they think they know about their fellows. Here was a man born to be a politician, and I don't think I need to say any more than that.

Timothy Cratchit came into the world poor, but that did not decide anything; the majority of the world is similarly shackled, and yet most struggle within the boundaries of morality. But Tiny Tim was different: like many of history's greatest criminals, he had been cursed with the gift to see his situation too clearly at too tender an age. He saw his father was an overgrown child, unequal to the task of raising his brood; his mother, on the other hand, was a sphinx of passivity, ignoring anything she did not wish to see; and about his siblings, the less said, the better!

Put simply, there was not enough to go around; and as the youngest, Tim

needed the good opinion of others to survive. What else could he do but inflate their affections? What else could he do but play upon their sympathy? In every outward aspect Tim strove to be kind, cheerful, sensitive, decent. And to give everyone's heartstrings that final pluck, at the age of three Tim decided to become crippled, too.

Nobody noticed that his crutch shifted arms, or that he was somehow strong enough to capture an escaped alligator, which subsequently became his own lethal pet. One time, Tim used the iron frame supposedly supplementing his withered limbs to maim a child thrice his size. (The boy's crime? Beating Tim at marbles.) Tim said it was an accident, and who could doubt a poor little crippled boy?

His family offered Tim their meals; Tim ate them. His father carried him to and from school on his shoulders; Tim enjoyed the ride. Whenever he thought someone might be catching on, or sensed a small decrease of sympathy, Tim was ready with a "relapse"—though what disease he had was never clear. The other Cratchits weren't the type to ask, or think to ask, or think.

In this way, he secured his boyhood, and stood at the head of his family. Had he not been committed to the easy way, Tiny Tim might've been a truly remarkable man, worthy in every respect. But Tim was determined to rise in the world, whatever it took. He waited for his opportunity in hiding, like a cunning beast of prey.

Ebenezer Scrooge was that opportunity. Tim did not believe in spirits—his Universe was uncaring and cruel, and did not contain ethereal beings that dispensed moral lessons. What Tim did believe in was money. And so, along with everyone else, he set about getting as much of that sweet Scroogian bullion as possible.

God, how easy it was! The old man was so sentimental, and there was always something more to buy for "poor little Tim"; Scrooge's outlay for new crutches alone was more than enough for Tim to buy the omnibus.

But it was another gift from Scrooge that allowed Tim to truly prosper: fame. As I have said, Scrooge's visitation was widely known, and no one came off better in those accounts than the humble, pathetic, good-hearted urchin Tiny Tim (it sickens me just to write it!). Scrooge was visited December 24th; by February 1st, every schoolchild in London knew and admired Tim. This made stealing their clothes a piece of cake.

Here's how it went down: Crippen would drive the omnibus to one of London's posh neighborhoods, and park it outside a particularly spiffy-looking school. As classes let out, the children would immediately see the sign on the side of the 'bus:

"Meet 'Tiny Tim'!
Urchin to the Stars! England's Favorite Cripple!
INQUIRE WITHIN!"

Naturally, students would stream into the omnibus, where Tim sat in the back, surrounded by sweets and toys. When the bus was filled, Tim would slip upstairs to the roof, locking the door behind him. Most of the time, the students wouldn't even notice, enjoying the carnival-like atmosphere. "Ooh, Sybil! Cholmondeley! We're moving!"

Crippen would drive the omnibus to a deserted region far from the school; then the captives (who were still busy playing, eating sweets and chatting), would be given a ultimatum: if they wished to see their families ever again, they had to strip off their clothes and leave them in the bins beneath each seat. There was always some crying, and Crippen occasionally had to twist an ear or two ("See what happens when you try to be a hero?") but most complied without comment. After they'd done so, they were released to wander back home in their underwear.

In this way, Tim quickly generated a fortune in the second-hand clothes trade. No one believed the stories of his victims, such was the goodwill generated by the original tale. And what kid wanted everyone to know that he'd been duped by a cripple? As usual, Tiny Tim had worked out all the angles.

It was a good living—a great one, in fact—but there were only so many upper-class children to fleece; much to Tim's chagrin, the rich did not reproduce as fast as the poor. So Tim had to branch out into other pursuits, if his criminal empire was going to grow. His first foray into this was the recent purchase of The Majestic Theatre, which Scrooge had unwittingly paid for (Tim had faked a fall down some stairs "attempting to save a beautiful kitten").

What Tim planned to do with the theater was unclear as yet. Crippen was encouraging him to torch it for the insurance, preferably with enough people still in it to distract the police. Tim wasn't sure, but he knew what sounded good: every actress' affections, it was said, were available for a fee. And just to give himself maximum range, Tim had assembled a very special troupe, where every actor was more than just a thespian—a pickpocket, perhaps, or a forger, a mountebank, a charlatan, a grifter, a ninja.

To keep salaries low, Tim allowed his troupe to live rent-free at the Majestic. As a result it had become a colorful place, with all sorts of dubious and eccentric types coming and going at all hours. The Majestic was never silent before three or four in the morning, and Christmas Eve was no exception: theater people follow older Gods, and wilder. Dionysus, the Lizard King, still lived at the Majestic.

So when Tim arrived, everyone was still up. Crippen hastily assembled them all, uncoupling some, pouring black coffee down the throats of others. "Everybody come to the stage!" Crippen yelled, pounding on one door after the other. "Master T's got a job for you!"

Perched upon Crippen's shoulders, Tim addressed the troupe. "Good evening, all. Merry Christmas."

"Merry Christmas," the troupe replied, in anything from a grunt to a giggle depending on their mental state.

"You all know Ebenezer Scrooge, don't you?"

"'Course we do," a girl with mussed make-up said.

"Ex-miser, now everybody's favorite mark," said an older man who stank of pomade. "Nobody's as trusting as a convert."

"Yes, well, there's been some talk—loose talk—that he's going back to his old penny-pinching ways," Tim said. "Naturally, we can't let that happen."

"But what can we do about it?" the girl said.

"Plenty," Tim said. "I've got a plan, but I need your help. Here's what we're going to do…"

Back in Scrooge's apartment, the old man lay in bed, awake. There was something about Marley's visit that bothered him, something not quite right. But after a half-hour without being able to put his finger on it, Scrooge was finally able to drift away.

Scrooge had been comatose for about an hour when he felt a sharp poke in the foot. Turning over, the ex-miser resolved to avoid the shepherd's pie at The Ball and Chain. The dish always gave him nightmares (and he occasionally found a file in it).

"Get up!" a voice said.

"Ouch!" This time the poke really hurt. Scrooge propped himself upon his elbows, and saw a shadowy figure at the foot of his bed. "Look, go away! Marley said there would be no more ghosts." Scrooge flopped back down. "One day off a year," he grumbled into his pillow, "That's all I ask…"

Scrooge's ankle was caught in a strong, chilly grip. "Come on," the voice at the end of the bed said. "Everybody's waiting."

The figure began pulling Scrooge out of bed from the bottom.

"Hey!" Scrooge said, now fully awake and perturbed. "Quit it!" He kicked, to no avail; grabbing onto the bedclothes was similarly useless, and Scrooge soon found himself on the floor in a pool of sheets. "All right," Scrooge said, slowly getting to his feet. "Just who the h—l are you? How did you get in downstairs?"

"I'm the Ghost of—" Crippen checked a greasy, crumpled note—"Christmas Past. Locked doors mean nothing to me."

"So Marley was wrong," Scrooge said,

relieved somehow. "Ghosts can still go through doors."

"Of course," Crippen said. (He'd smashed the lock with a paving stone.)

"Have you seen Marley? He looks different, doesn't he?" Scrooge went to light a taper.

The figure said in a stern voice, "No candles, please."

"Was Marley wrong about the other ghosts? I'm going to be up all night, aren't I?"

"Marley is crazy," Crippen said. "We all make fun of him. Now, put on some clothes, we're going on a journey."

"But last year—" Scrooge stopped himself; even in the gloom he could see that the ghost was annoyed, and this ghost was nobody you wanted angry. Though small, it was menacing, scorpion-like; and it was swinging a sand-filled sock. As he dressed, Scrooge attempted to chat it up.

"You're new, aren't you?" Scrooge simpered. "I like you much better than the spirit last year. Old, young, million arms, no arms, light coming out of its head—what a freak!"

Crippen was silent. He'd dumped himself into a chair and was studying his fingernails with a look that suggested they'd wronged him somehow, and he was looking forward to giving them the beatdown they so richly deserved. This was Crippen's expression for all occasions. When Scrooge was nearly finished, Crippen got up and left the room without a word.

"So, we're flying again?"

Crippen didn't answer, tromping down the stairs heavily.

"Okay, no problem. Walking's fine." Scrooge followed, pulling on his greatcoat. "Though I must admit I rather liked zipping around without feeling the cold…" They got to the front door. "What happened here?" Scrooge asked, handling the smashed lock which now hung loosely from the side of the splintered door.

Crippen didn't say anything, and continued to walk to the hansom cab parked out front.

"Hey!" Scrooge said. "We can't just leave! My house is completely open—somebody will rob it!"

A figure smelling of pomade opened the door of the cab, and called to Scrooge. "Why not let them take it all—as a Christmas present?" the driver suggested in a plummy, overcheerful voice.

Scrooge disliked him immediately; he was preening and perfumed, which Scrooge found unpleasant in man or ghost. Scrooge cast a glance back at his door, which was now swinging in the winter wind. "Look, this neighborhood is loaded with robbers, squatters, roving drunkards…It's only a matter of time before—"

"Time? What is time to an immortal spirit like me?" the ghost said. His features were jowly, rouged and entirely insipid. "Hurry up and step inside. My feet are freezing."

Scrooge gave up; he knew better than to argue with a spirit.

The instant the door was closed, the cab sprang forward. Scrooge fell against the creature, who certainly felt like a man. None of these spirits made any sense!

"You're not a ghost," Scrooge ventured boldly. "Since when do ghosts wear lilac aftershave?"

"I beg your pardon!" the creature said. "I am the Ghost of Christmas Past!"

"Then who is he?" Scrooge asked, pointing at the driver.

"Also myself. I can take many forms," the Ghost said.

Scrooge leaned out the window, attempting to see if the cab was driving itself.

"It's no use doing that," the Ghost said. "The moment you take your eyes off me, I transform into him, and vice-versa. Now close the window!"

Scrooge sunk back into his seat, frustrated. "I have to use the bathroom," he lied petulantly.

"Hold it until we arrive. It's not far."

The spirit was true to its word; within seven minutes, the cab stopped. "All ashore that's going ashore!" the spirit said.

Scrooge stepped out of the cab quickly, getting snow up his trouserleg. But he was nonetheless grateful, for the heavy scent of the spirit's hair oil was nauseating in the extreme. He found himself in front of a door—it was the stage door of the Majestic Theater, but there was no way for Scrooge to know that; neither miserdom nor his new career had afforded much time for attending plays. Above the door hung a crude sign which read, "This Way to the Spirit World."

Scrooge paused, feeling for the hundredth time that evening that the spirit world had really gone downhill in the last year, and that he'd rather be home in bed. He was about to express these sentiments in a particularly forceful fashion when the spirit behind him urged him forward.

"Hurry, hurry, we don't have all night."

Scrooge looked behind and saw the figure from his bedroom and the spirit that reeked of aftershave and pomade. Both at once. Standing next to each other. "Wait, there's something fishy—"

The pomaded one gave Scrooge a push through the door, then the other spectre added a gratuitous and very unspectral kick to Scrooge's backside.

The old man was immediately in pitch black. His other senses sharpened, Scrooge could smell paint and freshly sawn wood.

"Hallo?" he called. "Is there anybody here?" There was no answer. "This is different from last year, fellows—that time, nobody just left me…or swore at me… or kicked me…"

Still no answer. Slowly, as he stood there in the darkness and silence, Scrooge's annoyance turned into trepidation. "I'm getting out of here," he said aloud, then began feeling for the doorknob—it must be right here. But try as he might, Scrooge could not find it; it was too dark, and he kept sticking his hand into spider's webs. Then he stepped on something crunchy, and the willies overtook him.

"Help!" he cried out. "Help!"

ZOE MATTHIESSEN

A door opened, and the chamber was flooded with light. "Calm yourself," a high voice said.

Scrooge could not make out the figure. The light was too much for the old man's eyes. He felt the spirit take his arm.

"Come with me."

The spirit was small—and familiar, somehow. Could it be Tiny Tim? Oh, no! Say it wasn't so—Tim had succumbed to his illness (whatever it was) and had passed on! Then Scrooge looked again: though they could be twins, this was not the Tim he knew and loved. Tiny Tim walked with a crutch, while this child was whole—small, to be sure, but hale and hearty. Also, Tim didn't wear a suit with wide lapels. Or a hat with a leopard band. Or carry a bejeweled pimp's goblet. Or call women "ho."

As the spirit led Scrooge on a circuitous route through the bowels of the theater, Scrooge's brain burned with questions. Perhaps it was poor Tim, but in his spirit form, when all our maladies and troubles have been lifted. Could it be Tim's ghost, visiting from the future? Scrooge shook his arm free. "Tell me, who are you, spirit? For good or ill, I must know—are you...?

"I am the Ghost of Christmas Past."

"You, too? Thank Heaven!" Scrooge said, almost sobbing with emotion. "I thought you were someone I knew, a dear, sweet boy of my acquaintance..." The more Scrooge thought of it, the more laughable it was. This slick character, Tiny Tim? Ridiculous. "Where are we going?" Scrooge asked buoyantly.

They went through a door onto a balcony. "Sit," the spirit commanded. "Are we going to see a performance?" Scrooge asked.

"Of sorts," the spirit said in a high voice. It pointed to the stage. "Now, look!"

The stage blazed into light. Then a actor came out from behind the curtain and spoke.

"Ebenezer Scrooge," the man said, "you have disregarded the warnings of the spirits—"

"That's not true!" Scrooge shouted. He turned to the child-sized spirit beside him, who was fingering a large pinky ring. "I swear it's not!"

"Even though you are surrounded by misery and want, your resolve is weakening!" the man continued. "You must keep giving! Unless you want to end up in...H—L!" A chorus of wails and moans echoed through the theater, sending a shiver up Scrooge's spine. Then the stage went dark.

There were sounds of people moving things around. Normally Scrooge would've been unimpressed at the absence of magic—this year's ghosts were really quite lackluster, maybe he should give some money to them. But some small residue of awe remained, so Scrooge stayed silent.

The small spirit leaned over. "Whatever Marley told you," he whispered, "don't listen. Don't be a chump—don't suffer eternal torment, just because some idiot misheard God."

Before Scrooge could answer, the stage was lit again. In the middle of it, a boy sat alone, reading a book. Behind him was the backdrop of a circus.

"That's me, spirit!" Scrooge cried aloud. "Poor, friendless, alone, with only my books for company...I don't remember the circus part, though."

"Oh, that's...um," Tim cleared his throat. Damn propmaster was hitting the opium again. "It was a long time ago, and you are old and forgetful."

"Yeah, but I think I would—"

Tim leapt onto his chair. "WRETCHED SINNER!" Tim shouted, his prepubescent voice skirling into the higher registers. "THE SPIRITS KNOW ALL! DO YOU DARE CONTRADICT..."

"Okay, okay," Scrooge said, unconvinced. "Simmer down. Jeez." These ghosts were all so touchy.

Scrooge sat in silence, as groups of children teased and mocked his younger self. Their coup de grace came when the boy was forced to eat raw toad guts. As he lay on the stage crying, a young female came out.

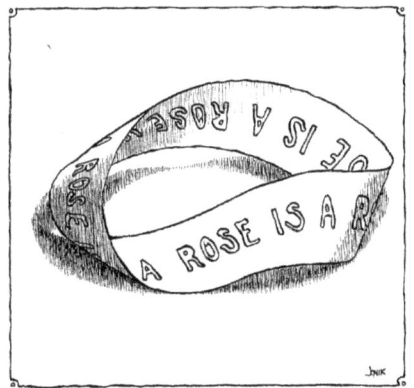

"Poor brother," the girl said, kneeling down and stroking his offal-caked cheek.

"Dear Fan," the boy said, voice quaking. "Dear, dear, Fan. Why do they all hate me so?"

"Who cares?" Fan shrugged. "They'd like you if you gave them some money."

"Would they?" the boy said, suddenly hopeful. "Would they really, truly like me?"

Scrooge stood up. "No, they wouldn't!" he yelled, thinking of the ruffians at The Ball and Chain.

Tim tugged on Scrooge's jacket. "They cannot hear you, Scrooge," he said.

It certainly didn't seem like that to Scrooge. Both performers had jumped a mile, and now seemed to be totally thrown by his outburst. "Would they really, truly like me?" the boy said again.

The girl paused, then hollered, "Line!"

"'No, not really...'" a voice whispered from the wings. "'They'd just be...'"

"No, not really," Fan said, picking up the thread. "They'd just be using you. But they wouldn't make you eat raw frog guts."

"Well," the boy said, "I guess that's something,"

With that, the stage went dark. When the lights came up again, Scrooge recognized the players immediately.

"Why, it's old Fezziwig," Scrooge said. "I apprenticed for him. What a kind, generous old fellow he was!"

"You think that? Then you learned nothing from your apprenticeship," Tim said.

"I do not understand, spirit."

Stifling a yawn, the spirit refused to explain. "Keep watching."

"Would you just tell me?" Scrooge asked. "You know what I hate the most about you ethereal beings? You're all so snotty!"

"What do you expect?" Tim said. "We know all and see all."

"Sure, but do you have to be such d—ks about it?" Scrooge's voice grew louder as he warmed to his topic. "Sure, it's easy for you spooks to tell me, 'Give it all away'–what do you need money for? You don't have to eat. You don't have to pay rent. I promise you this," Scrooge said, "one night of going hungry and all you shades would sing a different song indeed."

"Excuse me," one of the actors called

"I'd like to donate my body to comedy."

up to them, "but we're trying to portray the most poignant moments of your life down here."

"Yeah," another added. "Least you could do is shut up."

"I didn't ask for this," Scrooge said.

"Anyway, I'm sure you're all getting Equity rates."

"We'll talk about it later," Tim called down to his employees, anticipating the fight. "Carry on."

The stage had about ten people on it, reenacting the Christmas revels at the Fezziwigs'. They were all dancing and swinging each other around wildly, and bellowing things like, "Jolly good quadrille!" and "You're stepping on my corns!" and "This is the best Christmas ever!" It wasn't exactly as Scrooge remembered it—once again, the backdrop suggested it was taking place at a circus—but after the way the Ghost jumped down his throat the last time, he wasn't about to say anything.

The fiddler was awful, but Fezziwig fairly loaded him down with coin. He did the same to everyone else present at the dance, including their dog.

"Why, he's almost Scroogian in his generosity," Tim whispered to Scrooge.

"More fool him," Scrooge griped. "Probably counterfeit."

"It does not matter," Tim said. "Do you see how happy everyone is, including Fezziwig himself? Do you understand why?"

"Sure," Scrooge said. "And I also get why he always paid such c—p wages."

"There are more important things than business," Tim said. "Love, for example."

The stage had been cleared, and only two actors remained—the young, gangly one meant to be Scrooge, and a young lady.

"You have changed," the woman said to the man. "You never buy me presents anymore."

"It's not I who have changed," the stage-Scrooge said. "It's Fezziwig. He's cut our pay. We will never be able to marry, unless I economize."

From the balcony, Scrooge hooted with glee at his stand-in's defiance. "That's right! You tell 'em, Scrooge!"

The young lady was unconvinced. "I don't think you need to worry yourself on that score," she said, "as I do not wish to marry a cheapskate."

"Sensible girl," Tim said to Scrooge. "Pity you let her get away."

"Have you ever met my nephew Fred's wife?" Scrooge asked.

There had been a final scene, drawn quite vividly and aimed quite cruelly, showing everyone having a good time on Christmas except for Scrooge. At its crescendo, Tim had whispered to him, "See what saving your money gets you?" but Scrooge had long since stopped paying attention. These Ghosts of Christmas Past had made their point, and as usual, they really had no idea when to quit.

Back home in his bed, Scrooge didn't feel well. His knee hurt, he felt nauseous from all the waking up and going back to sleep, and his backside was sore from being kicked, twice. After all his hard work over the previous twelve months, the ghosts were certainly treating him a lot worse this year!

As he rubbed his rear-end, Scrooge pondered the events of the evening. He weighed what Marley had said, and then what the multiformed Ghost of Christmas Past had shown. They had certainly gone to a lot more trouble than Marley had, which had to count for something... Lying there waiting for his feet to warm up again, he really didn't know what to do. But he knew what he needed, and that was eight hours of good, refreshing, uninterrupted sleep.

NO REST FOR THE SAINTLY, EITHER.

Fred stopped at The Ball and Chain to return the "flair"; once inside, however, he realized there is no place on Earth more depressing than a prison-themed bar late on Christmas Eve, so he hurried home. Once there, he related his activities to his wife—which earned him not only dinner, but a basin of hot water, to wash the dried porridge out of his hair.

"This is wonderful!" Mrs. Fred said. "Fred, I never knew you had it in you. This is the best Christmas ever!" She put on her coat.

"Where are you going?" Fred asked.

"Over to Scrooge's, of course." Mrs. Fred got a dreamy look. "Bathing in money," she said. "How's that for a new Christmas tradition?"

This made Fred nervous; he wished to mimic the previous year in as many details as possible, and that meant letting Scrooge sleep, then awake a changed man. "Wait, dear," he said. "He's an old man. He needs his rest—I think I gave him quite a scare…"

"Wait, nothing! I want to feel the Queen's tiny metallic portrait against my nethers!" she said, and slammed the door.

Head still dripping, Fred scurried to the window. "Be careful!" he called into the cold, his voice pluming into the frigid, quiet night. "At his age, I don't know how much more Christmas Scrooge can take!"

By this time, it was well past midnight, and while the snow had eased a bit—it too observed the holiday—the wind had not, and Mrs. Fred cursed it as she walked. But she soldiered on, warming herself with thoughts of the untold riches that were about to be poured over her until she cried, "Enough!" And she would not cry that, not ever.

Scrooge must be fantastically wealthy, she thought, otherwise why would a trio of spirits have bothered with him? Yes, the old man must've set by a staggering store of gold, in all those years of misering, she was sure of it. Even though it was only in her mind, that gold radiated as much warmth as any fire could—no amount of mud-streaked slush could quench it, nor any chill breeze beat it back. And so she walked on.

The truth was that Scrooge's year of charity had eaten away a substantial portion of his fortune. But even this would've been replaced, and more perhaps, by new money—had the activities of the counting-house not been curtailed by two forces.

The first was Bob Cratchit's sandbagging, of which I have spoken before. But the second, and just as important factor, was Scrooge's fame. With every fawning article in the press, clients left Scrooge & Marley for other firms. Even assuming that the spirits were real (and most of Scrooge's colleagues in trade did not) no hard-headed man of business could possibly trust a gentleman in the grip of… something. What if the next crop of spirits counseled less-than-sound accounting practices? Or reducing the workday from eighteen hours to a mere fourteen? Could arming the rabble be far behind?

Scrooge's colleagues at the Exchange had seen it all too often: formerly dependable sorts who, late in life, had lost their heads over some trifle—religion, a pretty young wife, pederasty—only to eventually emerge as if from a trance, sheepish and chastened. And, as often as not, stone broke.

No, no, this would not do—this Scrooge fellow had to be curtailed, before others picked up his taint. So they cut ties with Scrooge immediately, switching their commerce to other firms. Of course they applauded him publicly, and if the walls of London's clubs could talk, it would be relayed that a few even admired Scrooge—in private. But business was business, and charity was charity, and "Scroogism" (as it was now called) could not be allowed to spread.

The businessmen of London needn't have worried; even if they had given Scrooge double the business, the ex-miser's charitable activities kept him more than busy. This left the entire operation in the hands of Bob Cratchit, who was neither up to the task, nor particularly wanted to be.

As I have said, Bob was a childlike man, and only the mute urgings of his procreative apparatus had tricked him into the role of husband and father. Just as Scrooge had drawn a lesson from the spirits' visit, Bob had drawn a complimentary one: if Scrooge was to be generous, Bob, and his whole brood, existed to provide a target for that generosity. The neatness of the arrangement proved its rightness to Bob—that, and the fact that he didn't have to work anymore. "I have always found loafing to be something I not only enjoy, but also do uncommonly well," Bob said to his ever-accepting wife. "I plan to practice this art for as many years as Scrooge has left, and more after that if possible. I am, my dear, an artist—who knows what sluggish vistas I might discover? Who knows what masterpieces of extended languor I might eventually achieve?"

Mrs. Fred passed the Cratchits' home on her way to Scrooge's apartment. Despite the lateness of the hour, their extensively renovated hovel was still brightly lit. If it had been any other house (and there hadn't been music pumping out of it), Mrs. Fred might've thought everyone inside was gainfully employed, doing needlework perhaps, or some other job whose wretched practitioners could not afford a holiday. But it being the Cratchits' place, there was a party going on, and her nature being what it was, Mrs. Fred was irresistibly drawn to it.

Not to join in, of course, nor even to scrawl "Merry Christmas!" on a slip of paper and slide it under the front door. No, what Mrs. Fred wanted—one of the few things she craved nearly as much as luxury—was feeling aggrieved, ill-used, done wrong. So Fred's wife wanted to see what Bacchic revels were taking place on Scrooge's dime. That way, she could feel morally superior, stolen from (for wasn't

HOW TO GET AT NIGEL
(OR SOMEONE LIKE HIM)

TWEET

YELL

THROW SOMETHING

PROD WITH BARGE POLE

KICK

NIGEL

CNH

A STOCKINGFUL...

...from P.S. Mueller

Scrooge's money now hers?), and entitled to gouge the irresponsible ex-miser for every last penny.

The Cratchits had not moved house. Tim's mother had a horror of "putting on airs." But as Bob's masterful leveraging of their son's sham infirmities swelled the family coffers, they had added to the original structure quite obsessively. Now, chez Cratchit was a vast collection of rooms outfitted with every modern convenience, encircling their rotting, rickety original quarters. The arrangement called to mind a wedding cake, with a festering rat hidden in its center.

Mrs. Cratchit insisted on living in the old, shabby part; the woman had saved and scuffled for so long that it was the only way she knew how to exist. Mrs. Cratchit was the opposite of Mrs. Fred—no increase in the family's bank balance could change her straitened world. The madness is never in the money, dear reader, but the mind.

Prosperity was not the only thing that Mrs. Cratchit ignored. She ignored the deterioration of her husband's character; she ignored the appearance of the older children in the scandal sheets; and most of all, she ignored the true nature of Tiny Tim. No matter how obvious it became that Tim was spending his days in anything but school, no matter how prodigious the boy's nefarious empire grew, or how ostentatious his ill-gotten bling became, his mother refused to acknowledge it.

Still, she was hardly the first mother to be blind to her children's faults. And we should not judge the boy himself too harshly either; without rascals, we could have no stories of redemption, and spirits would have nothing to do on holidays.

Fred's wife was not so generous to Tim as she peered into the window of the Cratchit's home. "Getting a lap dance, at his age!"

Mrs. Cratchit was knitting some scant feet away. "Tim, you haven't told me your new friend's name," Mrs. Fred heard her say. "Isn't she cold without a shirt?"

Peter Cratchit was passed out on the settee, in the thrall of something unwholesome, while the head of the household was demonstrating to the rest of their children how to use a beer-funnel. Another group (Tim's thugs, Mrs. Fred assumed) was clustered around the piano, making up dirty carols on the fly.

Crippen was reading a dog-eared pamphlet entitled, "Make £££ Selling Opium to Schoolchildren." Yes, it was true—Crippen could read.

Mrs. Fred heard something; out in the yard some feet away, a bedraggled woman swore and pawed at the air, chasing spirits only she could perceive. This was a common occurrence, and not just on Christmas Eve: Junkies were sprawled about the property, laying higgeldy-piggeldy like so many discharged and discarded Christmas crackers.

This, too, was Tim's doing. Over the past twelve months, so many illicit substances had been consumed in the Cratchit home, with such vigor and in such profusion, that said compounds had penetrated the very structure itself. Thanks to Tim's minions, word got around that the abode dispensed a rather sizeable "contact high," so degenerates of every stripe now hung about the property, licking it for a fee. Afterwards they tarried hollow-eyed, unable to walk, insensible to heat or cold, humans made phantoms through chemical submission. Mrs. Fred turned back to the window, thoroughly appalled. Within, without, wherever she looked, it was a scene authored by Scratch himself.

But the worst thing—in Mrs. Fred's eyes, at least—was the Cratchits' furniture. It was so much nicer than hers. And that wasn't all: the Cratchits had a piano! Beer-splashed and out-of-tune, to be sure, but a piano nevertheless. She didn't have a piano…And to think: these freeloaders weren't even Scrooge's flesh and blood!

"Disgusting!" Mrs. Fred said, after she'd filled her tanks, main and auxiliary, with envy and resentment. "Wait'll I tell Mr. Scrooge! That party will end, and quick!" She stomped off, double-time.

When Mrs. Fred arrived at Scrooge's apartment, she was impressed by how strongly her husband had apparently pressed the issue. Fred had smashed the lock and thrown open the door, like a barbarian sacking a citadel! No wonder Scrooge had agreed to let the money flow. Stepping over the small snow drift that had collected in the foyer, she made her way upstairs to Scrooge's chambers. Then she knocked on the door.

Scrooge lay in his bed, hoping that once tonight, ignoring something would actually cause it to go away. But his poor luck held; Fred's wife knocked again.

"I guess I'm just a 'glass half-full' type."

He wrapped a pillow around his head, but Mrs. Fred would not be denied. "Mr. Scrooge!"

"Don't you ghosts ever sleep?" he cried out, throwing his pillow at the door.

"I'm not a—" Fred's wife caught herself. Though she had thought to approach Scrooge as herself, now she realized that more money might be forthcoming if her origin was supernatural. He seemed to really go for that.

"Oh, miserable man!" she said at top volume. "I have come to show you the wickedness of your ways!"

"You and everyone else," Scrooge grumbled.

Fred's wife walked into the room, and Scrooge complained about the draft.

"Get out of bed," Mrs. Fred said. "We have someplace to go, you and I. I am the Ghost of Christmas Past."

"Hah! Somebody screwed up—you lot were here an hour ago!" Scrooge rolled back over defiantly. "Go get sacked and leave me in peace."

"Oh, sorry," Mrs. Fred said. "I'm Christmas Present. I always forget."

Scrooge turned to face her, opening one eye. "You're not the Ghost of anything. You're what's-her-face, my nephew's pet shrew."

Mrs. Fred let that one go. "Ebenezer Scrooge, you have only half-learned the lesson we tried to teach. But because you are not as wicked as you one were, I have tried to be less fearsome this time. I have assumed the form of someone you know and love."

"Shows what you know," Scrooge sneered sleepily.

"Up where we are," Mrs. Fred said, "we all think she's a lovely person. She's smart, and kind, and beautiful, too. You could learn a thing or two from her, especially about how to treat your relations." Scrooge was silent for a while. He was so very tired, and this year's crop of spirits was so very stupid. Finally, he spoke. "You're not leaving, are you?"

"Not after traveling this far, no."

Sighing heavily, Scrooge threw off the blankets. He thought this might happen, so he was fully dressed underneath. The old man swore quietly as he put on his shoes. "I suddenly understand the appeal of Judaism," he said.

"You are in the presence of a ghost, mortal!" Mrs. Fred said. "Most people would be terrified."

"Familiarity breeds contempt."

"All right, then—flattered," Fred's wife said as they went down the stairs. "How many people have spirits watching over their moral progress?"

"They're welcome to—sweet tricycling Christ!" A fresh gust of icy wind hit Scrooge's face, and he had a powerful urge to go back inside. "I really don't think this is necessary," he said to Fred's wife. "I got what the last spirit was trying to say: spread your money far and wide, give it to anybody who asks."

Mrs. Fred blanched, looking truly ghostly. "Oh, my heavens!" she said. "That is exactly the wrong message! You are so very fortunate I have come!" She grabbed his hand and began steaming towards the Cratchits at top speed. "There's something you must see."

Scrooge hung back. "How about we go back upstairs and you describe it to me?"

"No! I must show you the effects of charity without wisdom, and you of all people must see the full measure of its destruction."

Scrooge's interest in this endeavor was vanishingly small, and growing smaller with each freezing second. But Fred's wife cared deeply, and this gave her better traction in the slippery conditions. She yanked Scrooge along mercilessly.

"Scrooge, each of us plays parent to that which we bring into the world," Mrs. Fred said. "You have given much over the last year, but much you have given has ended up in the wrong hands."

"And, who, in your opinion, are the right hands?" Scrooge said. "Wait—I think I know."

"Your nephew and his wife would be an excellent choice."

"I'm getting too good at this," Scrooge said. "And where are you taking me?"

"To the Cratchits', so that you may see the effect wrongheaded charity has in this wicked world."

"Of course," Scrooge said. All at once, the entire evening made sense. "This is just too absurd. I should dump it all into the sea, just to spite you all."

"What?" the faux-ghost asked.

"'Lead on,' I said."

I can hear you now, dear reader, claiming that it would've never taken you so very long to figure out the ruse. This is easy for you to say. Remember that Scrooge had already suffered through one Christmas Eve filled with genuine apparitions. His sense of reality thus shaken, it was only logical (in a certain way), to expect that the same day a year later would be filled with even more ghosts dispensing even more lessons. Some part of Scrooge was hoping for just this occurrence. Plus, his vision wasn't great. And also, there was the chronic drunkenness I mentioned before. Taken together, it makes perfect sense.

And now it was all ruined. Scrooge was terribly disappointed—last year's glimpse into eternity had been replaced by a grubby, all-too-human melee over some cash. He stopped, preparing to denounce Fred's wife right there in the snow; but then, his brain hatched a counter-plan.

The longer they walked, the tighter Mrs. Fred grabbed Scrooge's hand; that comment about tossing money into the sea had spooked her, to her very core. Finally, the old man shook his bruised fingers free. "You know, for a spirit, you really leave a mark."

"Ssh!" Fred's wife said, creeping up to one of the Cratchits' windows. On tip-toe, peering over the sill, she was delighted at the scene of utter depravity. There was casual sex and loud music and gambling, but these sins were just the beginning. Everyone was using the Lord's name in vain. Crippen was slurping the fog of oblivion from a monster bong fashioned from a London bobbies' helmet. Tiny Tim was sassing his father, and pouring the contents of his pimp-cup onto the carpet. Mr. Cratchit didn't even notice, for he was busy deep-kissing someone not Tim's mother. Peter Cratchit was walking around in circles, high on patent medicines, and whipping himself for fun. The other, younger Cratchits were all naked, tattooing each other and huffing unlit gaslamps. And what was Mrs. Cratchit doing, you ask? Why, ignoring it all—and baking cookies.

Mrs. Fred motioned for Scrooge to join her. Scrooge crept over and looked inside.

"And on Christmas Eve!" Fred's wife clucked. She could hardly keep from giggling.

Scrooge put his plan into effect. "I don't see what your problem is, you old prude," he snapped. "That's just how the holiday should be celebrated. Check out the guy in the crotchless reindeer costume."

Mrs. Fred was speechless. Her jaw fell open almost as wide as Marley's had. (The real one, I mean.)

"Spirit, I want to thank you for bringing me here. I see now the error of my ways," Scrooge said. "There's only one way to dispose of my fortune: I must give it all to the Cratchits."

"But...but...that makes no sense," Mrs. Fred said. "You can't!"

"I can," Scrooge said, "and what's more, I will. You've shown me that I can't hope to untangle the conflicting wishes of the spirit world. And since my soul is already fricasseed, I might as well throw my lot in with the other sinners." He walked away.

Mrs. Fred was stunned. "Where are you going?"

"Duh," Scrooge said. "To join the party!"

"This is crazy," Fred's wife said. "You're crazy."

"If I'm crazy, then you're a figment of my imagination. Shoo!"

Fred's wife was completely unmanned by the situation, and began to scamper in the direction of home. Maybe Fred would know what to do.

Just in case he didn't, Scrooge tried to plant the seed. "You can tell the last ghost," he called after her, "to save his breath!"

After she'd turned the corner, Scrooge proved himself to be as good as his word: he walked right up to the Cratchits' door, and knocked. It took some real pounding to be heard over the music, but someone finally answered.

"Yeah?" Crippen said, all hooded eyes and weedy languor.

"I've come to complain about the noise," Scrooge said, pushing past. "There isn't enough of it."

Mrs. Cratchit was the first to hear Scrooge's voice, and the only one in a condition to speak coherently.

"Like what you've done to the place," Scrooge said when she appeared. "I've always been a fan of the Taj Mahal look."

"M-mister Scrooge," she said, all aflutter. "What a surprise seeing you here... at four in the morning."

"I couldn't sleep," Scrooge lied. "Ghosts had me up and down all night. No matter—is everyone here? I have an announcement that can't wait."

"I think everyone's up," Mrs. Cratchit said. The last time she'd seen Bob, he was passed out in a pool of his own sick. Happened every time he drank coconut rum.

Suddenly there was a loud laughing scream, and a woman in a thong ran between Mrs. Cratchit and Scrooge.

"That's Tiny Tim's new..." Mrs. Cratchit struggled for an appropriate word. "Governess."

"Ah."

Tim himself appeared, in hot pursuit. "Where my b—h at?" he said.

"Hello, Tim," Scrooge said. "I'm Uncle Scrooge, remember me?"

Tim didn't respond, trying to look tough. Given his size and general scrawniness, it was difficult.

"No matter," Scrooge said. He wanted to keep things moving—he suddenly had a lot to do in the hour or two of darkness that remained. "Mrs. Cratchit, please assemble your family in the parlor. I will make my announcement, then leave you to enjoy the rest of your holiday in peace."

Five minutes later, Scrooge stood in front of a semi-comatose Cratchit clan, surrounded by their equally impaired servants, retainers, and general hangers-on. "After the events of this evening," Scrooge said, "the details of which I will not bore you with—"

"More ghosts?" Crippen said mid-inhale, thinking their earlier gambit had worked.

"Yes, more ghosts," Scrooge said, then continued. "I have decided to give all my money to my sole heir, my nephew Fred and his wife, Shrewtastic."

Everyone sprang to life. Crippen moved toward Scrooge with murderous intent; in the right hands, a bong can be lethal. Scrooge saw the look in his eye and said, "That won't do you any good—I've already made out my will." Scrooge looked at each person in turn—Bob, Mrs. Cratchit, Tim. "Do any of you have questions?"

"But...why?" Bob asked, hurt.

"You have got to be kidding," Scrooge said. Stepping over a passed-out reveler, he walked towards the door. "Also, Bob," Scrooge added, "you're fired. Merry Christmas!"

TIM'S SECRET.

As soon as the door closed behind Scrooge, Tiny Tim declared, "I'm gonna bust a cap in that guy."

"What good will that do?" Mrs. Cratchit was distraught. This was something she couldn't ignore, and while it was all well and good to deny prosperity, she'd gotten used to the privilege. "He's already done a will."

"Wills can be changed," Tim said. "Right, Mr. Ligature?"

An older man sat up from the couch, dislodging an aspiring actress. Years ago, he had looked distinguished, but now he just looked seedy. "Indubitably, Master T."

"Dry your tears, mother," Tim commanded. "Father, put down that straight razor. Liggy here is one of London's pre-eminent forgers. He did a fake will for our savior Jesus Christ—and it stood up in court, too."

"But will I have to get rid of my sundries-girl?" Mrs. Cratchit's one luxury was a servant whose job it was to walk besides her from morning until night, wearing a lumpy garment which contained every conceivable household item. The poor thing resembled a sweaty potato.

"No, mother," Tim said. "No one is getting fired tonight, or any other night. Mr. Ligature," he said, "start writing. 'I, Ebenezer Scrooge, being of sound mind and body…'"

Meanwhile, some distance away, Fred and his bride were similarly shocked by the turn the evening had taken.

"Fred, you've got to do something," Mrs. Fred demanded.

"What would you suggest I do?" Fred replied. "The old goat's made up his mind."

"Well, make him unmake it," she said. "You're his flesh and blood."

"Quit saying that." Fred had broken out something strong, and was swigging from it. "Seems to me that everything was okay," he said, "until a certain person got involved."

"Oh, you shouldn't've said that," Mrs. Fred said, her voice menacing and low. "That's another year of celibacy for you." Fred took another gulp. "Who says I've been celibate?"

Normally this would've earned him a session with the thimble, but his wife had bigger issues to attend to (and he was out of range). "Please, Fred," she asked, "go talk to him. You'll be able to convince him. He likes you."

"It's still dark out," Fred said. "I'll do it tomorrow."

"No!" Fred's wife said. She reached into a drawer, and pulled out a piece of paper. "Go over there right now, and show Scrooge this!" It was Scrooge's last will, which named Fred his sole heir. "You tell him we'll fight! We'll say he was insane—that Christmas Eve always makes him insane!" Fred's wife let that sink in, but it had no effect, so she changed direction. "Tell you what. If you go now, I'll have something waiting for you when you come back. Something you haven't had in a very, very long time…"

Fred was officially over Mrs. Fred. "I'd prefer breakfast." He grabbed a fresh bottle, and left.

When Scrooge returned home, he headed directly for his bed. But not to sleep.

Instead, he took the bronze bust from the Prince of Wales, and some pillows, and arranged them to look like his sleeping form. It was passably realistic, with the gaslamps turned down low.

"That'll do," Scrooge said brightly. "After all, we're not dealing with geniuses." Chuckling at the mayhem he was about to cause, he took some of his counterfeit money—collecting it had been his only hobby, before the spirits had come along—and threw it into a sack. Just as he placed the sack by the door, he heard someone entering downstairs. "Whoop! Hallo!" Suddenly Scrooge felt wonderful; he should mess with people more often, it did wonders for his mood. The ex-miser had just enough time to leap into the fireplace and shimmy up the chimney. Bracing his feet on two protruding bricks, he perched there like a deranged vulture, just out of sight.

A moment later, Fred stuck his head through the door.

"Uncle?"

There was no answer, so Fred walked over to the bed, and sat on its edge. "Uncle, it's me, Fred."

Fred was quite fantastically drunk; Scrooge could smell his breath from inside the chimney.

Over on the bed, Fred was getting worried. The shape wasn't moving. "Uncle?" he said uncertainly, then reached out a finger and gave the shape a poke. He drew back; it was cold, as cold as the grave.

"FRED!" Scrooge shouted from the chimney.

The old man timed his moment well; Fred was so startled he fell off the bed.

When Scrooge heard him hit the floor, it was all he could do not to laugh.

"U-uncle?"

"I was your uncle," Scrooge intoned, pleased at how the chimney gave his voice a nice eerie echo. "Now, I have gone over to the other side. I'm dead, Fred—and without my reclamation completed!" To emphasize this last point, Scrooge gave a wail.

"But that can't be so!" Fred said, terrified. "Think of all the people you helped!"

"Not enough! Not enough!" Scrooge said. "Only the worthy ones counted! Perhaps if I hadn't been constantly distracted by your deceitfulness—I knew about your Italian Escape Fund, and your wife's badgering…But no!" Scrooge was actually freaking himself out a little. "You—and your wife—have condemned me to H—l!"

"Oh god! Oh god! Save me!" Fred said, cowering. He'd never quite believed his Uncle about the spirits, but now he had no doubt. "What can I do?"

"Nothing!" Scrooge said. "You must live with the knowledge you hindered a good man—your flesh and blood—and sent him to eternal torment."

Fred brought his head from the floor. "Now, Uncle, be fair—you weren't that good. At the end there, I'll admit you were a prince, but before then? A grade-A s—theel."

"How dare you disrespect the dead!" Scrooge moaned. "Sa-a-ay you're sorry!"

"I won't. It's the truth."

"Gee," Scrooge said, "that's too bad. I was going to give you that sackful of money by the door. Just to show there are no hard feelings."

"Really?"

"Yes, really! My time here is short, but I must tell you one more thing—"

"Uncle, why can't I see you?" Fred asked. "You could see your ghosts, right?"

"Didn't I just tell you my time was short?" Scrooge said crossly. "Don't waste it with a bunch of stupid questions!… Fred, listen to me: it's not too late for you—you can still change. Go get a job. Lay off the sauce. And for God's sake, divorce your wife!"

"I don't much like the first idea," Fred said, "nor the second. But I must admit the third one has real merit." Between the liquor, and the forced celibacy, he was horny enough to ravish Scrooge's bust. "We haven't had sex in years."

"TOO MUCH INFORMATION!" Scrooge's voice boomed.

"'Member when you gave me a hundred pounds to establish a free bunion clinic?" Fred said. "That was the last time."

"NOT LISTENING! NOT LISTENING!" Scrooge said, making a loud humming noise. Then Scrooge stopped. "You pushed me too far, Fred. I've just put a curse on that money."

"Hey!" Fred said. "Why'd you do that? I was going to spend it."

"Too late now," Scrooge said. "Give it to your wife. Tell her to spend it. Bad things will happen, I promise."

Fred chuckled at the prospect of causing his wife grief. "Well, that's better than nothing, I guess."

"Now, GO!" Scrooge boomed, making Fred's laughter catch in his throat.

"Uncle…?" Fred ventured quietly. "About your will…"

"GO!" Scrooge said. "LEAVE THIS PLACE, AND SPONGE NO MORE!"

The effort of this made Scrooge cough a bit, but he was able to hold it until after his nephew had scurried downstairs, clutching the bagful of counterfeit money.

Ten minutes later as he was making up another bag, Scrooge heard Crippen and Tiny Tim talking at the bottom of the stairs.

"Aren't you coming with?" Crippen said.

"If you carry me on your shoulders."

"Get stuffed, farter."

Ten seconds later, the weedy manservant burst through the door to Scrooge's bedroom. "Get up, Scrooge!" he yelled. "I'm the Ghost of Kicking Your A—e!" Crippen saw the shape on the bed, and rushed towards it. But before he could swing his sand-filled sock, Scrooge's voice boomed from the chimney.

"STOP, EVIL MAN!"

Crippen stopped, all right. He stood there, flabbergasted.

"Who's that? If anybody's hiding up here, they better come out or I'll—"

"You cannot reach me where I am," Scrooge said, "nor can you harm me any longer. I am dead, Crippen. You're speaking to Ebenezer Scrooge's ghost."

Crippen, like most criminals, was a bully; but given his pitiful physique, the prospect of facing something more powerful than a seven-year-old child made him distinctly uneasy. Furthermore, all the lousy things he had done gave Crippen a lively sense of guilt and dread; this, too, was an occupational hazard. Both factors now spewed forth, mixing to form abject terror.

Uttering a wordless cry, Crippen turned and ran—but not before grabbing the sack of coin Scrooge had very thoughtfully put by the door.

After Crippen had pounded down the stairs, Scrooge shimmied his way down the chimney. Lucky Crippen was such a scaredy cat, Scrooge thought, as he removed the bust and pillow. Outside the sky was lightening, and with every passing moment, his ruse looked more fake.

"So, did you plant the will?" Tiny Tim asked, as Crippen stood there panting on the stoop.

"I forgot."

"Well, go back up, then," Tiny Tim piped menacingly.

Crippen shook his head emphatically. "Your uncle's dead, and his ghost is up there!"

"Bulls—t!" Tiny Tim reached up and swiped the crumpled will from Crippen's hand. "Gimme that. And that m—rf—r isn't my uncle!"

Monkey-quick and as sure as a dancer, Tim climbed the stairs, taking care that no one saw how easily he did so. When he reached the door to his uncle's chambers, his manner transformed itself—his usual swagger was gone, replaced by a kind of dew-eyed self-abasing forelock-tugging that only can be properly described as

"emetic."

"Good morning, Mr. Scrooge!" Tim knocked on the door politely. "I've come to wish you a Merry Christmas!"

"Come in."

Scrooge didn't sound like a ghost, nor look like one either. That superstitious idiot, Tim thought, making a mental note to sack Crippen. But he'd do it after the first of the year—there were tax advantages.

The old man was sitting on the edge of his bed. "Come closer, my boy," he said warmly. He patted the bed. "Over here, by me."

All smiles, Tim hobbled over.

"Did you make it up those stairs all by yourself?"

"I did, Mr. Scrooge," Tim said. "That's how much I wanted to wish you a Merry Christmas."

"That's awfully kind of you, Tim," Scrooge said. "Come closer, so I can see you more clearly. These old eyes, like the rest of me, are frail. And the light is weak yet; the world is still asleep."

"Why do you have a hairbrush, Mr. Scrooge? You only have old man's fringe."

"Hairbrushes have other uses, too, Tim!" Quick as a flash, the old man grabbed the deceitful urchin. Tim tried to struggle, but a year's worth of vitamin-free dissolution had made him as weak as an early morning breeze. Scrooge had no trouble laying Tim crosswise across his lap. Rolling up a sleeve, he began to spank Tiny Tim vigorously.

"You've had this coming for twelve months, you rascal! I was too indulgent with you, but now the scales will be balanced!…Steal people's clothes, will you? Pretend to be a spirit, eh?…Girls in thongs? Didn't think I knew about lap-dancing, did you?…Go ahead, call me foul names, you poisonous little twerp!" Pants-on spanking was good, but Scrooge wanted more. He ripped down the boy's trousers, exposing his bare b—m. There, tattooed across the boy's backside one word per cheek, was the following:

Thug Life.

Scrooge was appalled. "Tim, you should be ashamed of yourself! Your mother must be so disappointed in you. I know"—Scrooge feigned a bright idea—"shall we see if I can remove that by hand? I don't know if it can be done, but let's try."

"MAGA Hari"

Scrooge whaled and whopped, until Tim's bottom was too red to make out the words. Pleased with his work, he let the sobbing mini-kingpin slide to the floor. Mumbling swears, the crying boy pulled up his baggy prison-styled trousers, and snuffled his snotty nose.

"Don't you dare wipe your nose on my sheets."

Defiant, Tim moved to do just that, but Scrooge lunged at him. "Boo!" Scrooge said.

"AHH!" Tiny Tim screamed, then scrambled towards the door. He paused once, to make a threat, but Scrooge lunged again and sent him running even faster.

Scrooge watched as Tim quite dexterously scuttled down the stairs. "God bless us, every bun!"

HAPPILY EVER AFTER?

Scrooge had never trusted banks, so he spent a lovely Christmas morning digging up all the coins he'd buried under the waiting room then decanting them into steamer trunks. In the afternoon, after signing over the insurance to a local orphanage, he hired a few neighbor kids to put the torch to his old countinghouse. They enjoyed it, and so did he.

By sunset, Scrooge was on a boat bound for the Continent, with more baggage than anyone had ever seen. This contained his entire remaining wealth, a considerable but not outlandish sum. The ex-miser had a propensity for seasickness, but this was more than counteracted by happy thoughts of his heirs—whoever the courts decided they were—being soundly and irrevocably screwed.

Scrooge's first stop was Switzerland, where his luggage went directly into a numbered bank account. Then, as all free spirits do, he felt himself drawn to Paris, where he planned to spend the balance of his days, kind, generous, anonymous, and happy.

Scrooge discovered that a year's worth of funding deadbeats had curtailed his guilt quite nicely. From now on, the old man had decided, he would tithe; let the Church puzzle out the wishes of the hereafter (and let them burn if they were wrong!). Scrooge had done his bit, and would do more, but now it was time for him to really live.

Thus that Michaelmas found our hero tucked away in a cozy bistro, eating delicious food and flirting with an attractive barmaid. A slight improvement from The Ball and Chain, Scrooge thought.

After the meal was over, Scrooge dallied, as was his new custom. He drank a cognac, and pondered the meaning of it all. "A life spent in service to others," he said quietly to himself, "is only as good as the others you serve."

A man at the table closest to Scrooge took note. "Are you a philosopher?" he asked.

"No," Scrooge said with a smile. "Just someone trying to figure out this world."

"If you find the answer," the man teased, "let me know."

The drink and the man's genial nature loosened Scrooge's tongue, and he told the stranger his entire story, from Marley's first visit to the affair with Tim's b—m.

"Bravo!" the man said, when Scrooge told him about spanking Tim. "What a little ratfink."

"You can't blame him, I suppose," Scrooge said with a sigh. "He's only a product of our times. Or perhaps he is a ratfink...After everything that's happened, I admit I'm more confused than ever. As long as man measures himself by what he has instead of what he is, charity is doomed to piddle along, a weak flowing trickle in such a thirsty world. Say what you will, friend: a man will not do anything contrary to his interests for long—even if you threaten him with everlasting torment."

"You know," the man said, "you might be interested in some ideas I've come up with, ways to solve just these problems, and make a better world."

"I'm all ears," Scrooge said.

The man—who was all beard—looked at him puzzledly.

"It means 'I'm listening.'"

"My name is Karl Marx," the man said, digging a coffee-stained brochure out of his pocket and handing it to Scrooge. The ex-miser listened politely as Mr. Marx began a long discourse about something he called "communism," and how it was destined to change the world.

To Scrooge—especially after the events of the last weeks—it seemed like a nice theory that would never work; but he was not so boorish to tell his new friend that. After about an hour, simply to get out of the conversation, Scrooge gave the man a donation.

"Thank you, Comrade Scrooge," Mr. Marx said, as they parted. "We will remember this, come the Revolution."

"Most assuredly," Scrooge said, not convinced. Still, the old man walked to his hotel pleased at his good deed. Comrade Marx's heart seemed to be in the right place...and after all, what harm could it possibly do? ᴮ

DON'T TEACH YOUR GRANDMOTHER TO SUCK EGGS
CLODS OF EARTHY WISDOM FOR URBANITES

BY RON BARRETT

ONLY THE GRAVE WILL CURE A HUNCHBACK.

WOULD IF I KNOW WHERE YOU FALL, THERE I LAY STRAW.

HAVING HELD A GOAT'S TAIL YOU CANNOT MAKE A FUR COAT.

YOU CAN HAVE SMOKED FISH BUT YOU CANNOT HAVE FISH SMOKE.

HE THAT HAS NO HEAD NEEDS NO HAT.

IT IS EASIER FOR THE WOMAN WHEN THE MARE GETS OFF THE CART.

A HANDLE ON A HEDGEHOG IS NOT WORTH A KLOPKY.

IT IS A WISE MAN WHO DOES NOT SPIT IN HIS SOUP.

IT IS GOOD THERE WHERE WE ARE NOT.

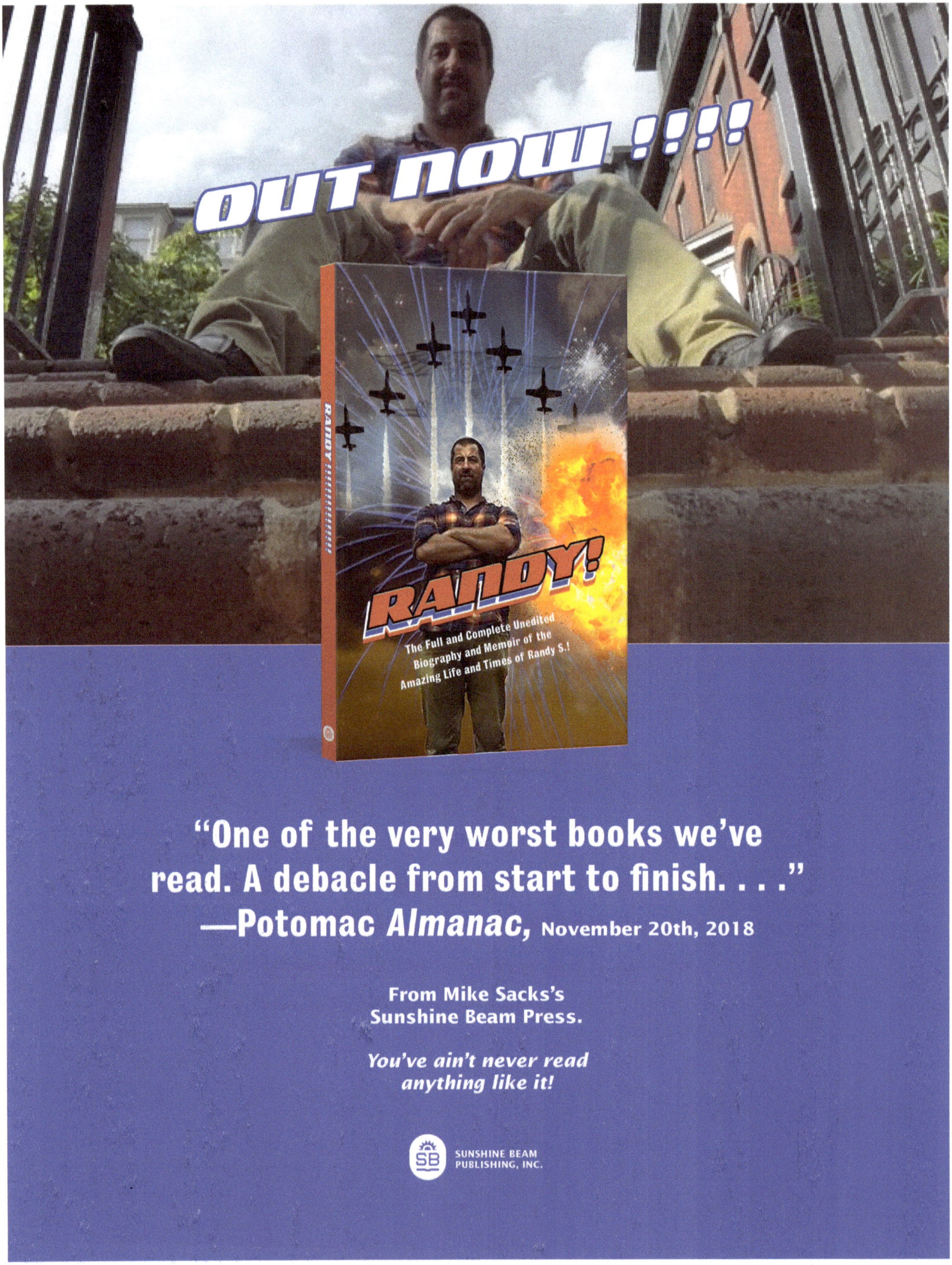
OUT NOW !!!!
RANDY!
The Full and Complete Unedited Biography and Memoir of the Amazing Life and Times of Randy S.!
"One of the very worst books we've read. A debacle from start to finish. . . ."
—Potomac *Almanac,* November 20th, 2018
From Mike Sacks's
Sunshine Beam Press.
You've ain't never read anything like it!
SB
SUNSHINE BEAM PUBLISHING, INC.

OUR BACK PAGES

LETTER FROM MELANIA

Season's Greetings, and an update on the thing we gave Eric's face • By Emily Flake

Dear Ones to Whom We Are Bound by Blood, or Blood-Oath,

My goodness, is it almost 2019 already? It seems impossible that the year so eagerly anticipated by the enemies of my husband, to whom I am sworn in body if not in soul, is almost over. We are almost two years into the Administration's first term, and I am pleased to see that the first small green shoots of seeds I planted long ago are starting to peek above the surface. Don't worry, all will be revealed in the fullness of time.

It has been a busy year for our blended family: Ivanka and Jared raising their family and smoothing the way for my ultimate plans, Don Jr. and Eric serving as our faithful dogsbodies and of course, Donald and myself running the country and its shadow-world counterpart. Of my own son, B-----n, we need not speak here. Who am I forgetting? Oh yes—the blonde one whose name begins with T. She is also alive.

Donald continues to make strides in the bending of reality to his will by the power of his words—it is a shame he is not more intellectually gifted, for he would be a truly powerful mage—important work if I am to execute my own vision. I myself am recovering nicely from the kidney procedure I had on my face and am feeling stronger than ever. Together we continue to shake the foundations of institutions all over the world, from democratically elected governments, to entire weather systems.

The daughter of the Czech whore continues to prosper under my tutelage. Her living children with the mannequin we forged for her are growing nicely, and hardly ever scream in the night anymore. And sacrificing the babies Donald put in her will be worth it in the long run! You cannot raise an army of vengeful souls without breaking a few human laws, as they say. Sometimes I think she even thinks her conversion to the Old God will be enough to save her and her family!

Don Jr. is an exemplary namesake in every way, from his parroting of falsehoods on social media to his casting aside of a wife. His brazen murder of the majestic creatures of this world bodes well for his ability to do what will be asked of him to our human subjects. As his father's flesh continues to weaken and rot, Don Jr. is looking more and more like an appropriate choice of consort when I begin my final ascent.

The thing we gave Eric's face caused us very little trouble this year.

Travel-wise, this fall I visited many countries in Africa. How glorious the riches of that continent! We may allow China to scoop out her material resources, but I am happy to report that the ongoing suffering of her people makes the souls there especially sweet to consume. And how trustingly they hand over their babies, when they feel they have no other choice!

In sadder news, you may have noticed that the recent "elections" showed some gains in the ranks of our enemies. This is unfortunate, but I remind you to take heart in the fact that even the most fervent idealism can be crushed under the boot of tyranny if only we all work together. That sparkle in the Cortez woman's eye will be out by summer, I promise you that.

In closing, I would like to wish every one of you a satisfying celebration of the Dark Times to come. *For every candle lit, let two be snuffed!*

Be Best,
Melania

P.S.: And to He Who Shall Not Be Named—I remind you: we have a fucking deal.

EMILY FLAKE is FLOTUS Whisperer for *The American Bystander*.

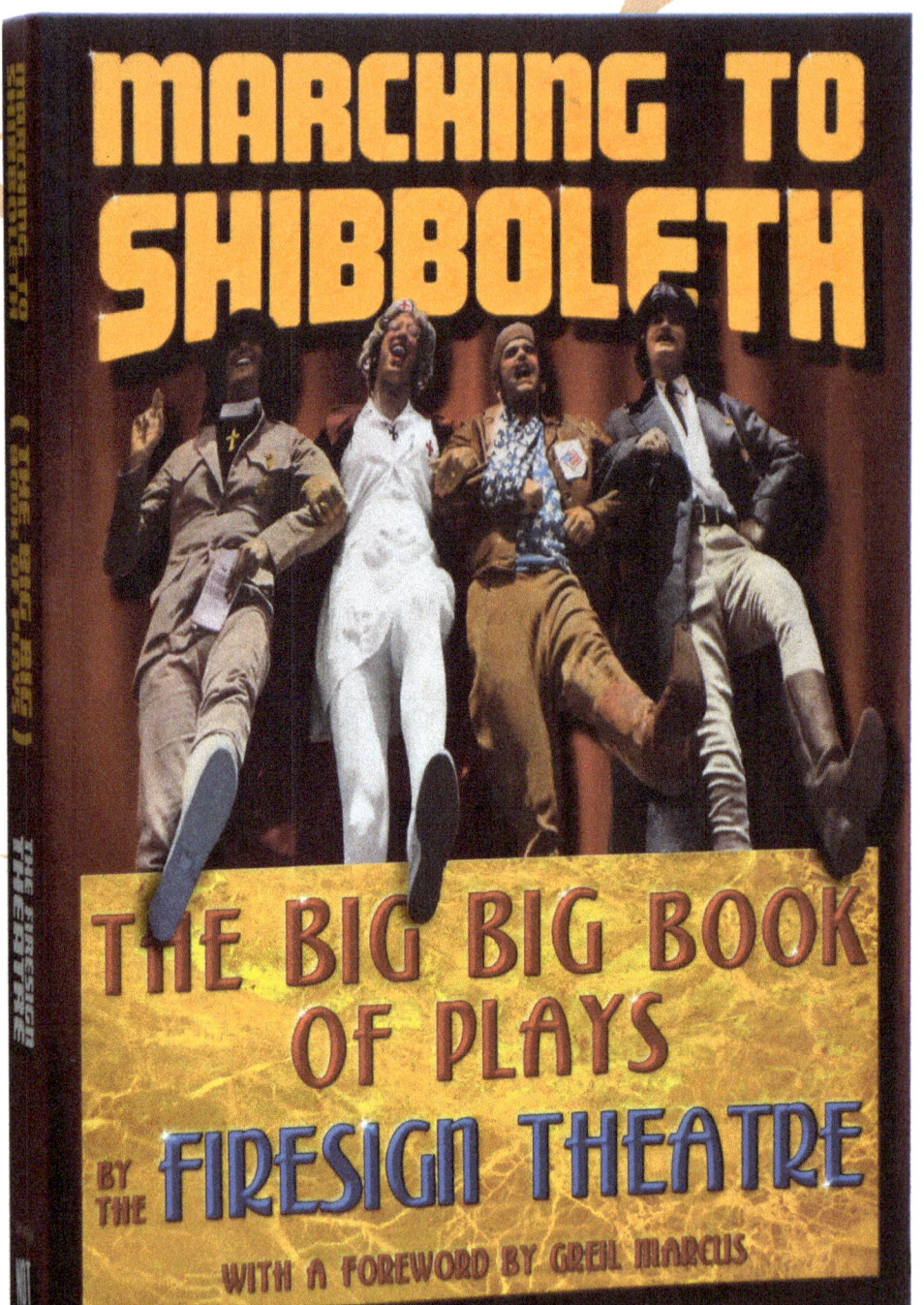

OUR BACK PAGES

JOAN'S OTHER KITCHEN

Matt and Vic, and traps and bunny rabbits • By Brian McConnachie

Baseball Is Hunting

When I drive that section of dirt road to and from work, there are often robins or swallows or crows standing or sitting in the road. As I approach, they scatter though some cut it pretty close. First disappearing under the car, seeming to be goners but then miraculously emerging, like the Blue Angels, banking off to the left and right.

It could be older birds training younger ones how to judge distance, mass and velocity and then put it all to the test. Admiring their skill and wanting to be helpful, I keep my speed at a constant 10 M.P.H. when I drive at them. (If this is what they're doing—I've quit watching the nature shows on public television at the insistence of Walter Wells, a former neighbor, who convinced me that they make it all up to match the amazing footage they've amassed over the years.) I've also considered the birds could just be pecking at the dirt, hoping for a worm or two, confident in their ability to scram when necessary.

But once beyond this stretch, when it turns into asphalt, my thoughts on their Ranger-camp bird- skills depart my mind, leaving my current thoughts mostly in the possession of Victoria Wells, former wife of said Walter, who both moved away some five years ago. My own ex had departed the region just before the Wells's had arrived. But now Victoria may have returned, which if true, is of disturbing concern to me. I believed I was over her but now can't stop thinking it was her I saw buying gas the other night.

BRIAN McCONNACHIE is Founder and Head Writer of *The American Bystander*.

I was stopped at a light while driving home from a meeting at the VFW hall populated by parents and parent/coaches who were considering a plan to extend the town's Little League season from July 4th through Labor Day.

Most parents who coach usually have a child on the team they coach. I'm not a parent and probably for that reason some parents have been urging me, and a few other childless locals, to please get involved. They want more impartiality and a less competitive atmosphere; they want an atmosphere where everyone cheerfully roots for everyone else.

The league's regular season ended on a disturbing note with a parent, from the visitor's side, muttering louder and louder; then he trotted out to the pitcher's mound, where his son had just walked in two runs, losing the lead. The boy's father started shouting.

"Okay, you wanted my attention, you got it. So let's get it out. Just what are you trying to do here? Disgrace me? Because that's exactly what you're doing and you damn well know it. Just wait till I get you home, pal—NO! You get this next batter out or you just better not plan on coming home!"

Not wanting to give this incident more attention than it caused, the episode was thereafter referred to as "that thing that happened with the guy." It was first used as an argument for *not* extending the season, suggesting we leave this business behind and start fresh again in the spring with some new rules in place. But a growing majority—a number of whom were at the game in question and so regretted their own inaction—now believed that by extending the season they would not be bending to that behavior. They would bury that thing that happened with the guy under an extended season of dreamy afternoons, cherishing non-competitive baseball games and nearby dappled sunlight.

Through the paused traffic and gas pumps, I saw only part of a woman's back but knew it was her. Her name had come up a few times lately. I'd heard she and Walter divorced. I was sorry about that. In spite of what my intentions toward her ultimately were, I always believed she and Walter had a beguiling relationship that co-authored some spirited battles of enviable passion.

I should have pulled in behind her, but was stuck in the outside lane with cars honking for me to move it. Also, we hadn't parted on the best of terms: indifference on her part and feigned indifference on mine. If someone had a question with her as some, or all, of the answer, I'd retreat behind a bewildered stare.

"Matt! What's her name? You know who I mean. Curly hair, over the top, perky. Always in motion. Flirts well with others. Married to that tall guy, the doper. He's a chemist for some big food corporation. C'mon. She was a tennis instructor. You know who I'm talking about —"

"Uuummm…No. I really don't…I don't, really." My passion for her made me self conscious, as I attempted to conceal all interest I held for everything remotely connected to her.

"Well guess what? I think she's moved back."

I had already become friends with Walter before I had met her. He had a range of odd interests and a playful feminine side. He'd drop by occasionally. We'd smoke a little dope that he'd provide, put on some tunes and speculate about lives lived at the edge of an expanding universe. He worked for General Foods but wouldn't say what he did there, which became a running joke.

"I make sure the frozen peas are frozen at the exact, right moment. 'The moment of readiness,' we like to call it," he'd say with a wink. Occasionally he'd bring up his buddy, Vic, mentioning trips they've taken together; but until I met Vic I had assumed Vic was male. When I did meet her and her tomboy nature, I saw their snug synchronization.

Sitting on the porch, Walter and I would let the conversation drift until it bumped into something we'd both enjoy contributing to.

"I was reading about the earliest Phoenicians where the children's toys had wheels on them, but the adults were still dragging rocks around in a net of ropes."

"When they finally straightened that out, did they acknowledge the kids with a holiday?" I asked.

"I think they were too embarrassed. But it freed them up to start working on their precious alphabet that they made the kids stay indoors memorizing on lovely Mediterranean afternoons."

"Were there other things the kids were keeping from their betters?" I said.

"Oh, yes."

"Like what? Frozen foods?" I said.

"Frozen foods, yes…that would definitely be one," Walter said. "We still use their secret formula, you know."

This idea—learning from play, "The child is father to the man"—stuck with me. It then joined up with another major ponderable, baseball. That's when I realized something so fundamental about baseball: Baseball is hunting. It's hunting as a game that has almost perfectly evolved. All the men in the field are traps. The pitcher is the hunter with the powerful, accurate arm. The catcher helps flush out the prey. The batter, the bunny rabbit, or whatever, has to get from one safe place to the next. The traps are set. Then the pitcher/hunter sets it all in motion. Everybody gets to be the traps and everyone gets to be the bunny. Except in the DH-corrupted American League version.

I thought Walter might get a kick out of this so I dropped in for a visit. My first to his house. We sat on the back porch and talked about the childhood influences that transcend our lives. Building to the reveal, I wanted to give the idea a modest preamble. "I was thinking," I began, "that probably all sports no matter what objective they have could be training for a particular function in later life. Such as, football is war. The soldiers capturing territory. Attacking, defending. And rugby is similar. I think. Not altogether sure about rugby. Running off with a big leather egg filled with milk chocolate? The spoils of war? It appears to be a rough struggle, so let's for the sake of war call it war.

"Then there are those contests that Red Smith called 'the back and forth sports': lacrosse, soccer, basketball, hockey, polo, water polo, which is a half of a back and forth sport. All those could be various"—I was reaching here—"sales positions?"

"Where are you putting tennis and all its paddle-wielding offspring like squash, ping-pong, badminton and racquetball?" he asked.

"Tennis is probably boxing at a safe distance. Actually, you could put it in with war; the artillery division. But we're getting off-track here. The rest are mostly individual achievement. Track and field, swimming, golf, horse racing," I said. "But of all sports, the most difficult, sophisticated, evolved, complex, elegant and violent, and the one that stands unique"—here I lowered my voice and raised my brows—"is baseball. Baseball is hunting. What is more ancient and universal than hunting?"

Walter thought for a while. "Then what is hunting?" he said. "I'm not sure I'm with you on this."

"Are you a baseball fan?" I said.

"Not really."

"Are you a sports fan?"

"I like tennis," he said. "I like the outfits."

Since it was new, I went slowly. There were certainly flaws but this day's version would merely introduce the overall thesis. Later, I'd do the polish.

"Think of all the players on the field as traps," I told Walter, as I heard someone inside the house. "It requires every bit of a man's instinct, knowledge, speed and strength. It's quiet, it's still, then—BAM! It explodes into orchestrated chaos that can happen so fast, a dozen things can go on at once…"

The door opened and out came a woman dressed in shorts and a green T-shirt with an emblem of crossed tennis racquets on it.

"Hey babe," she said.

"Hey babe," Walter said. "Didn't hear you drive in."

"Hell-o, there. Is this your imaginary friend? It's Matt, right? Hi. Good to finally meet you and see you exist. Walter has been telling me about you. I'm the wifie, Victoria."

She came towards me. I rose, and staring at her, mostly missed her extended hand but we caught and pinched the tips of each other's fingers.

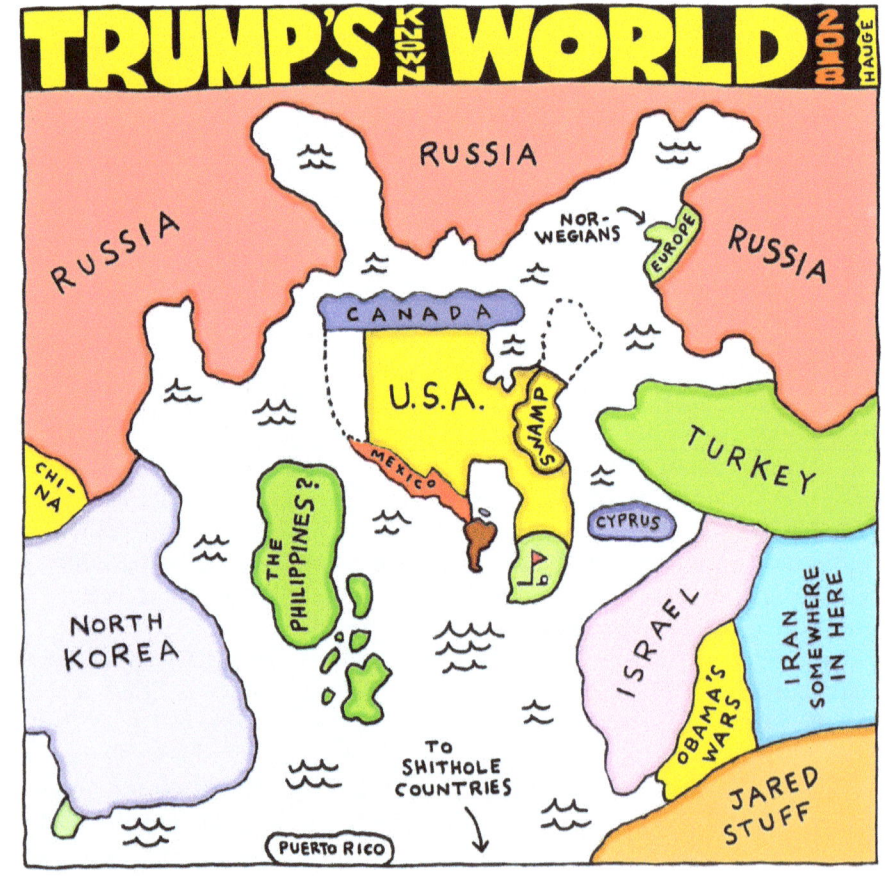

"What are you guys up to?"

"I was just saying to Walter—"

"Matt? Has someone offered you a drink? You don't have a drink. Let me get you something. Today's Friday. That's a gin day for me. I'm going to have gin and tonic. In fact, I think it's all we have," she said adding, "Did you get to the store today, babe?"

"I asked him if he wanted a drink, babe. He said he didn't. Didn't I ask you? I'm not totally worthless as a host, am I?" said Walter. "But I did go to the store."

"I'm fine, really," I said. Thank you."

"You sure? The train's leaving. It's the gin-town express. Yes? No? What are you guys talking about?" she said, heading back into the house.

"Matt thinks baseball is an ancient endeavor. Like hunting," Walter answered.

"I knew it was prehensile," she said. "Keep talking but louder so I can hear you. But please, not about baseball. OK?"

She then told a story, out the kitchen window, in considerable detail, about her father taking her to a baseball game and how she didn't like a minute of it. She preferred football or tennis. I thought, what a shame because she'd look great in a baseball cap, a ponytail bouncing out the back as she wildly cheered the runner rounding third. Then she brought up tennis, and I never got any further with my baseball-as-hunting thesis.

As nice as it was to have such an attractive and friendly neighbor, I initially kept my distance. I found Vic would interrupt the interesting to rephrase the obvious. Or she would monopolize a conversation she had interrupted by offering what she didn't know about a topic that was no longer being discussed because she had shoved it onto a corner and blocked anyone who would try to retrieve it for the better common interest. She was quick and proficient at this. And I found her to be randomly short-tempered and intolerant of Walter when he tried to cure her of this. Occasionally she'd fire back a "Shut up!" that felt as hurtful as a slap across the face. But then, like the electricity suddenly going back on, she'd resume talking as if hadn't happened.

So for a while, whenever I saw Vic approaching, like a child needing to hide favorite toys from a reckless sibling, I'd quickly wrap up my end of a conversation with Walter and be on my way.

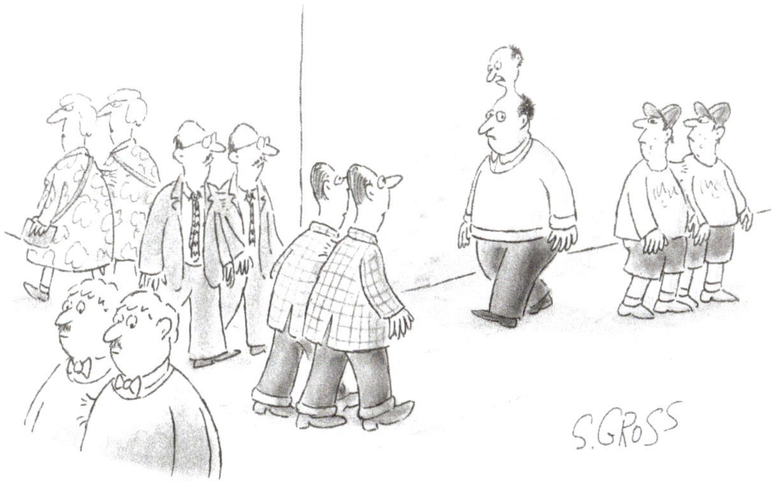
S.GROSS

"Why can't we be normal Siamese twins like everybody else?"

Traditionally many families headed off during July or August. But this year fewer families had those plans and that meant there were more than enough kids to populate six teams.

The games were seven innings long. The coaches, there were at least two, would pitch to his or her own team for the first three innings. When the coaches pitched to their own team, strikes counted but balls did not and a team could only bat around once.

I become a co-coach for the Dodgers with Peter Kloit who manages the dairy department at the Shopwellrandom. Mostly, he worked with pitching and batting.

Among our notable players was the barrel-chested Gino Salvatore, who only liked batting. To him, fielding was like cleaning your room—for wussies. He would plant himself in the outfield like a teamster with his arms intractably folded across his chest. A ball would practically have to roll over his foot—with parents, coaches and teammates screaming at him—before he'd pick it up and lob it to the cutoff man.

There was Sean Delaney, at second base, a thin child with the efficient bony framework of a potential marathon runner. He was the only boy among four older sisters all known for their dexterity at Irish step dancing. At second, he'd often be on his toes, hopping from foot to foot, in constant motion as if keeping time with the fiddles, flutes and war drums that were unceasingly banging away in his head.

There were the twins, Andy and Paul Brewer, who played first and shortstop respectively—and were good at it. They also pitched. A&P were handsome and inseparable and full of grandmotherly advice for their teammates on matters of personal hygiene, traffic crossings and the value of chewing food throughly. They were the team's biggest boosters who wept dramatically when we lost and went leaping, into deranged paroxysms of joy whenever we won. (Which was about half the time.)

At third base was Zed Krouse, who had the most natural talent, but only a casual interest. Zed would sometimes play barefoot and wear his mitt on his head and stand with his hands in his pockets and his back to the plate looking off at whatever else he found more interesting—which might be anything else other than the game he was playing. Zed had a growing artistic temperament. Somedays he'd put in a great effort and other days not. We let him be. Coach Kloit and I agreed he was a good example of "picking your fights."

Behind the plate was George Weigel, who had the bulk and fearlessness that suggested a real future as a catcher. He mumbled a fair amount. I suspected it was an inaudible narrative of the game currently underway; could he be eye-ing a broadcasting career if the catching didn't pan out?

Being raised indifferently by a single

America's LIVE Japanese gameshow

BATSU!

Now Playing: New York City & Chicago
Shows Tues-Sat • Tickets: www.batsulive.com
"Hilarious, strange and kind of sick" — Thrillist

International Waters
A comedy quiz show where land laws don't apply.
a podcast from maximumfun.org

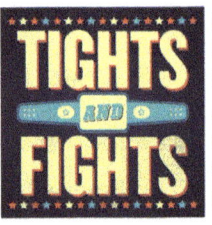

Cultural analysis. Drama. Feats of strength. Spandex.
A weekly podcast about professional wrestling.
From maximumfun.org

A Chartered, non-profit body established in 1972, with the aim of aiding in the study and perpetuation of heraldry in the United States and abroad.

VISIT OUR WEBSITE
AMERICANCOLLEGEOFHERALDRY.ORG

mom was Clifford Blake. Young Clifford. Master Blake. He was a plumpish boy of privilege with soft cherubic looks and curly black hair who had no instincts for, or interest in, this confounding, dangerous and pointless activity that his mother had thoughtlessly sentenced him to. Clifford had a small plastic mitt that more resembled a yellowing hand infection than standard baseball equipment. He held this gently over his heart and then over his face whenever the *ping* of a bat and shouting announced the ball was in play and possibly en route, determined to hit him in some soft, unprotected place where the sting of pain lingers far longer than the laws of physics should mercifully allow. But Clifford was the most obliging boy on the team. He tried with all effort to do everything I asked of him, while his sad, wide eyes searched for the hope that Life will go on, and all the perils of hardball would one day be safely inert in his diary. Then he would at last be able to joke about the ordeal—as he'd heard a number of self-deprecating adults often do on various subjects as he, dressed in a child's tuxedo, served them warm *hors d'oeuvres* at one of his mother's popular cocktail parties. Though Clifford's bad habits were deep, and his fear of the ball deeper still, he did improve. His willingness to persevere made me admire him more than anyone else on the team. Initially, Clifford would get out of the way of the ball, and when it bounced safely past him, he'd give chase. Yelling at it to stop, he'd throw his mitt at it—which was swiftly followed by the realization he valued his mitt more than he wanted the ball, thus redirecting his pursuit. His mistakes and their solutions kept him one busy boy in the outfield.

It was during our fourth game that Clifford caught a ball. It was a high fly he was simultaneously trying to get nearer to and away from, but in doing so, found himself directly under. For a moment the ball appeared wedged between his neck and shoulder. Then, like a wandering goiter seeking toasty sanctuary in the depths of Clifford's underwear, it vanished.

"Don't move!" his teammates yelled.

The umpire gave it a fair amount of time to reappear out his pant's leg and thump to the ground. When it did not, he called the batter out and a cheer went up, "Clif-*ford*! Clif-*ford*!"

Over a short amount of time, my objections to Victoria grew inconsequential. I didn't care if she talked too much about nothing, she was fun to be around. The three of us were spending more healthy weekend time together, hiking, kayaking and sailing on Shepard's Lake. Then came the evening when the climate between us changed, or so I believed.

She had invited me for supper with another couple. While shaving and thinking about what I'd wear, I realized how much my vanity had been aroused, and how I looked forward to seeing her and absorbing her possessive, welcoming hug.

Their porch chairs were lined up facing west. We sat on the deck with our drinks watching the sun, like a golden coin, deposit itself into the back hills of Massachusetts—while opposite, keeping the balance, a creamy, pumpkin moon ascended. We talked about the errors of the Town Board compounded by the Zoning Board. Then about the exploding deer population, and the ever-escalating cost of coyote urine and their even more costly and foul derivatives.

As Victoria placed a refill next to me, she ran her hand across my shoulders igniting a fuse that sent something utopian up my spine. Without turning, I reached around to pat her hand just as she removed it, leaving me patting myself.

During dinner, I told a story about a raccoon chasing me. It made her laugh. She jumped up from her seat and gave me a hug and a kiss on the cheek. I looked at Walter as he was lowering his head.

At the door, saying our good nights, there was a brief but lip-y good night kiss between us. As I was getting into my car, Betsy, the other woman, said as she walked by, "Be careful, she's a cat."

Walter also cautioned me. "It's not what you think. Don't misunderstand her. People sometimes believe her affection is for them. It's not directed at anyone in particular. It's her nature. It's for everybody. Men, women, children, dogs, trees and plants. Everyone but cats. To think it's more personal is a mistake. She doesn't have many women friends; ;nly Betsy, which is regrettable. But she tries."

Among the fundamentals, concentration came first. We called it the 'The Big C.'

"What do we need?"

"The big C!"

"When do we need it?"

"Now!"

The first time we yelled this, just before a game, the opposing coach came over. He told me his wife was undergoing chemo, so would we not chant that?

"Sorry about your wife," I told him. I hadn't thought about the other big "C." I made a note to come up with another chant. And a second note to explain to the boys that baseball is hunting which maybe could give them an edge. If they never win another game, they'll always have that.

Then I remembered Arthur Miller's famous line: *Attention must be paid.* There were two ways to go with this: "What did Linda Loman say?" Or, "What did Mrs. Willy Loman say?"

We went with the latter.

I'd set them up and they'd shout, "Attention must be paid!"

"When must it be paid?" I'd yell.

"Now it shall be paid," they'd scream in a voice of wild boyhood, then bit off a *"YEAH!"* to seal the deal.

It was lumpy at first, but it smoothed out with repetition. I can't really say why, but I liked that our team was further distinguished by a theatrical reference to *Death of a Salesman*.

That opposing coach, the same one who objected to our earlier chant, came over and wanted to know what this new one was about. Since our last game, I'd learned his wife had only had a small "c" —a basal cell carcinoma removed at her doctor's office, a minor procedure.

Now this coach wanted to know "who this Mrs. Willy Loman is." He was like a cop slowly gathering evidence. I was about to tell him when I thought, no, if I told him, he'd find other objections. Willy Loman, for one. Things aren't going well for Mr. Willy Loman, so what does he do? He offs himself. Is that the message we want our Little Leaguers to carry into their promising futures?

Fundamentally, I think he just didn't like us having an unregulated chant, one he didn't get to pass official judgment on.

"So, who's this Mrs. Willy Loman?"

I told him Mrs. Loman recently donated a new research wing to the county hospital, and we were giving her a shout-out as we do at the start of our games to all who advance medical research. I know it'll come back to bite me.

The last time I tried to passionately explain my baseball-is-hunting theory was to Victoria. I wanted to bring her over to the enlightened side; I *knew* she could appreciate it.

Driving by one fine day, I saw who I believed to be Walter lounging out on the back porch. It was Vic, who never lounged anywhere—and was wearing a powerful bikini. I had never before seen her so undressed. The clothes she usually wore were always sizes too large. I was almost giddy by this figure she'd been concealing, a tummy that begged to be petted and stroked.

"Hey," I said. "Didn't realize it was you back here."

"Hey Matt. How have you been? I'm knocked out. I hit the wall. I'm calling it quits for the day," she said. "I'm just going to lie here and do nothing. What are you up to?"

"Um, not much. I just thought I'd say, hi and oh, I'm glad you're here. I just remembered something I really wanted to do..."

I really wanted to start kissing her stomach. And toss in a mess of zerberts as well. Get her laughing and wiggling and begging I stop.

"I never finished telling you my baseball is hunting theory ..."

"That's right. You like baseball, don't you?"

"I'm sure if you understood it you'd really enjoy it."

"You go ahead and tell me about your baseball. I'm all yours."

"Baseball is chess and everything else is checkers! No truer words," I said.

"My father taught me how to play chess. We ought to play one day. Okay, lay it on me," she said shutting her eyes.

"Well, baseball is hunting," I began.

"As in hunters and gatherers?"

"No. It's only about the hunters. I suppose there are gatherers like bat boys, ticket takers, vendors and such—but they don't affect the outcome."

"So what happened to the gatherers? Did the hunters run them off? I want to learn this," Vic said, stifling a yawn.

"Let me start again."

It took only a short while for her to get deep inside me, but years for her to grow out—if that's even happened. This was not something I pursued. It just happened. She reminded me of my first teen love; she had the same exuberance. On top of that, Vic strongly resembled my ex-, and—dear God—she had the same birthday as my mother!

She was the last thought I'd have at night, and the first one impatiently waiting for me in the morning—waiting to offer me more impetuous advice I should employ to speed along my misplaced passion and crash it into something nearby.

I would dwell upon her flaws and carry them around like buckets of ice water to douse myself with, but they wouldn't take. I could only find delight and more excitement in them that made the pain more torturous.

I dreamed about Victoria. I was in an art class and she was to be the figure model. Upon hearing that, I pushed my way to the front to set up my easel right next to where she'd be posing. But then realized this looked a bit lecherous. I began retreating a little further back. Then a little more. And a little more. Then it was too far. I was at the back wall and everyone else filled in. It was crowded. Then a big, "Oooooo!" went up and I couldn't see a goddamn thing. I did hear her laughing and flirting with the guys up front and enjoying herself as much as they were.

One afternoon as I entering the park, I started thinking of places where I'd most likely run into her. I wondered if I should frequent some of those places when I heard someone behind me, and felt a hand slip into mine. It was Clifford. It felt most awkward and pleasant.

Last week there was a chocolate layer cake left on my porch. It looked like a child had made it or it had been dropped. The note read: "Thank you for helping Clifford. You've done heaps for his confidence, signed, Connie B. P.S. Cocktails and Dancing. Friday the 16th. 7 P.M. Hope you can come." It was my first invite to her legendary home.

"We have to concentrate more. Right, coach?" Clifford said, nodding emphatically.

"Why don't you run on ahead and get some more practice in?" He started away then paused. "What is it, son?"

"I was wondering before: do hippopotamuses think rhinos are unicorns?" Clifford smiled.

"Go on now," I said.

"Maybe it's where they got the *idea* for unicorns."

As I watched Clifford run off to engage in the unique seriousness of baseball, I resumed guessing where I might run into Victoria and what I'd say when it happened. "Hey! I think I know this guy," might work. But—it shouldn't be rehearsed.

For the most part, Peter Kloit was the hitting and pitching coach (I was the fielding coach). Most of the kids had trouble getting around on Peter's pitches; he'd throw fast. But that meant when they did get ahold of one, they took it for a ride.

On this day I noticed the other team was slow to show up. I thought it might be a good time to have a talk with our guys.

I called the team in. We all took a knee.

"I want to tell you something important about baseball that not many people know. Gather around. Can you all hear me? This might help you see the game more clearly. It might make you better players.

"When the other team is up and we're out in the field," I continued, "do you ever think about who you are?"

"…We're the…Dodgers?" someone offered.

"Anything else?"

They looked at each other for clues. Then a smile lit Clifford's face.

"We're Mrs. Willy Loman!" he shouted. A few more voices meekly endorsed this odd but reasonable response.

"No," I said. "When you're out there in the field, you're all *traps*, set to catch the batter. The batter has to run through the traps. Like a bunny. And you're the bunny-hunters. You're the traps that catch the bunny. Because baseball, when all is said and done, is hunting!"

"What kind of traps?" someone asked. "Like bear traps?"

"Don't get hung up on the traps. Don't get literal on me," I told them. "You can't let anyone get by you and get safely on base."

"Are the bases traps?" said Gino.

"What's 'literal' mean?" someone asked.

"Did somebody do something to the bases?" Gino asked Zed.

"Listen," I said. "It doesn't matter what kind of traps. What is important is that you know baseball is hunting," I said, "and we're going hunting."

"Coach, are we going to need permission slips?" asked one of the twins. "If you want, we can help collect them," said the other.

"I know! I know!" said Sean. "Can we be those traps where you dig a big hole, cover it over with twigs and leaves, and put spikes in the bottom?"

"Yeah! That's so cool." A few of the boys did imitations of being impaled on wooden spikes trying to stretch a single into a double while twitching to death.

"Guys. Stop!"

"What about Have-A-Heart traps?" said Zed. "We have some in our garage. I don't think a person can fit in one."

"We'll try this later," I said. Coach Kliot stepped in and gave out the batting order and some tips for today's game.

I joined the procession of cars that stretched for almost a quarter of a mile, to a cleared field where teenagers in black pants and white shirts directed the parking. I'd been here once before as a tourist, but not as a guest. I'd heard for tax reasons the house is open to the public four days a year. (It's also available for non-profit events.) The house, which is on the National Registry, is a twenty-room American Gothic mansion built around 1850 by a prominent D.C. architect, and sits on about a hundred acres. The current owner, Connie Blake, got it in a divorce settlement.

There was a bar setup halfway between the parking field and the house. I got myself a drink, then looked around for someone to talk with. There were no faces I recognized. I went in the house and took a meandering tour of the first floor and spotted Peter Kloit and his wife, Pam, who appeared momentarily trapped in the butler's pantry where the caterers were storing boxes of food and liquor.

"Hi, you two," I said.

"Hey, Matt, how are you?" he said. "You know Pam."

"Hi, Pam. I think if you can climb over that carton you can come out this way."

"Wow. Some joint, huh?" Peter said.

"It's amazing," Pam said. "Imagine taking care of a place this size. Just cleaning part of the downstairs would take a week. Does she and the boy live here by themselves?"

"I think there's also an older daughter from an earlier marriage," I said.

"Hey, you'd never guess what happened. There was a chocolate cake at our door with a note inviting us here," Peter said.

"How about that," I said.

"It was good," he said.

We headed out on the veranda where there was live music and two more bars. It felt like a grand wedding. Swing standards were playing softly. A number of women were dancing with children and each other.

"Which one is Connie Blake? Do you know? I have to thank her for inviting us," said Pam, "and tell her how great her house is."

"I'd heard she doesn't make an appearance at her parties until they're well under way," I said. "Two or three hours in."

Peter piped up. "Matt, before I forget, I'm not going to be able to make our game tomorrow. Can you handle it by yourself? I've got some family business to deal with. Sorry to do this to you."

"No problem." I welcomed it.

I was watching the dancers and then saw young Clifford, in his tux, serving *hors d'oeuvres* to a group of people at the edge of the dance floor. And there among them, at last, was Victoria. She took a *hors d'oeuvre* from Clifford's tray, made a fuss over him, and gave him a long affectionate hug.

I crossed the floor and came up behind her as she turned around. She was almost expressionless but then she grabbed my belt buckle and shook me with it. Then smiled.

In all the time Victoria was married to Walter, she never once wore make-up—but this evening, she was in full war paint. She was hunting. It suited her.

"I think I know this guy. Hi there, you," she said. "I was wondering when we'd run into each other. Actually I saw you a few times in town but decided to leave it alone."

"Really? Why is that?"

"I was probably in a hurry," she said.

"Well, tell me what you've been up to," I said.

"Well, to begin with, I'm leaving tomorrow evening. For England. For a month. Can you believe that? But I'll tell you what, meet me tomorrow at the slip on Shepard's Lake. Two o'clock. In the boathouse. We'll steal some quality time together. We deserve it, don't you think? Maybe even take a swim."

"...Okay," I said.

"Sorry I can't talk now. I need to get back. I'm actually working here. Long story, but I'll see you tomorrow."

As I watched her leave, I was suddenly empty of any reason to stay. I headed home, head packed with her. She wants to meet me at Shepard's Lake, which means she wants to be alone with me. I dwelled on that for a while.

It wasn't until I got home that I realized the Dodgers had a game tomorrow and Peter would be away. Two o'clock would be cutting it close. If we start right at noon and finish by two, I wouldn't be that late.

I arrived early, and for a half hour was the only one there.

The Dodgers were slow showing up. By the scheduled start of the game, I had half a team; we didn't have enough players.

There was nothing to do then but postpone or forfeit. Pick another day. The umpire gave us another fifteen minutes. Just when that time was up, two SUVs arrived with the rest of the Dodgers and some parents.

George, our catcher, came over. "Hey, Coach! I told my Dad what you said, that baseball was hunting, and he said he liked that idea. He'd like to talk to you about it. My dad loves baseball. This is the first game he's been able to come to. I'll go get him..."

"We've got to get going here, George..." I said weakly, but George ran off. He returned with a man in bright pants, a white shirt and golf shoes.

"Jeff Weigel." He extended his hand. "Never heard that before but yes, hunting, it makes sense. You've been giving this some thought, I suspect—"

"Nice to meet you, Jeff." I began backing away.

"Hold on, there's Mort—you've got to talk to this guy. *Mort!* He's a real fan. A stats guy. I want to see his reaction. Do you mind? Mort, get over here. You got to meet Coach and hear this," said Jeff.

"Jeff, I have some stuff to do..."

"Wont take a minute. Hey, did you read that Willy Mays bio? *Mort!* You're holding Coach up. Here he comes..."

"Sorry, hi," said Mort.

"He's a real fan. Tell him what you said about baseball is hunting. Tell him what you mean by that. He'll get a kick out of it. Mort, listen to this guy. He knows the inside."

"Well, baseball is hunting and...all the players on the field are traps...all the traps get set before each pitch..." I said.

"I like the sound of that. I'd love to hear more," said Mort.

"Guys..." I began.

"Okay, you're in a hurry. But after the game let's talk about this. We're not going to let you get away," said Jeff.

For the first time, I had the team to myself. When the kids saw me take the mound, they cheered. I was the coach who threw the fat lazy grapefruits, not the hard stuff. Everyone on the team, including Clifford, could wallop what I threw.

"Hooray for Coach!"

"We all bat around!"

"Big inning, everybody!"

"Get ready to do some damage, guys," I yelled. "We're gonna move this along."

First up was Zed. I held the ball up and away so he could get a good fix on it. I looked like I was throwing darts. The first pitch was wide; Zed chased it and missed. The next was inside and made him jump back. "Good eye, good eye," his teammates cheered.

The next pitch was right at Zed, and as he jumped away, the ball hit his bat and dribbled down the third base line. He ran safely to first.

Andy was up next and the ball hit him in the shoulder as he twisted around to get away from it. The next pitch went at his head and bounced off his helmet. The next bounced in front of the plate and hit him in the ankle as he tried to jump over it. After dodging the next one, he swung and hit a ball a foot over his head for a single. Men on first and third.

I had never thrown so poorly. I had to concentrate.

I hit Sean in the thigh and the arm. I hit Gino in the chest who then struck out on purpose just to get out of there.

Paul, of the twins, froze as he watched the arc of the ball coming right at him. At the last moment, he twisted around and took it in the middle of his back, the thump echoing inside the hollow of his thin ribs. On the next pitch, Paul dropped the bat, fell to the ground and buried his head in his arms. The ball bounced off his helmet.

The parents, understandably, began voicing some concerns. I wasn't throwing that fast but granted, these were their kids I was hitting with a hardball. It had to look worse than it was.

"Quit hitting the kids, ya crazy shit-head bastard," someone yelled. A number of parents yelled back, "Hey! Language! Language!"

I wanted to yell, "It looks worse than it is, believe me," but that would just open up a debate. I had to ignore them and concentrate.

The umpire came out to the mound.

"Having some trouble? Want a break, let someone else try for a while?"

I had never seen a coach take himself out of a game and there was nobody else. This was a fluke. It would pass. "I'll be all right."

"Out doing the town last night?" he said.

"Yeah, something like that," I lied.

I was past the point of thinking about it too much. I knew I was throwing too softly; if I used more speed, I'd be more accurate. They could handle it. I had to stop thinking about the plate. I had to stop thinking about the ball. I had to stop thinking about everything I could stop thinking about.

Next up was Clifford Blake with his sad, angelic eyes saying, "I know I'll get hit but please don't make it hurt too much." The suffering on the boy's face would have been inspiration to any religious painter in search of the ideal Saint Sebastian. But for me on that day, it provoked anger.

"Lose the attitude, Clifford. Quit looking at me that way. Suck it up," I yelled at him.

Then I wound up.

The cries from the stands as the ball left my hand said two things: first, it was faster than anything I'd thrown that day, which I knew; and second, they were expecting the worst. The pitch sailed past George's mitt and wedged in the link fence backstop while Clifford was already safely in the fetal position halfway back to the dugout. How he got there that fast still baffles me.

As the game progressed, I regained control and they started knocking them out of the infield. The score was tied eight to eight in the fifth inning and remained so until the bottom of the thirteenth. With Sean jigging away on first, Geno tagged one over the right field fence. And the game was finished. It was half past three.

Keeping their promise, Jeff and Mort cornered me and we had a talk adding to the growing evidence that baseball is, in many ways, like hunting.

When I got home that day, there was a notice from the county announcing they were going to pave the stretch of dirt road which meant the work-out birds, most likely, will be relocating.

I'll miss them.

I'll miss them along with the exhausting anticipation of one day running into Victoria again, knowing that if I obsess about it, it won't happen.

But until then, if ever, I have enough material to improvise upon: the woman who wanted to meet the man, deep in the woods by the lake on a summer's afternoon, with the promise that something surprising might happen. It was in her voice; it was in her eyes. He could actually feel it. It was already physically upon him. And there would be a good amount of dappled sunlight. ◗

OUR BACK PAGES

WHAT AM I DOING HERE?

Our intrepid traveler travels to Rio TK TK • By Mike Reiss

Rio Stole My Heart. And Wallet.

I once had a new boss who invited me to his home for dinner. When I arrived at the appointed time, my boss had completely forgotten who I was and why I'd come to his home. He and his wife were in their underwear, watching TV and eating take-out. They stared at me like I was a crazy stranger who dropped into random homes looking for free meals. I slowly backed out and, in the thirty years I worked with this man, I've never mentioned it again.

Rio de Janeiro is like my boss.

In 2017, 6.6 million people visited Rio and the city wasn't ready for any of them. There are no information stands, no tourist centers, no currency exchanges. No one speaks English—they don't even speak Spanish! Brazilians speak Portuguese, a language spoken outside of Brazil by one-sixth of one percent of the world's population. Even other South Americans visiting Rio are out of luck.

This is not to say Rio de Janeiro is the worst place on earth. (Honduras is.)

But Rio is the worst place on earth that you think is going to be fun. (Grandma's house is a close second.) It looks great in the movies. There's that giant Christ the Redeemer statue on top of a mountain. Only it's not all that giant—you've seen bigger figures inflated on top of car dealerships. It's made of poured concrete and is about the blandest looking Jesus you'll ever see. The name is a tip-off—Christ the Redeemer? You can just picture this Savior sitting home clipping coupons.

Nearby is Rio's other major tourist

What am I doing in Rio? Even Jesus is shrugging.

disappointment—a mountain called Sugarloaf. A sugarloaf is a lump of sugar shaped like a mountain. So, despite its colorful name, Sugarloaf is basically a mountain shaped like a mountain.

What was I doing here?

My wife and I had come to Rio for Carnivale, that glittering fiesta of massive debauchery. I'd expected it to be spilling out into the streets, with parties and parades everywhere, like Mardi Gras in New Orleans. But Carnivale is a private ticketed event, held in a special stadium. Outside that arena, you'd have no clue anything was happening.

There were signs for a Celebration in the Park, but, in typical Rio fashion, the organizers lost interest once the signs were posted. Hundreds of angry tourists showed up for what should have been called "Nothing in the Park." As I fought my way through the crowd, I got squashed up against a ferocious-looking woman. I apologized; she snarled back. It was only when I emerged from the mob that I realized the woman had torn the pocket off my pants and taken all the money I had.

I walked ten feet to a policeman who was sunning himself on the hood of his patrol car. He was actually using a tanning reflector, something I'd only seen as a prop in 60's bikini comedies. I told the cop I'd just been robbed. He looked at me, baffled: did I know him? Were we friends? Why was I bothering him with my problems?

"She's still there!" I said, pointing to her. "The black woman. The really ugly one!"

"They are all ugly," he said and went back to tanning. Not just a lousy cop, a racist too. I hope he got melanoma.

I'd been to a hundred countries, many of them hellholes, some of them war zones. But this was the first time I'd ever gotten robbed. The second time, actually— the first was two hours before. I'd used an ATM that had been rigged to steal credit cards. Luckily, there was an emergency phone handy. It was broken.

Crime, of course, is the one area where Rio really delivers. The city's wealthy tourist area is surrounded by *favelas*, a ring of shanty towns up in the hills. The Brazilians handled this problem the best way they know: cosmetic surgery. They painted the slums in bright day-glo colors. They're still a nest of poverty and hopelessness, but now they look like a package of Starburst candies. Problem solved.

They even give walking tours of the *favelas*. "The people here are very poor, but they never steal from each other," chirped our guide. "We steal from you—the tourists! How many of you have been robbed since you got here?" There were twelve of us in the group—eight raised their hands.

There was no escape from crime, even at a costume contest we attended. There were women in elaborate confections of feathers and spangles. One guy came as Big Ben (he was, in fact, the only clock in Rio keeping correct time). Another was dressed as the entire city of San Fran-

MIKE REISS is Intrepid Traveler for *The American Bystander*.

cisco, with glittering lights and moving cable cars.

And the winner was…a woman (or possibly a man) dressed as Evita. S/he wore a white dress and had blonde hair. That's it. The judges had clearly been bribed and the crowd knew it. The fancy dress ball ended in violence. You can't spell 'riot' without R-I-O.

But the real costume ball in town was Carnivale—it's a non-stop parade that lasts from nine P.M. till dawn, two nights in a row. I missed the first evening, having caught a terrible stomach ailment from something I ate. Or touched. Or looked at. I sent my wife off alone, at night, into a strange and truly dangerous city. (I'm a great husband.) I stayed in bed, shivering, sweating, and watching TV. The only thing on was *Suddenly Susan*, dubbed into Portuguese. If you don't remember this show, it was a Brooke Shields sitcom based on the premise that there's nothing remotely funny about Brooke Shields. When that episode ended, another *Suddenly Susan* began. I scrambled for the remote, but it squirted from my sweaty hand and rolled under the bed. I was too wracked with chills to get it, so I lay there all night, watching a *Suddenly Susan* marathon. The only thing worse than watching six hours of this show in Portuguese would have been watching it in English.

I dragged myself out of bed for the second and final night of Carnivale. Thousands of Brazilians participate, representing dozens of Rio neighborhoods. Every group dances to its its own special samba, and every samba sounds exactly the same. Their outfits all look similar too—giant contraptions of plumes and sequins. It looks and sounds like a massive invasion from the planet Fabulous.

Carnivale costumes can cost up to fifty thousand dollars each, and the poor people of Rio pay for it themselves. What could have been their child's college education is spent on an outfit they wear once, as they swagger down the mile-long promenade. When they reach the end, they throw it away, right where they're standing. From glamor to garbage in five seconds. By sunrise, several city blocks were piled high with spangled headdresses and feathered brassieres.

It was surreal.

It was also the greatest show I'd ever seen in my life. Carnivale was worth all my suffering: the robberies, the diarrhea, the rigged costume ball, and the twelve episodes of *Suddenly Susan*. I was hooked, so I came back to Rio for the 2014 Olympics.

Once again, the city invited the world to a party they forgot they were throwing. They'd had four years to plan, but seemed to throw it all together in the last couple of days. Many venues were unfinished; others were visibly crumbling while the events took place. Spectators agree it was the worst Olympics of the past, say, 3000 years. Oh, and I got robbed again. B

"The doctor would like you to pee into this chalice."

"IF BARRY BLITT IS ANYTHING IT'S BRILLIANTLY PROVOCATIVE."

—JAMES RAINEY, *LOS ANGELES TIMES*

Blitt
by Barry Blitt
THE NEW YORKER

"By turns fascinating and entertaining . . . The beauty of [Blitt's] art is that it rarely needs explaining. You just *get* it."

—*MOTHER JONES*

A gorgeous, hilarious, and provocative compendium of the award-winning artist's illustrations for *The New Yorker*, *The New York Times*, *Vanity Fair*, and more.

- Featuring more than 100 never-before-seen sketches and unpublished illustrations with insightful and satirical annotations by the artist
- Including original essays by Frank Rich, Françoise Mouly, Steve Brodner, David Remnick, and Steven Heller
- Gorgeously designed, an essential coffee-table book for discerning political spectators and fans of comic art alike

ON SALE NOW

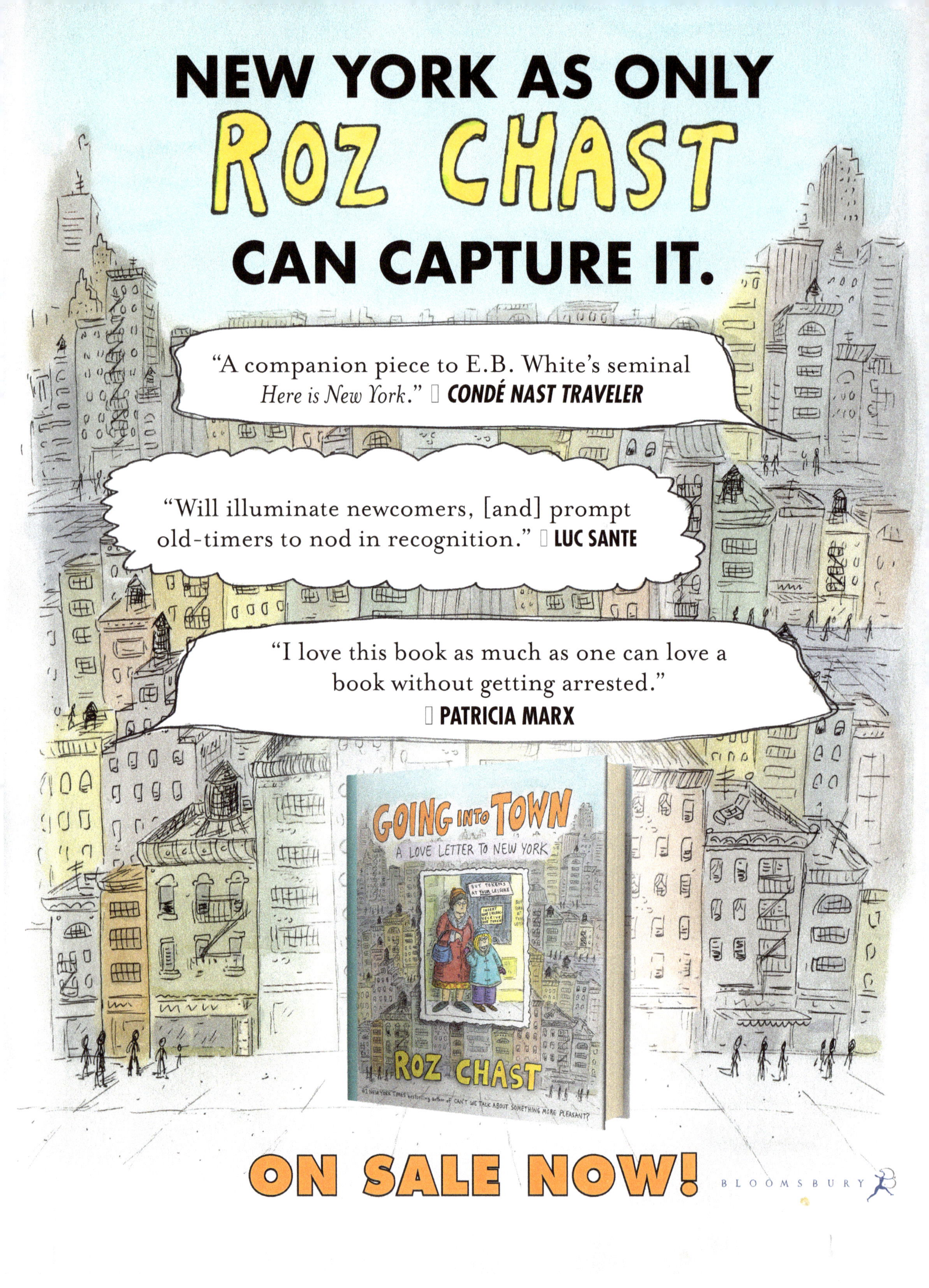
NEW YORK AS ONLY
ROZ CHAST
CAN CAPTURE IT.
"A companion piece to E.B. White's seminal *Here is New York*." — CONDÉ NAST TRAVELER
"Will illuminate newcomers, [and] prompt old-timers to nod in recognition." — LUC SANTE
"I love this book as much as one can love a book without getting arrested." — PATRICIA MARX
GOING INTO TOWN
A LOVE LETTER TO NEW YORK
ROZ CHAST
#1 New York Times bestselling author of CAN'T WE TALK ABOUT SOMETHING MORE PLEASANT?
ON SALE NOW!
BLOOMSBURY

ERRATA

To err is human, to admit divine • By Steve Young

Page 4: The Moon should not have been described as "the Earth's only natural satellite." Though it may look natural, it has had a lot of work done.

Page 7: That may in fact be how that guy spells his name, but come on, that's fucked up.

Page 8: "When you're a Jet, you're a Jet all the way, from your first cigarette to your last dyin' day" is not correct. According to the *Official Jets Gang Manual*, your first cigarette marks the beginning of a three-month probationary period, after which you may or may not be a Jet all the way.

Page 11: The Statue of Liberty was misleadingly described. Its presence in New York Harbor has been confirmed by science; it is not an "urban legend."

Page 22: Instead of the long tedious thing about history and politics and whatnot, there should have been pictures of adorable baby animals. Right? Seriously!

Page 25: "Alopecia" was not the most popular name for baby girls in the late 1940's. It has never even been in the top twenty.

Page 33: The recipe for Red Velvet Cupcakes should have been attributed to *Ladies' Home Journal*, rather than the Book of Leviticus.

Page 39: The opposite is true: biologists have proven that in fact mold and mildew do NOT like to be lumped in together.

Page 44: The claim that the legendary "Nazi Gold Train" merely carried the metaphorical gold of friendship is unproven, and frankly, stupid.

Page 51: According to one of our editors, Dan, it's *person*-splaining, not mansplaining.

Page 56: The advice for escaping from a car that has plunged into water was incorrect. Do not "honk your horn to summon friendly mermaids."

Page 60: Unfortunately, further research has determined that the Strategic Petroleum Reserve cannot be rented out for birthday parties or bar mitzvahs.

Page 66: Licorice may not be many people's favorite flavor, but there is no evidence to suggest that it's "the work of the Devil."

Page 68: The band Paul McCartney was in after the Beatles was called "Wings," not "Courtesy Flush."

Page 73: The drawing to show scale and relative sizes was incorrect. Even the largest prize-winning pumpkin could not contain the city of Tulsa, Oklahoma.

Page 74: The coupon expired in 1959, and in any case, Edsel is out of business.

Page 79: "Foots" is not the plural of "foot" in Delaware, or for that matter in any U.S. state.

Page 82: The claim that "Abraham Lincoln's Gettysburg Address included a shout-out to Todd Bellinger" is not supported by historical evidence, and has apparently been promulgated by someone named Todd Bellinger.

Page 85: We're pretty sure there was something wrong on this page but now we can't figure out what it was. Take everything on this page with a grain of salt.

Page 88: The phrase "dishwasher safe" is a misnomer. Nothing is actually dishwasher safe. Safety is an illusion. Everything in this world dies, decays, disappears. Laws, institutions, and friends and family cannot protect you, or your plates and glasses.

Page 96: The assertion that "This page intentionally left blank" is wrong because it's not blank; it contains that assertion. Mindfuck!

Page 100: The phrases "robber baron" and "rubber barn" should have been transposed.

Page 103: This material is basically correct, but was supposed to be in a different magazine.

Page 108: There is no truth to the assertion that "FDR ran for President just to get on the dime."

Page 109: What does it matter; nobody reads that far anyhow.

This page: This page should have been titled "Erotica," not "Errata."

SHAKESPEAREAN HOLIDAY GIFTS

CROSSWORD #6

BY MATT MATERA & ALAN GOLDBERG

SHAKESPEAREAN HOLIDAY GIFTS

All the world's a page, and all the men and women merely puzzlers. Answers on page 97.

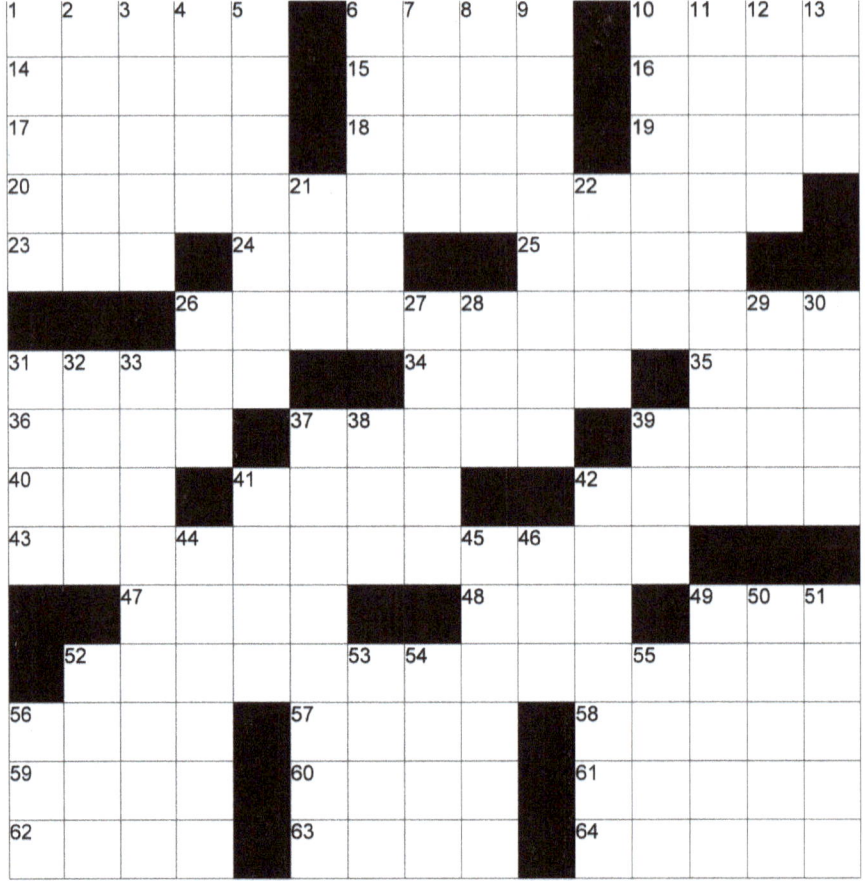

2018

ACROSS

1. Cathedral surrounding
6. Hybrid fruit probably not named by a marketing whiz
10. Hath, to the Bard
14. Straighten, as hair
15. Not a crossword, but usually themed
16. Movie star Jackie who said, "Anyone who thinks I'm not scared out of my mind whenever I do one of my stunts is crazier than I am."
17. Meeting place for Timon of Athens?
18. Places, everyone!
19. It's sometimes prehensile
20. Best gift for a moody indecisive Dane?
23. One on a roll, often?
24. One half of a score
25. Primo
26. Perfect present for a mad king who doesn't want to bring a flesh-and-blood Fool onto a rainswept heath?
31. Pride of lions?
34. Not e'en once
35. Resistance icon?
36. Provide a phony alibi for, say
37. For many kids, the good doctor
39. Mother Earth
40. *Shakespeare After ___* (Majorie Garber book)
41. Most popular avocado worldwide
42. Goldfinger actor Shirley
43. Great gift for a hunchback king desperate for a horse?
47. Schools of thought
48. Non-prescription, for short
49. Pre-fury, post-annoyance
52. Excellent gift that lets lovestruck teens text about when they're going to fake death?
56. *The ___* (1953 faith film)
57. Crow's nest supporter
58. Cohere
59. 1/300th of a lethal dose
60. Pain in the neck?
61. Not how you want your neighbor to be at 3 A.M.
62. "The ___ the limit!"
63. Soothsayer in *Julius Caesar*, for one
64. Birdhouses?

DOWN

1. Pain in the neck?
2. Like same-sex marriage in America
3. Science suffix
4. "Sorry, not ___" (response to a failed effort to make a South Asian dress?)
5. Some horseracing bets
6. Connection to a satellite
7. Ocean spirits?
8. Macduff's lake
9. Apes or parrots
10. Fuel specification
11. Dagoo and Tashtego's "office"
12. Ace
13. Show parodying *Celebrity Jeopardy* (Abbr.)
21. Brussels-HQ'd predecessor org.
22. Nobelist specializing in quantum physics
26. Sister publication to *Ebony*
27. Occupied
28. *Legend of Zelda* console, for short
29. Neil Young protest song
30. Bishop or Cyclops
31. How Joe Friday addressed women
32. With aplomb
33. She went around world in 72 days
37. Citrus fruits popular in Louisiana
38. New New Yorker's study, often (abbr.)
39. Like participants in the Stonewall Riots
41. Internet coding language
42. Bewitch
44. Specks in the sea
45. *Kiss Me, Kate* composer
46. Romantic endgame, in fanspeak
49. Low-budget film
50. One of three notable R's
51. Annual sports awards
52. It's possible for just one to spoil the broth
53. *Arsenic and Old ___*
54. First black male Wimbledon champ
55. Smell you later
56. Campers